ＵＭＧＹＵＸ

The Samaritans

To Andi—
w/ great
excitement!

Steve

𐡔𐡌𐡓𐡉𐡌

The Samaritans

A Biblical People

Edited by

Steven Fine

BRILL

Leiden – Boston
2022

PUBLISHER
BRILL
Plantijnstraat 2
2321 JC Leiden
The Netherlands
brill.com

Every effort has been made to contact all copy-
right holders. Any omissions or errors are entirely
unintentional and details can be addressed to the
publisher.

ISBN 978-90-04-46690-6
EISBN 978-90-04-46691-3

EDITOR
Steven Fine

DESIGN
Peter Yeoh, New York and London

cover DESIGN
Pieter Kers

COVER AND FRONTISPIECE
The Passover Pilgrimage to Mount Gerizim,
2020 (Photograph by Eitan Bino).

המרכז ללימודי ישראל
Yeshiva University Center for Israel Studies

museum of the Bible

Michael Scharf Publication Trust
Yeshiva University Press

BI
MU
Bibelhaus
ErlebnisMuseum

This book is printed on acid-free paper.

MIX
Paper from
responsible sources
FSC® C004472

PRINTED BY DRUKKERIJ WILCO B.V. - AMERSFOORT, THE NETHERLANDS

Contents

Figures

Foreword

I am most pleased to introduce *The Samaritans: A Biblical People*. The YU Israelite Samaritans Project, which this volume celebrates, enhances our understanding of Jewish history in profound ways. Samaritan history has long been intertwined with Jewish history—from biblical times to the present. Their traditions and texts shed light on ours, and ours on theirs. The Samaritan will to survive gives greater context to our own struggles through the ages, and their modern rebirth gives hope to all people of good will. The modern integration of these ancient people into the State of Israel affords greater texture to all that Israel stands for and hopes to be. The YU Israelite Samaritans Project brings together renowned scholars from around the world to focus on these issues, and more, with the goal of both expanding academic engagement with the Samaritans and raising public interest in their—and our—past. This multifaceted project ranges from scholarship to exhibition, documentary film to a cookbook and popular engagement. Our undergraduate students on both campuses and our graduate students at the Bernard Revel Graduate School of Jewish Studies have been deeply involved from the start. Visits by major scholars and creative talents have added excitement to our campuses. This is YU at its best: harnessing deep scholarship, a broad range of media, educational innovation, complexity, and our hallowed past as we build for the future.

Through the YU Israelite Samaritans Project carried out by our Center for Israel Studies, Professor Steven Fine has focused us—our collegium of scholars, our students, and our community—on all aspects of Samaritan history and Samaritanism as they enrich the study of the Jewish past. Dedicated to the study of Israel "in all of its complexity," the YU Center for Israel Studies has sponsored our first documentary, *The Samaritans: A Biblical People, ha-Shomronim: Edah. Torah. Har.*, by filmmaker Moshe Alafi in partnership with the Israeli New Fund for Cinema and Television; this beautiful volume; and the exquisite exhibition that this book celebrates. We are thrilled to partner with the Museum of the Bible for this important exhibition, which encapsulates our shared commitment to all things biblical far and wide.

The YU Center for Israel Studies is an invaluable resource not only for YU and our community, but for our shared intellectual and cultural life on an international scale. I congratulate Professor Fine, who has created this delightful entree into the world of the Samaritans. We especially appreciate the vision and stalwart support of our friend Tzili Charney, who, through the Leon Charney Legacy Fund of the Center for Israel Studies, has supported our documentary, this volume, various educational materials, and the audiovisual aspects of the exhibition. Tzili's participation is especially heartwarming, as Leon ז״ל (Yeshiva College, 1960) originated New York's landmark "Good Samaritan" law.

On behalf of Yeshiva University, I thank all involved in this marvelous project.

Ari Berman,
President of Yeshiva University

Greetings

HIGH PRIEST ABDULLA WASEF

SAMARITANS PRESIDENT

الكاهن الأكبر عبدالله واصف السامري

رئيس الطائفة السامرية

Peace be upon you from Mount Gerizim-Beit El, the Blessed Mountain!

On behalf of the Samaritan community in the Land of Israel, I congratulate all the participants in the Samaritan Project of Yeshiva University. To viewers of the documentary, for visitors to the international exhibition and for readers of this in-depth volume, may the blessings of the Lord be upon you! I wish great success to all those involved in this sacred work, which brings the story of the Israelite Samaritan community to the entire world.

May the Lord bless you and keep you.
May the Lord make His face shine upon you, and be gracious to you.
May the Lord lift up His countenance upon you, and give you peace.

Aabed-El Ben Asher,
High Priest of the Samaritans

June 6, 2021

0.1 Greetings from Aabed-El Ben Asher (Abdulla Wassef), High Priest.

0.2 The Passover Pilgrimage to Mount Gerizim, 2020. Left to right, front: High Priest Aabed-El son of Asher, Ishmael son of Uzi ha-Dafni, Nadav son of Uzi ha-Dafni. Back: Amram son of the priest Pinḥas, Ramzia wife of Ishmael, Uzi son of Ishmael son of Uzi ha-Dafni (Photograph by Eitan Bino).

Preface

YU CENTER FOR ISRAEL STUDIES

Many thanks go out to the high priest Aabed-El ben Asher ben Matzliah and the Samaritan Community Council for their trust and many kindnesses. Benyamim Tsedaka of the A.B. Center for Samaritan Studies in Holon twice visited our New York campus, catalogued the YU collection of Samaritan manuscripts, and served as a special advisor for both the documentary and the exhibition. Benny, Abood Cohen and Moshe Alafi helped us to identify the members of the Samaritan people who appear in the illustrations of this volume. We have been privileged to work with Moshe and his creative team of filmmakers, especially Tamar Gan Zvi, Moshe Huri, Dror Lebendiger, and Ronit Tsedaka, on both our splendid documentary and the marvelous exhibition videos. We are especially grateful to each member of the Samaritan community who appeared in our productions, shared their knowledge with us, or who stood behind the cameras, smiling. Blessings to you all!

We thank our Academic Advisory Board for its trust and support: Joseph L. Angel (Yeshiva University), Yosef Blau (Yeshiva University), Selma Botman (Yeshiva University), Helen Evans (Metropolitan Museum of Art), Laura Lieber (Duke University), Menachem Mor (University of Haifa), R. Steven Notley (Nyack College), Reinhard Pummer (University of Ottawa), Lawrence Schiffman (New York University), and Avigdor Shinan (Hebrew University of Jerusalem). We are grateful to our partners at the New Fund for Cinema and Television (NFCT), Dorit Inbar, Ron Goldman, and Orel Turner, for their support, excitement, and professionalism.

Institutions the world over have shared their resources with us, a kindness for which we are profoundly grateful. These include the A.B. Center for Samaritan Studies, Holon; the Archaeological Museum of Thessaloniki, Greece; the Bernard Museum of Judaica of Congregation Emanu-El of the City of New York; Bibelhaus Erlebnis Museum, Frankfurt; the Bible Lands Museum, Jerusalem; Boston University, School of Theology Archives; the Ephorate of Antiquities of the Cyclades, Greece; California Museum of Photography, University of California, Riverside; the Center for Jewish Art of the Hebrew University of Jerusalem; Hebrew Union College–Jewish Institute of Religion's Klau Library, Cincinnati; The Jewish Museum, New York; the Hebraic Section of the Library of Congress, Washington, DC; the Israel State Archives, Jerusalem; the Israel State Photographic Collection, Jerusalem; Library of the Jewish Theological Seminary of America, New York; the Magnes Collection of Jewish Art and Life, Berkeley; the Museum für Islamische Kunst, Berlin; National Archives of the Netherlands, Amsterdam; National Library of Israel, Jerusalem; Tel Aviv Museum of Art; University of Sydney Library; Yad Ben-Zvi Institute, Jerusalem; Yeshiva University's Mendel Gottesman Library; and Yeshiva University Museum. Special thanks go out to the Israel Antiquities Authority. Private collectors have been most generous in allowing us access to their collections. We thank the Gross Family Collection, Ramat Aviv; Leah and Steven Fine, New York; Roger Harrison; David and Jemima Jeselsohn, Zurich and Binyamim and Miriam Tsedaka, Holon. Contemporary Samaritan life is illustrated thanks to the beautiful photography of Moshe Alafi, Eitan Bino, Ori Orhof and Zev Rothkoff. We are proud to have partnered with the Jewish Art Salon, led by Yona Verwer, as we together enlisted and then worked with an amazing group of Jewish artists who reflected on the relationship between Jews and Samaritans in ways that only artists can.

Scholars around the world have been unflinchingly openhanded toward this project. We especially thank Moshe Florentin, David Gilner, David Hendin, Abraham Tal and Vladimir Levin. Stefan Schorch graciously allowed us to use his truly beautiful Samaritan font, *Samaritan Bethel*, which is based upon the script of the renowned thirteenth-century scribe Abu l-Barakat (Abi Barakata). Matthew Chalmers and Reinhard Pummer read the entire manuscript, saving us from errors large and small. For decades, Reinhard has patiently answered all of my questions, with kindness and cheer. We are especially grateful to the authors for their excitement, expertise, and, most of all, for their marvelous contributions.

YU students, graduate and undergraduate, have been brought into Samaritan studies through coursework and special programs over more than a decade. Students in my Spring 2020 graduate seminar, "The Samaritans: From the Bible to Modern Israel," read, discussed, and improved each contribution to this volume, and were also involved in the acquisition of artifacts for the exhibition—even when our face-to-face work was interrupted by the COVID-19 pandemic. David Selis, the Leon Charney Doctoral Fellow of the Center for Israel Studies and the assistant curator of this exhibition, has been deeply involved in all aspects of object selection, conceptualization, and the preparation of this volume. Baruch-Lev Kelman, the Dr. Joseph and Faye Glatt Research Associate of the Center for Israel Studies helped with translations, editing, and research, and adeptly prepared the index for this volume. Rebecca Zami, a Charney Research Associate, helped with editing and research. Ilona Moradof, Ilana Benson, and Bonni-Dara Michaels (YU Museum) and Paul Glassman, Tina Weiss, Zvi Erenyi, and Shulamith Berger (YU Libraries) were supportive in every possible way. Many thanks go out to my YU colleagues and creative partners, Joseph Angel, Joshua Karlip, Jess Olson, Ronnie Perelis, Shay Pilnik, and Jacob Wisse. The Michael Scharf Publication Trust of Yeshiva University Press, led by Stuart Halpern, joined with Brill in producing this volume, for which we are grateful. I thank my marvelous editor, Katie Chin and the people of Brill Academic Publishers for their exemplary professionalism and kindness in producing this book. I make special mention of Emma de Looij and Erika Mandarino, who saw our volume through production, Michael Helfield, who copyedited the volume, and Peter Yeoh, who designed it so beautifully.

We are most pleased to partner for this exhibition with the Museum of the Bible. Working with the people of MOTB has been a delight at every stage, from conceptualization to execution. I am particularly pleased and proud to have teamed up in curating the exhibition with Dr. Jesse Abelman (PhD Jewish History, Yeshiva University, 2021), who is the curator of Hebraica and Judaica at the Museum of the Bible. This joint project could not have been a more pleasant experience. Our exhibition will open at Bibelhaus Erlebnis Museum/Frankfurt Bible Society in Frankfurt, Germany in the Spring of 2023. Veit Dinkelaker and Silvia Meier of Bibelhaus and Benedikt Hensel of the University of Oldenburg will bring our project to a European audience, which is most exciting.

As always, we are deeply appreciative of Ari Berman, our president, for his full support of our work, and Selma Botman, our provost, for her trust and wise counsel that makes everything possible. Our funders have stood behind this project from the beginning. The Dr. Joseph and Faye Glatt Program will ensure the future of our vibrant Center, and has made it possible for YU students to grow professionally through this project. In 2017, Tzili Charney established the Leon Charney Legacy Fund of the YU Center for Israel Studies. This inspired gift, born of our shared commitment to understanding and presenting Israel in all of its amazing complexity, has made this project possible. With Tzili's encouragement, this gift supported the work of filmmaker Moshe Alafi in creating the inspired exhibition videos; the participation of our amazing student fellows; and the Center's sponsorship of *The Samaritans: A Biblical People, ha-Shomronim: Edah. Torah. Har.*, and this volume. As always, thank you Tzili!

Our project comes at a propitious moment. Samaritan studies has experienced tangible and important growth in recent decades. This is thanks to a small but dedicated international group of scholars and their project of establishing Samaritan Studies as an interdisciplinary field of study. This community includes historians, philologists, biblical scholars, Talmudists, archeologists, folklorists, and cultural anthropologists. These scholars revived the study of Samaritanism, creating the tools of this new discipline—from the publication of text editions, translations, language studies, and lexicons, to the collection and synthetic analysis of primary sources, to the discovery of previously unimagined archeological finds and fieldwork among contemporary Samaritans. They have studiously published the results of their labor in ways accessible not only to scholars but also to a wider readership interested in the Samaritans past and present. The Samaritan Studies community has presented its work in monographs, articles, handbook volumes, periodicals, and created bibliographies of previous scholarship. They even created *A Companion To Samaritan Studies* to help the novice through the complex thicket that has naturally developed around Samaritan Studies, a field that encompasses 3,500 years and multiple languages.[1] This effervescence is enriched by the Samaritan community. In turn, I believe and hope that it has enriched the Samaritans. Members of this small people have created text editions, translations, histories, and cookbooks—some of them in English. For over 50 years, *A.B. – The Samaritan News* has brought together academic scholars with the Samaritans themselves, creating a living, ever-expanding archive and agent of this amazing development. The Samaritan Studies community is welcoming and kind. That this volume came together in less than ten months is a tribute to the commitment of scholars to this joint project. In short, Samaritan Studies is a textbook example of a small discipline creating knowledge, a community, and an infrastructure meant to last generations. The YU Israelite Samaritans Project rests on the foundations of this prodigious accomplishment and celebrates the work of the many scholars who have dedicated their lives to it. This volume is dedicated to two giants of Samaritan Studies: Reinhard Pummer and Benyamim Tsedaka.

Steven Fine
Dean Pinkhos Churgin Professor of Jewish History
Director, Yeshiva University Center for Israel Studies
Director, YU Israelite Samaritans Project

---

1   Crown et al., 1993.

Preface

MUSEUM OF THE BIBLE

It is my great pleasure to collaborate with the YU Center for Israel Studies on *The Samaritans: A Biblical People*. The Museum of the Bible and Yeshiva University are natural partners. The Museum's mission is to invite all people to engage with the transformative power of the Bible. Yeshiva University exemplifies that mission with its motto, *Torah u-Madda* ("Torah and secular knowledge"), representing the combination of ancient wisdom grounded in the Bible and the wisdom of the modern world.

The Samaritans, too, represent this combination. A small people struggling to maintain their biblical traditions in an often-hostile world, they have adapted themselves to new circumstances over the millennia of their existence. I am excited about this opportunity to help tell their story to the world and to help our guests understand better this biblical people. Our collections contain significant Samaritan objects, including a twelfth-century Samaritan Torah Scroll. The YU Israelite Samaritans Project has given us the opportunity to place those objects in the context of the Israelite Samaritan people's history in order to tell this unique story in a way we could not have on our own. By bringing *The Samaritans: A Biblical People* to Museum of the Bible, we are able to provide a global audience for this groundbreaking exhibition and a venue for the ongoing presentation of the story of the Israelite Samaritan people.

Jesus in the Gospel according to Luke presents the Good Samaritan as the paradigmatic example of the fulfillment of the commandment in Leviticus 19:18, "Love your neighbor as yourself," a scriptural directive shared by Jews, Christians, and Samaritans. The history of these three religious groups has been intertwined for as long as all three have existed. We are all neighbors, even if our relationships have not always been good. This collaboration is a step down the road of neighborly love for all of our communities, and I hope that we will continue to engage together with our biblical traditions. I thank Professor Steven Fine for bringing this project to our attention and to everyone who contributed to the project.

Jeffrey Kloha
Chief Curatorial Officer
Museum of the Bible

Contributors

Aabed-El Ben Asher is the High Priest of the Israelite Samaritans.

Jesse Abelman is Curator of Hebraica and Judaica at the Museum of the Bible. Abelman's research focuses on the cultural, legal, and intellectual history of medieval Ashkenazi Jewry. His recently completed dissertation explores violence between Jews in high medieval Europe.

Golda Akhiezer is Associate Professor in the Department of Israel Heritage at Ariel University. Her interests include the history of Eastern European Jewry, Karaism, and Jewish historiography. She is the author of *Historical Consciousness, Haskalah and Nationalism among Eastern European Karaites* (2018).

Moshe Alafi is the Producer of *The Samaritans: A Biblical People, ha-Shomronim: Edah. Torah. Har.* He is a member of the Israel Documentary Filmmakers' Forum and the Israel Film and TV Producers Association. He is a senior lecturer at the Maaleh School of Television, Film and the Arts in Jerusalem.

Joseph L. Angel is Associate Professor of Jewish History at Yeshiva University, focusing on Jewish literature and history in the Greco-Roman world, with a special interest in the Dead Sea Scrolls. He is preparing a volume on Hebrew prayer manuscripts called the *Songs of the Sage.*

Ari Berman is the fifth President of Yeshiva University. An intellectual historian specializing in medieval Jewish law and philosophy, his first book, *The Ger Toshav in Halakhic Literature of the High Middle Ages*, is nearing completion.

Daniel Boušek is Associate Professor of Hebrew Studies at Charles University in Prague. He received the Alexander von Humboldt-Stiftung Research Fellowship (2016–2018) for his work (with Stefan Schorch) entitled the *Masu'il al-Khiluf: The Samaritan Polemical Treatise against the Jews.*

Matthew Chalmers is Visiting Assistant Professor in Religious Studies and Director of Undergraduate Studies at Northwestern University. His recently completed dissertation is entitled *Representations of Samaritans in Late Antique Jewish and Christian Texts* (2019).

Steven Fine is the Dean Pinkhos Churgin Professor of Jewish History at Yeshiva University and Director of the YU Center for Israel Studies and the Israelite Samaritans Project. In 2013, he received the Samaritan Medal for Samaritan Studies.

Reuven Gafni is the Head of the Department of Land of Israel Studies at Kinneret College. A historical geographer, he focuses on the Jewish settlement map in Eretz Israel from the early nineteenth century and on synagogues and Jewish liturgy in Eretz Israel in modern times using an interdisciplinary approach.

Jeffrey P. García is Assistant Professor of New Testament and Second Temple Literature at Nyack College and Academic Coordinator for the Center for the Study of Ancient Judaism and Christian Origins. He is the author of *Understanding the Gospels as Ancient Jewish Literature* (2018).

Katharina E. Keim is a scholar of rabbinic literature and author of *Pirqei DeRabbi Eliezer: Structure, Coherence, Intertextuality* (2017). Her "The Samaritan Correspondence of Moses Gaster" brings Gaster's correspondence into conversation with his manuscripts and archives.

Jeffrey Kloha is Chief Curatorial Officer at the Museum of the Bible. A scholar of New Testament literature, Kloha was previously Provost and Professor of Exegetical Theology at Concordia Seminary in St. Louis.

Richard McBee is a painter and writer on Jewish Art and a founding member of the Jewish Art Salon. He is a member of the team that curated *Jewish Artists Encounter Samaritan Culture,* a project of the YU Center for Israel Studies.

Laura Lieber is Professor of Religious Studies at Duke University, and directs the Center for Jewish Studies and the Elizabeth A. Clark Center for Late Ancient Studies. Her most recent book is *Jewish Aramaic from Late Antiquity* (2018). Lieber's *Classical Samaritan Poetry* will appear shortly.

R. Steven Notley is Distinguished Professor of New Testament and Christian Origins at Nyack College and director of the El Arab Excavation Project. His works include *Sacred Bridge: Carta's Atlas of the Biblical World* (with A. Rainey, 2006); with *Parables of the Sages* (with Z. Safari, 2011).

Dov Noy ז״ל was the Max Grunwald Chair of Folklore and Hebrew Literature at the Hebrew University of Jerusalem. A close friend of the Samaritan community in Israel, Noy profoundly influenced the development of Jewish Folklore as an academic discipline in Israel and abroad.

Reinhard Pummer taught the History of Religions at the University of Ottawa, Canada, for many years. His publications include *The Samaritans in Flavius Josephus* (2009) and *The Samaritans: A Profile* (2016). In 2016, he was awarded the Samaritan Medal for Samaritan Studies.

Stefan Schorch is Chair of Biblical Studies at Martin-Luther-Universität Halle-Wittenberg and an Honorary Member of the Academy of the Hebrew Language (since 2016). He is preparing a critical edition of the Samaritan Pentateuch, beginning with Leviticus (2018).

Yitzchak Schwartz is a cultural and intellectual historian focusing on nineteenth-century religion and popular religious thought. A Doctoral Candidate at New York University, his dissertation explores attempts to define and redefine Judaism by American Jews during the mid- to late nineteenth century.

David Selis is the Leon Charney Doctoral Fellow at the Bernard Revel Graduate School of Jewish Studies of Yeshiva University, and Assistant Curator of this Samaritans exhibition. His research focuses on the history of the Hebrew book and modern Jewish cultural history.

Haseeb Shehadeh, born in Kufir Yasif, taught Hebrew and Arabic for four decades at the Hebrew University, the University of Helsinki, and elsewhere. His publications include *The Samaritan Pentateuch in Arabic* (2011). Shehadeh was awarded the Samaritan Medal for Samaritan Studies.

Israel Sedaka ז״ל was Deputy Director of the Israel Government Coins and Medals Corporation and served as Secretary of the Samaritan community in Holon. An artillery officer in the Israel Defense Forces in his youth, Sedaka was a communal scholar of great repute and an editor of sacred texts.

Shana Strauch Schick is a Leon Charney Fellow of the Center for Israel Studies at Yeshiva University and teaches at Herzog College in Israel. Her first book, *Between Thought and Deed: Intention in Talmudic Jurisprudence* (2021), examines the role of intentionality in Talmudic law.

Dina Stein is Associate Professor of Hebrew Literature at the University of Haifa, Academic Head of the Dov Noy Israel Folklore Archive and author of *Textual Mirrors: Reflexivity, Midrash, and the Rabbinic Self* (2012). She is currently engaged in a project on modern folktales and rabbinic narratives.

Introduction:
From the Heights of Mount Gerizim

STEVEN FINE

The day of the Passover sacrifice, the *qorban*, is the most honored and greatest day for the Samaritan community. My father and older brothers told us that on one of the sacrifice days there remained only half an hour [before the end of the time prescribed for the sacrifice on Passover eve], and they had no sheep to slaughter. They could not find sheep anywhere in the city [of Nablus]! This distressed them greatly and they prayed to God. They asked: "What should we do, there are no sheep!"

Suddenly, from a distance, they heard bells ringing, coming closer. They saw a shepherd coming, and he had an entire flock of sheep! They asked him: "Will you sell them to us?" He said to them: "Yes, I will sell them to you. How many would you like?" They took two or three sheep and said: "We will take them now, and bring you back the money later." They came to slaughter the sheep at the time of the sacrifice.

Suddenly, a group of evil men came upon them, many in number, and threatened ominously. They said: "You will not sacrifice the *qorban* today." My father said to them: "If I do not sacrifice the *qorban* today, I will no longer be considered a Samaritan."

Suddenly, horsemen arrived from somewhere, saw what was happening, threatened the evil ones, and chased them away. The Samaritans managed to sacrifice the *qorban* on time, ate it, completed the ceremony, and later went looking for the shepherd to pay him. They were not able to find him. They were very happy to have been able to fulfill the commandment, offering the Paschal sacrifice.

There has never been a time when the people of Israel did not sacrifice the Passover *qorban*!

— Badri Cohen

Badri Cohen lives in the Samaritan community of Kiryat Luza, near the summit of Mount Gerizim, above modern Nablus, biblical Shechem. The wife of a communal prayer leader, a *ḥazzan*, and daughter of a high priest, Badri is herself a leader of the Samari-

tan people (Figure 0.3). The story translated here from her spoken Arabic was collected and edited by filmmaker Moshe Alafi as part of the YU Israelite Samaritans Project. Badri's tale is set in a simpler, even mythic, time. It happened when "she was perhaps one year old," and before the Samaritan Passover was transformed into a tourist attraction during the early decades of the twentieth century. It encapsulates the spiritual and historical experience of the Samaritans, a window into this tightly patriarchal culture, as told to Badri by her "father and older brothers." These *kohanim*, elite members of the priestly class caste, we are told, were leading participants in this unfolding drama.

The tale takes place in the city of Nablus and upon holy Mount Gerizim, the "blessed mountain," which is believed by the Samaritans to have been "chosen by God" above all others (Figure 0.4). It is set at Passover, the high point of the Samaritan calendar, when the entire community ascends to the peak of Gerizim to slaughter, roast, and eat the Passover sacrifice—the *qorban*. Badri today lives near the sacrifice compound (Figure 0.5-6). She was filmed in the community center, which was built between the sacrificial compound and the synagogue. The entire Nablus Samaritan community relocated here as a result of difficulties experienced in Nablus during the Intifada of 1987.

This is a tale of deprivation, persecution, faith, and deliverance —typical of stories passed from generation to generation by "the people of Israel"—as Badri refers to the Samaritans. These descendants of the biblical Northern Kingdom of Israel, the capital of which was in *Shomron*, Samaria, refer to themselves as the *Shemarim*—"the guardians" of the Torah. In this way, they transform the geographical designation used by outsiders, *Shomronim*, "Samaritans." Their will to "keep" the biblical commandments, especially to perform the Paschal sacrifice atop the Holy Mountain, is central to their identity.

Three events appear "suddenly" in our highly structured narrative. Each marks a "sudden" transition, seemingly out of the blue. In the first, a shepherd appears, his presence announced by bells worn by his sheep to track their locations. He supplies sheep for the sac-

© STEVEN FINE, 2022 | DOI:10.1163/9789004466913_002

ⵣⵎⵇⵢⵝⵕ 1

0.5   Passover Prayers on Mount Gerizim.
Photograph by the American Colony
Photographic Department, 1914 (G. Eric
and Edith Matson Photograph Collection,
Library of Congress).

   ꚋꚏꚍꚍꚏꚅ

0.6 The Passover Sacrifice, Burning the Entrails, Kiryat Luza, Mount Gerizim, 2015 (Photograph by Ori Orhof).

0.7 El-Khirbe Synagogue Mosaic, fifth century (Museum of the Good Samaritan, photograph by Steven Fine).

rest on Mount Gerizim. Stefan Schorch continues this focus upon "the blessed mountain" with a warning: "'Woe to Those Who Exchanged the Truth for a Lie, When They Choose for Themselves a Different Place': Samaritan Perspectives on the Samaritan–Jewish Split." It was this biblical "parting of the ways," Samaritans believe, that set the northern Israelites and the southern Judeans on vastly different trajectories—Samaritans venerating Mount Gerizim, and Jews venerating Mount Zion and Jerusalem.

Our volume then turns to ways that Jews interacted with the Samaritans in the Greco-Roman world, from the Hasmoneans to the end of antiquity. Joseph L. Angel opens with "'Kinsmen' or an 'Alien Race?': Jews and Samaritans from the Hasmoneans to the Mishnah." Relations between Jews and Samaritans were decidedly complex during this period, ranging from warlike contempt and destruction of the Samaritan "Temple" on Mount Gerizim by John Hyrcanus I in 111–110 BCE, followed by the destruction of the Jerusalem Temple in 70 CE, followed by positive acceptance of the Samaritans by early rabbis. This complexity is further explored by R. Steven Notley and Jeffrey P. García in "'But a Samaritan … Had Compassion': Jesus, Early Christianity, and the Samaritans," which interprets this relationship through the prism of the early followers of Jesus of Nazareth. Finally, Shana Strauch Schick and I bring us to the end of this long period with "'Do You Have an Onion?': Rabbis and Samaritans in Late Antiquity," reading rabbinic texts edited under Christian Rome and early Islam against the grain to uncover complex and very human relationships between rabbis, regular Jews, and Samaritans.

The next two articles focus on the inner life of the Samaritans during late antiquity and beyond, with emphasis on the ancient synagogue and the Samaritans' celebration of the fall festival of Sukkot ("Tabernacles"). In "'A Place in which to Read, to Interpret and to Hear Petitions': Samaritan Synagogues," I present this institution from its earliest appearance during the Hellenistic period to the present read through the lenses of Samaritan literary sources, archeological discoveries, and modern fieldwork (Figure 0.7). In "Sukkot in the Garden of Eden: Liturgy, Christianity, and the Bronze Bird on Mount Gerizim," Laura Lieber marshals late antique literature and poetry to explore the complexities of Samaritan life under Christian Rome and the continuing implications of that experience for the Samaritan celebration of Sukkot.

The profound changes in the lives of Samaritans, Jews, and Christians that were wrought by the coming of Islam is the subject of Daniel Boušek's "'This Covenant of Peace for the Samaritans': The Prophet Muhammad's Encounter with a Samaritan, a Jew, and a Christian." Stories of this pact are told by all three communities, this "covenant" guaranteeing their status as "peoples of the book"—and hence their survival. For Samaritans, this status has always been precarious. Jesse Abelman then turns to Jewish interaction with the Samaritans in "'These Are the Jews of Shomron who Are Called Samaritans': Jews and Samaritans in the High Middle Ages," which explores day-to-day interactions during this period that are preserved in Jewish sources. Finally, Matthew Chalmers brings us into the Early Modern period and to the brink of the twentieth century with

0.8 Jacob son of Uzzi, "This is the Image of the Holy Tabernacle," Tabernacle Drawing, Nablus, early twentieth century. A note in English in the left bottom corner identifies the artist as "Jacob son of Shafeek son of Jacob, the high priest in Nablus (The Bernard Museum of Judaica of Congregation Emanu-El of the City of New York).

ײﬦﬤ﬩ﬡﬧﬦﬡ

"'Do You Have the Chronicles of the Kings of Samaria?': Jewish Knowledge, Christian Hebraists, and the European 'Discovery' of the Samaritans."

Our sources multiply once we reach the nineteenth century, when European interest in the Samaritans exploded. We set the stage with Reuven Gafni's "Two Minorities on the Brink: Jews and Samaritans in Nineteenth-Century Nablus," which describes the complexities of survival for Samaritans during this period, how they dealt with the threat of extinction, and the aid they received from both Europeans and the chief rabbi of Jerusalem that helped them avoid this fate. This event profoundly changed Jewish–Samaritan relations, preparing the way for Zionist support decades later. In "'The Priest Salama Son of Ghazal and the Tailors': Palestinian Arab Justice and the Samaritans," Haseeb Shehadeh presents a thick description that encompasses both the complex world of its nineteenth-century protagonist in Ottoman Nablus and of a twentieth-century Samaritan storyteller under British Mandatory Palestine, and under Jordanian and Israeli rule. In "And We Shall be One People": Abraham Firkovich, Karaism, and the Samaritans," Golda Akhiezer introduces one of the most colorful characters to encounter the Samaritans during the nineteenth century. Akhiezer explores Firkovich's fraught and fascinating relationship with both the Samaritans—whom he saw as kinsmen—and other Jews. Yitzchak Schwartz then describes interventions in Samaritan life by American Protestants near the turn of the twentieth century in "Samaritans on the American Protestant Mind: William Barton, Edward Warren, and the American Samaritan Committee." Finally, in "'Joined at Last': Moses Gaster and the Samaritans," Katharina E. Keim presents modern Jewish cultural interest in the Samaritans through the lens of one of the most important Jewish scholars of his age, who corresponded extensively with the legendary high priest Jacob son of Aaron (Figure 0.9).

The next cluster of articles explores aspects of the Samaritan experience with Zionism and modern Israel, bringing our exploration to the present. The late Israel Sedaka's article, "To This Day the Samaritans have Never Left Shechem and Mount Gerizim: Izhak Ben-Zvi, David Ben-Gurion, and the Samaritans," presents relations between the Israeli Samaritan community from an Israeli Samaritan perspective. David Selis and I then explore the profound changes caused by the 1967 Six-Day War through the Passover sacrifice ceremony. In "Passover, 1968: Johanna Spector, Israeli Civil Religion, and the Ethnographic Study of the Samaritans," we present this transition as experienced by American ethnographer Johanna Spector. Dina Stein then explores the real complexities of Samaritans becoming modern Israelis with "Samaritan Stories in the Israel Folktale Archives: Poetics and Cultural Exchange in Modern Israel." Changes in the relationship between the Samaritans and the modern state were profound and expressed in the ways that they told and recorded their precious stories. This complexity is further shown in "A 'Samaritan Renaissance': The Tsedaka Legacy and the Samaritan Community in Israel," in which I translate pieces of an obituary written by the late folklorist Dov Noy for Samaritan leader and scholar Ratson Tsedaka, a primary agent in the formation of modern Israeli Samaritan culture. I then continue with the work of Ratson's sons, Benyamim and Yefet, who, like their father, are essential bridges and agents of contemporary Israeli Samaritan culture. This section closes where our volume began, with six stories told to us by contemporary elders of the Samaritan people, collected by Moshe Alafi and preserved here for posterity.

In the final section, Moshe Alafi and I reflect upon our work together. We begin with Moshe Alafi's "Reflections of a Documentary Filmmaker," which presents Alafi's personal experiences while embedded with the Samaritans throughout this project. In 2020, at the height of the COVID-19 ordeal, a remarkable international group of Jewish artists assembled virtually, studied the content of our project and then set out to create art. In "Contemporary Jewish Artists Encounter Samaritan Culture: A Visual Essay," Richard McBee and I curate some of the works these artists produced. We close this volume with my own reflections, called "Why the Samaritans?" In it, I consider questions that I have fielded from people of diverse backgrounds, and share my personal experiences and responses.

Though I have divided our articles into thematic groups in this introduction, the volume itself presents a single (if multi-lane) "path" through the thicket of sources and approaches that make up Samaritan Studies. Our collective contribution intentionally crosses temporal boundaries in our attempt to capture the uniqueness of each source and moment, and, at the same time, to express the bonds that connect Samaritan culture and our own. Is this volume a complete history of the Samaritans? Absolutely not. There is so much more to say! Like a Samaritan chronicler, who updates his work even as he "copies" it—"forgetting" recent strife and emphasizing recent successes—we began at the beginning of Samaritan sacred time, and, with him, have moved forward with our own stories, interests, and scholarly methods to (and from) our own moment (Figure 0.10, 11, 12).

0.9 Ephraim Moses Lilien, *The Samaritan High Priest*, 1906-1914 (Tel Aviv Museum of Art, Gift of Schocken Family).

0.10 Naila daughter of Yasmin and Uri Tsedaka studying the Torah in the Supplementary Afternoon School with Teacher Ḥefetz Marḥiv, Kiryat Luza, Mount Gerizim, 2019 (Photograph by Moshe Alafi).

0.11 Yitzhak and his son Pinḥas Cohen Study the Torah in the Holon Synagogue (Photograph by Moshe Alafi).

labat	ל		alaf	א	
meem	מ		bit	ב	
noon	נ		gaman	ג	
singat	ס		dalat	ד	
een	ע		iy	ה	
fee	פ		ba	ו	
tsadi	צ		zen	ז	
koof	ק		eet	ח	
reesh	ר		teet	ט	
shan	ש		yoot	י	
taf	ת		kaf	כ	

0.12 The Samaritan Alphabet, used for both Hebrew and Aramaic, with contemporary Samaritan pronunciations (Steven Fine).

0.13 Oil Lamp with Image of a Scroll on Two Staves, Inscribed in Samaritan Hebrew, "Blessed is His Name Eternally," *Barukh Shemo le-Olam,* Samaria (?), late third-late fifth century CE. Bells (?) suspended from a horizontal above the scroll. Left: Torah shrine with a curtain pulled to the right (?); Right: amphora resting on a tripod (David and Jemima Jeselsohn Collection, Zurich, Switzerland).

1

"The Consolation of Souls, the Assurer of Hearts, and the Certainty of Truth": The Abisha Scroll

STEVEN FINE

Pinḥas, his son and successor [son of Eleazar son of Aaron the high priest] was a strong ruler, widely esteemed and very distinguished. It was he who worked out the calculation of the dimensions of the latitude of Mount Gerizim, viz. 14 hours and five ninths of an hour, in the days of his father in the thirteenth year of the kingdom of Israel in the land of Canaan.

It was in the above-mentioned year that Abisha son of Pinḥas wrote out the Holy Book which is now to be found in Nablus, under God's protection, in the safekeeping of our lord the high priest Pinḥas, may God repeatedly bless him and lengthen the number of his days, by whose means God made known its whereabouts, after its disappearance and its being hidden from his predecessors in the high priesthood. This is the good news—if God so wills it—which will reveal the return of the *Radwan* [the period of Divine favor] in his day and in the days of his children who are steadfast in the service of this Book which is the consolation of souls, the assurer of hearts and the certainty of truth handed down by means of the Samaritan community—may Almighty God give them increase. In this year, it was again uncovered on the Sabbath of the Feast of Tabernacles, This was a marvelous occasion, All the assembled present witnessed the *tashqil* [the colophon] which it contained. It commences at "and it will be (that the Lord your God) will bring you" which follows "Hear O Israel" and is as follows:

> I, Abisha, son of Pinḥas son of Eleazar, son of Aaron the priest upon whom be the *Radwan* of the Lord and his Glory I wrote out the Book of Holiness at the entrance to the Tent of Meeting on Mount Gerizim in the thirteenth year of the dominion of the sons of Israel over the land of Canaan, to its borders around it. I give praise to the Lord.

This illustrious Book represents the *Radwan*. Whoever is sincere in seeking something in its presence, or if absent from it asks its help with heart and soul, he will be heard, and his needs will be satisfied. We beseech Almighty God to help us through its special dignity, its blessing and the blessing of its ministers and their noble descendants.

— *The Chronicle of Abu l-Fath*, Chapter 9[1]

The Abisha Scroll—*Mikhtav Abisha* in Hebrew—rests on a silk cloth embroidered with dedicatory inscriptions. It is set on a low wooden stand. Standing beside it is a Samaritan priest—usually the high priest—bearded and robed, with a red hat on his head. Sometimes two priests appear, one on each side of the scroll; in other photographs, the single priest is sitting. The Torah scroll is open, its ancient Hebrew letters—preserved today only by the Samaritans—visible but not readable. The priest's face is stern and serious, as is appropriate when approaching God's revelation—and *de rigueur* in nineteenth- and early-twentieth-century portraits. This gravitas is enhanced by the shining brass container that protects the scroll and the lavish textiles embroidered in an exotic script in which it is wrapped and upon which it rests. In a real sense, the priest and the scroll are a single inseparable icon.

Drawings and then photographs of the priest with the Torah Scroll were spread across the world in print, projected on walls from glass magic lantern slides, mailed as postcards, and experienced with three-dimensional realism when viewed on stereoscope slides (Figures 1.1, 2). On a relatively early visit to the Samaritan synagogue in Nablus, biblical Shechem, in 1855, Mary Elizabeth Rogers recalled that, after being shown the Abisha Scroll by the high priest Salama ben Tabia (reigned 1787–1855), "at my request Selameh sat down for a little while, holding it in his hands, that I might sketch it and him."[2] In 1869, German-British artist Carl Haag visited Nablus, creating a much copied painting of "The High Priest at Nablus Holding the Pentateuch" (Figure 1.3). The Christmas Supplement of the London Illustrated News of December 18, 1869, describes the Scroll and painting in great detail:[3]

> The artist visited the synagogue of the Samaritans at Nablus during his visit to Palestine; and being much impressed by the noble bearing and handsome, intelligent, expressive Semitic countenance of the high priest, Amram, sought an introduction through his friend, Dr. George Rosen, then accredited as Prussian Consul to Jerusalem, but at the time staying at Nablus. The result was that Mr. Haag was not only permitted to take his easel into the synagogue for the purpose of sketching the place, but

the Kahaen [priest] stood in person, in his robes and the Pentateuch in his hand, to enable the artist to make a large finished study of him.

The article claims that "the picture is consequently authentic, equally as regards the portraiture and accessories." This is certainly correct, showing the historic 1509/10 Torah curtain (Figure 2.3) and a Torah case that the Samaritans call "the ark [aron] of the breasts" owing to the nine protrusions on its sides.[4] The article suggests that Amram son of Salama (reigned 1855–1874) held the Abisha Scroll, which is incorrect. With the level of access he clearly had, Haag certainly chose the "ark of the breasts" for its highly articulated and interesting surface decoration. Samaritans often showed outsiders seeking Abisha other, less precious, scrolls.

Pilgrims of all sorts would make their way to Nablus to visit the Samaritans during their passage between Jerusalem and the Galilee. Perhaps the most famous was Albert Edward, the Prince of Wales (later Edward VII). On April 12, 1862, Albert and his entourage observed the Passover sacrifice. He reported in his diary that "six sheep were killed." The next day, Bertie, as he was called, reported that he "went into the synagogue where some of the same people [we] saw yesterday showed us 3 very old scrolls of the Pentateuch on parchment." The Abisha Scroll was photographed by the accompanying photographer, Francis Bedford—apparently for the first time (Figure 1.4).[5] All of this royal attention certainly helped raise the profile of the Samaritans across the English-speaking world. This visit was likely arranged by James Finn, the British Consul in Jerusalem, who was something of a self-appointed protector of the Samaritans.

Images of the Scroll spread widely. Tourist literature, especially Mark Twain's best-seller *The Innocents Abroad* (1867), mediated the experience.[6] Like most visitors, Twain focused on the Abisha Scroll, though with his typical wit: "Carefully preserved among the sacred archives of this curious community is a MSS. [manuscript] copy of the ancient Jewish [sic] law, which is said to be the oldest document on earth. It is written on vellum, and is some four or five thousand years old." Nothing but bucksheesh can purchase a sight." Satisfying European curiosity, Samaritans clearly valued the income from such visits, and, perhaps more importantly, the protection afforded them by the biblically inspired European powers.

SEEING THE ABISHA SCROLL

Looking at these images, Samaritans see the elders of their community beside their most important Torah scroll—both statements of authority and something close to family portraits—lovingly curated in their homes, at the Samaritan Museum on Mount Gerizim and in Benyamim Tsedaka's weekly magazine, *A.B. – The Samaritans News*. The priest watching over the Scroll is a cipher for everything Samaritan. Samaritans do not identify themselves by locale, as the people of Samaria. Rather, they are the *Shemarim*, those who keep and "guard" (*shomer*) the Torah—and there is no Torah scroll more emblematic than the Abisha Scroll.

Westerners have had very different visions of the Samaritans. Modern European contact with the Samaritans began during the

Samaritan Highpriest and scroll.
Samaritanischer Hoher Priester und Gesetzes-Rolle.
Grand Rabbin Samaritain et décalogue.

1.1 *Samaritan Highpriest and Scroll*, Jacob son of Aaron (reigned 1874–1916), Postcard, Edition Fr. Vester and Co., Jerusalem, no. 41, after 1907 (Collection of Leah and Steven Fine, New York).

seventeenth century. From first contact until nearly the present, Samaritans were seen and often treated as living "fossils" of the biblical past—the "Good Samaritan" of the Gospels incarnate. Twain well reflects this attitude: "I found myself gazing at any straggling scion of this strange race with a riveted fascination, just as one would stare at a living mastodon, or a megatherium that had moved in the grey dawn of creation and seen the wonders of that mysterious world that was before the flood." Through photography, people who could not make their way to the Holy Land could see what Twain saw, often mediated through Twain's popular travel log itself.

For Western Christian scholars, the Samaritan Pentateuch (Samaritans recognize no other book as scripture) has functioned since the Enlightenment as evidence for scripture beyond the Jewish Mas-

1.2 "Samaritan High Priest and Old Pentateuch Roll at Shechem, Palestine," Jacob son of Aaron (reigned 1874–1916), Stereoscope slide, Keystone View Company, Underwood and Underwood Publishers, ca. 1900 (Courtesy California Museum of Photography, University of California, Riverside. Gift of Mr. and Mrs. Arnold M. Gilbert).

oretic text. It has been taken to substantiate biblical readings found in the Septuagint translation of the original Hebrew of the Bible into Greek. Long ago abandoned by Jews, since antiquity the Septuagint has been the standard text of the Old Testament of the Orthodox Church. European and American libraries eagerly purchased Samaritan books—through illegitimate and legitimate means. The impoverished Samaritans reluctantly sold them. During the second half of nineteenth century, they earned a meager livelihood by copying and selling manuscripts for this market. Again, Twain: "Speaking of this MSS [the Abisha Scroll] reminds me that I procured from the high-priest of this ancient Samaritan community [Amram son of Salama], at great expense, a secret document of still higher antiquity and far more extraordinary interest, which I propose to publish as soon as I have finished translating it." Secret or esoteric knowledge is often ascribed to the Samaritans, their books, and their Hebrew script—amulets written in Samaritan script by priests are sought after even today. Many of the Samaritan books and artifacts assembled in our exhibition were originally procured in similar purchases, and souvenirs were created to fulfill tourists' appetites at various levels of expense. More than four thousand books were sold. Despite the concerted efforts of Western book collectors, the Abisha Scroll has never been for sale. It has been and continues to be vigorously protected.

Secularizing Western Jews looking at these same photographs might have been a bit more reticent. Traditional enmity between Jews and Samaritans has led to complex relations. Samaritans referred to Jerusalem with the taunt *Arur Shalem* ("Cursed Shalem")—even in books sold to Jews. Since antiquity, Jews have called Samaritans *Kutim* ("Cutheans")—mostly rejecting the Samaritans as members of the people of Israel. Curious about differences between Jewish and Samaritan texts, both biblical and postbiblical, modern Jewish scholars turned to Samaritan studies beginning around 1851 with Raphael Kirchheim's *Karme Shomron.* Differences between the Samaritan Torah and the Jewish Torah were downplayed by *fin-de-siècle* Jewish culturalists, nationalists, and reformers eager for relationships with the Samaritans and their high priest. These people saw in the latter a biblical sage with a very Jewish-looking scroll—a living leader of the "ten lost tribes."

Some Protestants and Zionists took the next step: befriending, corresponding with, and providing economic support for the then destitute Samaritans. Some knew the priests of our photographs personally—especially the high priest Jacob son of Aaron (Figures 0.9, 1.1, 2, 8, 15.1, 16.4, 23.4, 5). A small number of nineteenth-century Christian scholars studied with the Samaritans for a number of months. Correspondents included the American Protestant E.K. Warren, who valiantly worked to help the community and had the Abisha Scroll photographed for the first time. Another was folklorist, rabbi, and early Zionist leader Moses Gaster, who corresponded with Aaron using a specially built Samaritan-Jewish typewriter (Figure 16.3). Izhak Ben-Zvi, later the second president of Israel

1.3 Carl Haag, *Kaheen Amram— The High Priest of the Samaritans*, 1869, watercolor (Israel Museum, Courtesy of Leicester Galleries).

THE ABISHA SCROLL ·ᛃᛘᛩᛑᛂᛝᛃᚱᛉ 19

(1952–1963), was also a major scholar of Samaritanism and benefactor of the Samaritans. Ben-Zvi befriended the Samaritans. As a young man, he helped to lessen a critical shortage of brides by helping Samaritans in Ottoman Jaffa find Jewish wives. During the Jordanian period (1948–1967), as a Knesset member and later as president of Israel, he helped procure life-saving funds for the community in Nablus through the American Jewish Joint Distribution Committee (at first through the Red Cross). Jacob son of Aaron knew them all during his very long forty-two-year tenure as high priest (1874–1916) and sought good advantage through these Westerners for the good of his community. He even made a fundraising trip to England—the second Samaritan to do so—and his memoirs were published in English. It is no wonder that the photogenic Jacob appears in so many of the early photographs. He was a media star!

THE SIGNIFICANCE OF THE ABISHA SCROLL

The story of the Abisha Scroll, ascribed to Abisha, son of Eleazar, son of Aaron the Priest sitting at the gate of the biblical Tabernacle thirteen years after the Children of Israel entered the Holy Land under Joshua son of Nun, is central to Samaritan self-understanding. Modern priests are his spiritual descendants. Samaritans believe that before 1624, when the last descendant of Aaron died, the high priests were physical descendants of Aaron, the brother of Moses. Scrolls and codices were written on animal skins prepared by priests who needed to be purified of contact with the dead through the ashes of the biblical red heifer (Numbers 19:2–6). Since then, without Aaronite priests, this mode of purification has ended. All books are written on paper, making scrolls and codices copied before 1624 all the more precious.

In that year, Levitical families that trace themselves to the biblical Uziel son of Kehat, Aaron's uncle, took up the priesthood. The "priest" photographed, then, is not from the family of Aaron and Moses. He is not a linear descendant of Abisha, Aaron's grandson. Contemporary high priests are stand-ins, the oldest Levites of a particular family. This distinction, obvious to all Samaritans, is often unclear to outsiders—adding yet another difference between what Westerners and Samaritans "see" when they look upon the venerated priests. In reality, Samaritans downplay this inferior lineage. The disruption of the priestly line of Aaron is another result of the current age of Divine *Fanuta* ("disfavor") and awaits redemption in a restored *Radwan*, a "time of favor." Still, the priest's authority comes with his high Levitical lineage, learning, liturgical function, and communal standing. While not a descendant of Aaron, the high priest acts and looks the part, and, most importantly, he is treated accordingly.

Images of the high priest together with the Scroll assert continuity from the priests who served in the biblical Tabernacle to the present, through the medium of the holy writ. The colophon (*tasqil*) of the Abisha Scroll, correctly transcribed by Abu l-Fath, asserts this continuity:

> I am Abisha, son of Pinḥas, son of Eleazar, son of Aaron the Priest, on them the favor of the Lord and his glory. I wrote this holy book in the door of the tent of meeting on Mount Gerizim in the thirteenth year

of the dominion of the Children of Israel over the land of Canaan to its boundaries roundabout. I praise the Lord.

The Abisha Scroll with its unique pedigree is the physical connection and guarantor of the Sinai revelation, and the high priest is its authoritative interpreter. This manuscript is a bridge from the idyllic biblical days of divine favor, the *Radwan*, through the current days of cursedness, the *Fanuta*, and on to a better eschatological future when the redeemer, the *Tahab*, will "return" and restore the Tabernacle from its hiding place on Mount Gerizim. The Scroll is a tangible and precious legacy. It is the physical presence of the age of divine favor, a scroll with the power to help those in need. The colophon of the Abisha Scroll is woven into the body of the Torah text itself, composed of letters separated out and read vertically down the manuscript column. It is intimately associated with the story told in the *Kitub al-Tarikh*, which is the starting point for this article. This chronicle of Samaritan history was edited by Abu l-Fath son of Abu l-Hasan in 1355 in Nablus at the request of the high priest Aaron. This chronicle was written at a moment of turmoil in the Holy Land. Crusader invasion, Islamic reconquist, and much slaughter had set the tenor of the age—which followed the equally tumultuous "Age of Transition" from Christian Rome to the new Islamic empire. After the Crusades, Jewish and Christian pilgrims developed renewed interest in the Holy Land, and (re)inscribed their stories upon it, sometimes engaging with the Samaritans. *The Chronicle of Abu l-Fath* unified the textual record of the Samaritan past into one Arabic-language history. A product of what scholars call the "Samaritan Renaissance" of the fourteenth century, this chronicle is a consistent history that grounds the Samaritans in their place and social position by consolidating historic memory. The Abisha Scroll grounds this narrative. Abu l-Fath begins by recounting biblical history from creation to Joshua and the settlement of the tribes of Israel in the Promised Land and then introduces the story of the Abisha Scroll. His hero, with whom he clearly identifies, was a pious scribe of the Torah, a priest of the line of Aaron, who copied and transmitted the Torah to future generations. Like Saadia Gaon's Rabbanite Arabic translation of the Pentateuch (a book read and copied by Samaritans), and Karaite and Christian commentaries on sacred texts and traditions, Abu l-Fath wrote in the prestige language of his day, Arabic. In an age when the fixing of scriptural manuscripts and accuracy was an obsession and guarantor of continuity, legitimacy, and authority for Jews, Christians, and Muslims, the Samaritans developed their own voice and cadence.

Beyond the desire for a more organized history for internal use, however, Samaritan survival depended upon them being classified as a "People of the Book" by the Islamic rulers, and not as idolaters. It was important, then, to have an authoritative rendering of their story in Arabic, one that included a covenant with Muhammad that is similar to those he made with Jews and Christians. "Peoples of the Book" held a protected if subservient status in Islamic law, and in principle were not subject to the persecution enacted against "idolaters." Samaritans have always had an ambiguous standing in this regard, and often suffered for this ambiguity. In 1842, for example, the community was saved from destruction by local Muslims through the intervention of a Jerusalem rabbi, who convinced the Turkish authorities that the Samaritans were, indeed, "a branch of the Children of Israel who acknowledge the truth of the Torah," and hence should be protected.[7]

The scribes of the Abisha Scroll spliced together some of the oldest and most worn fragments of medieval manuscripts of the Torah that they possessed into this one complete manuscript. Moses Gaster, who saw the Scroll, says that "it consists mainly of a mass of patches, held together by a backing."[8] At least six distinct scribes wrote or repaired the Scroll over at least eight hundred years. Two of them are mentioned by name, one of whom is Hassebi son of Joseph son of Abraham, who wrote the last column of the Torah in the sixteenth century. Restoration continued through the eighteenth century, and some columns were patched in the nineteenth. Historian Alan D. Crown suggests that a large part of the manuscript was written in Nablus around 1149 CE and may be the work of a scribe known as Mitpasia son of Metuhia.[9] Already during the first half of the nineteenth century, Western scholars doubted the antiquity of Abisha. Twain correctly reported that "its fame is somewhat dimmed in these latter days, because of the doubts so many authors of Palestine travels have felt themselves privileged to cast upon it." None of this was relevant to the Samaritans and their devotion to the Abisha Scroll.

The complete Abisha Scroll is the work of generations of scribes, a work of assembling and repairing manuscript fragments into a unified whole over many lifetimes. The earliest Samaritan chronicle known as the *Tulidah* (twelfth century) engages the sorry state of the Abisha Scroll, explaining that an earthquake hit the Holy Land as the Samaritans were conducting a festival procession up Mount Gerizim—clearly a sign of divine disfavor. The high priest carrying the Scroll, the *Tulidah* tells us, was struck with illness, and the Scroll case fell open. This metal case, called an *aron* after the Ark of the Covenant (*aron ha-berit*), was stored in the biblical Tabernacle—hidden by God on Mount Gerizim. The Scroll was lifted by the fast winds at the summit of "the blessed mountain" (as they call it) and ripped. Only the Books of Numbers and Deuteronomy survived this traumatic ordeal. On the following Sukkot festival, the restored Abisha Scroll was exhibited to the community on the Sabbath, and the colophon, the *tasqil*, was seen by all. Sukkot is the biblically ordained festival of the dedication of the Tabernacle, re-dedication clearly being the intention of Abu l-Fath in his story. This story resonates with the discovery of "the scroll of the Torah in the Temple of the Lord" discovered in the time of Josiah, King of Judah, that sparked a major religious renewal in Jerusalem (2 Kings 22:8). Abu l-Fath's story of antiquity and discovery, read together with the *Tulidah*'s tale of loss, well expresses the multigenerational project of maintaining and preserving the Abisha Scroll, and explains the visibly poor state of the restored manuscript. The history of the Scroll parallels the composition of its literary sister, *The Chronicle of Abu l-Fath*, which also brings together fragments of Samaritan memory from a number of manuscripts into a unified narrative of biblical proportions.

THE SAMARITAN PENTATEUCH

The Samaritan Torah, of which the Abisha Scroll is an early manuscript, has been preserved since the Middle Ages in numerous scrolls and later codices. It is substantially the same as the Masoretic text preserved by Jews (the earliest copy of which dates to the ninth century) and the Hebrew text that stands behind the Septuagint (third century BCE). That said, there are many places where the Samaritan text differs from both of these ancient Jewish textual witnesses. Since the discovery of the Dead Sea Scrolls, beginning in 1947, scholars have come to understand that the biblical text was somewhat fluid during the later Second Temple period, and that versions related to the Jewish Masoretic, the Greek Septuagint, and the Samaritan texts existed simultaneously and were used broadly during this period. The Samaritans preserve a version that supports and reinforces their historical claims. Thus, "the place that the Lord will choose" of the Masoretic and Septuagint versions of Deuteronomy is "the place that God has chosen"—Mount Gerizim—in the Samaritan version. Where for Jews, Mount Zion in Jerusalem was "chosen" by the time of David—and so the anticipation of a chosen mountain is embedded in Jewish versions—for Samaritans, Mount Gerizim had been "chosen" by God already in the time of the Patriarchs. According to Genesis 12:6–7, at Shechem Abram "built an altar to the Lord who had appeared to him … and had given that land to his descendants." The Masoretic text and the Septuagint preserve a version of Deuteronomy 27:4 that designates Mount Ebal, on the northern side of modern Nablus, opposite Mount Gerizim, as the place where twelve stones, plastered and inscribed with "this Torah" were to be set up, an altar built, and sacrifices offered. The Samaritans preserve a version that places the stones and the altar on Mount Gerizim, the "mountain of blessings"—the one that God "chose" as His own. Samaritans write Mount Gerizim as one word, *Hargerizim*. This spelling appears as early as 2 Maccabees 5:23 and 6:2 (late second century BCE), on an inscription from the island of Delos, and on a piece of papyrus written in early Hebrew script that was discovered on Masada[10]— but does not appear in later Jewish texts. This conflation of "Mount" and "Gerizim" into one word is a Second Temple period phenomenon. It parallels the New Testament Armageddon, *Har Megiddo*—Mount Megiddo, the place of the final battle of Revelation 16:16. By late antiquity, though, the single word version was a distinctly Samaritan form, an identity marker. Almost none of the differences between the Samaritan Pentateuch and the other biblical versions began with the Samaritans. They were part of the common heritage of Israel, which was preserved in its diversity by these three traditions, and our knowledge was enriched by the Dead Sea Scrolls. The versions chosen and preserved by the Samaritans fit the theological and cultural ethos of their community.

The Dead Sea library preserves fragments of biblical scrolls in the Paleo-Hebrew script that we associate with early Samaritan writings. Occasionally, Jews used this script on coins, in inscriptions, and to signify the special holiness of the Divine name, the Tetragrammaton. Samaritan script is a continuation of this ancient script for their sacred texts, for their marriage contracts, and for more secular purposes. To make the story more complicated, Samaritans occasionally used the later Persian period square script adopted by Jews for their

1.5 Pilgrimage to Mount Gerizim, Passover, 2020 (Photograph by Ori Orhof).

1.6 Pinḥas Cohen of Holon on *Givat Olam*, the "Eternal Hill," where the biblical Tabernacle rested on Mount Gerizim, Passover morning, 2019 (Photograph by Moshe Alafi).

1.7 Passover Prayers on Mount Gerizim, Cantor Matzliaḥ (Najah) Cohen waves a Torah scroll as a sign of blessing. The scroll case was donated by Ḥefetz and Yiftaḥ, the sons of Marḥiv the Marḥivi and produced in Nablus, is a homage to the *Ark of the Images* that houses the Abisha Scroll (Photograph by Eitan Bino).

sacred texts for correspondence. Dedicatory inscriptions found in their Sacrificial Compound on Mount Gerizim (called a temple by non-Samaritans and rarely by Samaritans) date before 111–110 BCE, when the Hasmonean John Hyrcanus I marched northward from Jerusalem and destroyed their holy place (an event that was celebrated in first-century Jerusalem), but apparently not after. A Samaritan tradition remembers that, during a Judean invasion led by "King Simon" (possibly Simon the Maccabee) the Samaritans fled, except for a small group that stayed in Shechem and was persecuted.[11] The Abisha Scroll, it is said, was hidden away in Shechem, buried in a clay pot for safe-keeping—reminiscent of the Dead Sea Scroll jars discovered in Qumran. The script choices of the Samaritans and the Jews were pretty much fixed by the first century. Both options were part of the commonly shared Israelite tradition; choice of script, textual differences, and even word spelling were adopted by Samaritans to express their distinctive version of Israelite religion, which, most importantly, included the centrality of Mount Gerizim (Figure 1.5).

Only once did the Samaritans implant their doctrine in the biblical text itself through an explicit addition to the text. Numbering the Ten Commandments differently from other communities, they included a unique tenth commandment:

It shall be when your God will bring you to the Canaanite land, which you are going to inherit, you shall set yourself up great stones, and plaster them with plaster, and you shall write on them all the words of this law. It shall be, when you are passed over the Jordan, that you shall set up these stones, which I command you this day, in Mount Gerizim. There shall you build an altar to the Lord your God, an altar of stones: you shall lift up no iron tool on them. You shall build the altar of the Lord your God of uncut stones; and you shall offer burnt offerings thereon to the Lord your God: and you shall sacrifice peace-offerings, and shall eat there; and you shall rejoice before the Lord your God. That mount beyond the Jordan, behind the way of the going down of the sun, in the land of the Canaanites who dwell in the Arabah, over against Gilgal, beside the oaks of Moreh, against Shechem (Nablus).

Visitors to Mount Gerizim today are shown the twelve stones of Deuteronomy 27, which were once plastered, they believe, and inscribed with "this Torah." They can see the place of the Binding of Isaac and the resting place of the Tabernacle (Figure 1.6), which is where Abisha wrote the scroll. On festivals, priests hold Torah scrolls high and bless the people (Figure 1.7, 8, 9). The Abisha Scroll, however, is kept safe in the synagogue on Mount Gerizim—lest this

1.9 "The Samaritans," Israel Postage Stamp. Designer: David Pessah. Image based upon an American Colony Photograph, 1914. First Day Cancellation, Holon, February 2, 1992. Legend: Deuteronomy 11:29: "You shall offer the blessing on Mount Gerizim."(Collection of Leah and Steven Fine, New York).

1.10 *The Tulidah*, a Samaritan Chronicle, ca. 1200; Nablus, 1872. Scribe: Jacob son of Marḥiv. The pastedown commemorates modern donations to the Nablus Synagogue (Yeshiva University, Mendel Gottesman Library, Joshua Finkel Collection).

fragile manuscript fall again and be damaged or stolen. It is never taken out of its glass case, even on major festivals, when it is used to bless the people in the synagogue. This reconstructed scroll is an apt metaphor for the imperfect state of the world from the great schism of the Israelite tribes until the messianic coming of the Moses-like *Tahab,* "he who will return" the *Radwan,* the age of Divine favor. Even in its imperfect state, the Abisha Scroll is seen by Samaritans as a bridge from Moses and Aaron to that "return." It is the guarantor of religious truth.

INTO THE MODERN WORLD

Nineteenth-century manuscripts of the *Tulidah,* written in a mixture of Aramaic and Hebrew (a dialect called "Samaritan" by Western scholars) in Samaritan script mention the Abisha Scroll toward the end. This mention was added in the very last phase of composition, as each generation updated the chronicle to include itself. One of these manuscripts is preserved in Yeshiva University's Gottesman Library in the Special Collections section. This text focuses on

the genealogy of the priests, from Aaron to the copyist's present. It appears near the end of the manuscript is a patch placed over an earlier text. It was important enough to break the flow of the manuscript. Written on the patch, we read the following:

In the [Islamic] year 1276 [= 1861] a good man rose and did good for all of the community of Israel who were in need. He is the father of Marḥiv and with him his brother Ḥovav, the sons of Jacob son of Ishmael of the sons of Tsafar. In that year they made [that is, donated] a large silver *aron* ["Torah case"], pure and fine, and in addition pomegranates [finials] similarly of silver, and a *masakh* ["curtain"] embroidered with silver thread, his name inscribed upon them. They also made a *beged* ["wrapping"] for our master, the holy writ, the writ [*mikhtav,* "scroll"] of Abisha son of Pinḥas. May the peace of the Lord be upon him. May God help us on account of this great act, and have mercy on us in consideration of the deeds of Abraham and Isaac and Jacob and our master Moses, the beloved. Amen. May they be remembered for good, those who do good. Amen.[12]

1.11 "Samaritan's Manuscripts — Nablus," Postcard, The Priest Pinḥas son of the High Priest Matzliah and the Priest Tsedaka son of the High Priest Jacob son of Aaron, Holy Land Views, Jerusalem, Jordan, 1962. This scroll and case were stolen from the Nablus synagogue in March, 1995 (Collection of Leah and Steven Fine, New York).

1.12 Roman Vishniac, The Priest Sadeq son of Abisha, Nablus, 1967, color slide (Magnes Collection of Jewish Art and Life, University of California, Berkeley, gift of Mara Vishniac Kohn).

Reflecting the continuing life of the Samaritan people, the *Tulidah* concludes with a description of contemporary piety and eschatological hope. Marḥiv son of Jacob, not a priest but an Israelite of the Tsafari clan, made a major donation to the synagogue in Shechem, and was roundly praised: he donated his specific *aron*—Samaritan for "Torah case" (what Eastern Jews call a *tiq*)—and *rimmonim*—Torah finials (because they are shaped like pomegranates), which are also called *rommemot* by the Samaritans—as well as a Torah shrine curtain embroidered in silver (a *masakh*) and a *beged*—a "garment" for the scroll itself. Similar treasures have been photographed with the Abisha Scroll for more than a century. In fact, the Abisha Scroll is kept in a brass *aron* dated 1522 inscribed with a schematic drawing of the Tabernacle, a visual reminder of its status as last remnant of the period of Divine grace before darkness set in when the Children of Israel split into competing nations. A dedicatory inscription that encompasses the upper register of the Torah container praises the donor, and calls it "the ark of the Holy of Holies."

Drawings and photographs of the Abisha Scroll, usually shown together with its priestly guardian, have been continually updated ever since the mid-nineteenth century (Figures 1.11-14). Over the years, priests died and were replaced by younger men, technology

1.13 Moshe Milner, "Samaritan Priest Zadok [Sadeq] ben Avisha HaCohen Holding a 2,000-year-old Torah Scroll in the Synagogue in Nablus," August 10, 1967 (Israel National Photograph Collection).

1.14 Yitzhak and his son Pinḥas Cohen in the Holon Synagogue (Photograph by Moshe Alafi).

improved, and sensitivity toward "Orientalism" as a concept increased, but the image has stayed the same. So embedded is this icon in our consciousness, that a visitor to the Samaritan Museum on Mount Gerizim today may pose before a mock Torah shrine, a rough facsimile of the Abisha Scroll resting on a low stand that is covered with an embroidered cloth. The proprietor of the Museum, the priest Yefet Husney Cohen, dressed in traditional garb (unusual on weekdays for contemporary Samaritans), is the host. Visitors are welcome to pose to the side of the scroll, with Husney (who jovially introduces himself to tourists as "the Good Samaritan") on the other. The presence of non-Samaritans is unheard of in historical photography. No traveler or Western scholar is shown in close proximity to the sacred scrolls, no doubt in order to maintain and/or create a mystique surrounding this precious artifact and its custodians. Today, however, both the visitor and the priest smile for the camera, as is expected for contemporary photographs of this sort.

To conclude, nineteenth- and twentieth-century photographs of the Abisha Scroll with its priestly guardian, taken by Westerners for Western consumption, well reflect the awe with which Samaritans themselves view the holy scroll and its continuing significance. The Abisha Scroll is a central cipher for the Samaritans, transmitting and "guarding" their sacred tradition from generation to generation (Figures 1.12, 13, 14, 15). The Torah of Torah scrolls, it is a relic that guarantees the truth and antiquity of Samaritan tradition. The Abisha Scroll is a transmitter of Divine grace, and thus able to answer prayers—both for those who stand in its presence and for people at a distance who merely think about it. Questions raised by Western scholars and travelers—people like Mark Twain—about the antiquity of this scroll or any other aspect of Samaritan tradition are not relevant to the Samaritans themselves—no more than Western studies of the Quran influence most pious Muslims, the authenticity of the Shroud of Turin for many Christians, and the authorship of the

Zohar for many Jews. Photographs of the Abisha Scroll with its priestly guardian, stereotyped as they now are, allow non-Samaritans a window into this fascinating tradition and its most significant single Torah scroll, the one that Samaritan tradition holds was written by Abisha, the son of Eleazar the son of Aaron the Priest at the gate of the biblical Tabernacle.

For Further Reading

Alan D. Crown, editor. *The Samaritans*. Tübingen: Mohr Siebeck, 1989.

Reinhard Pummer. *The Samaritans: A Profile*. Grand Rapids, MI: Eerdmans, 2016.

Ephraim Stern and Hanan Eshel, editors. *The Samaritans*. Jerusalem: Yad Ben-Zvi Press, 2002. [Hebrew].

Benyamim Tsedaka, and Sharon Sullivan, editors. *The Israelite Samaritan Version of the Torah: First English Translation Compared with the Masoretic Version*. Grand Rapids, MI: Eerdmans, 2013.

———

1   Ed. Stenhouse, 44–45.

2   Rogers, 1862, 266; 1868, 42.

3   See also Rogers, 1862, 323, 325.

4   Yaniv, 1997, 208-213.

5   Albert Edward, Prince of Wales, 1862, 99-–96; Bedford, 1862. See Selis and Fine, below.

6   Twain, 1869, 552.

7   Discussed by Gafni, below.

8   Gaster, 1925, 108.

9   Crown, 1975.

10 Pummer, 2016, 53.

11 Adler and Séligsohn, 1903, 35–36.

12 Yeshiva University Gottesman Library Special Collections, Ms. 752; see Tsedaka and Selis, 2021.

1.15   Prayers before the Abisha Scroll, Synagogue, Kiryat Luza, Mount Gerizim, 2017 (Photograph by Ori Orhof).

2

The Samaritan Tabernacle:
From Sinai to the Mountain of Blessings

REINHARD PUMMER

The Samaritan nation too was not exempt from disturbance. For a man who made light of mendacity and in all his designs catered to the mob, rallied them, bidding them go in a body with him to Mount Gerizim, which in their belief is the most sacred of mountains. He assured them that on their arrival he would show them the sacred vessels which were buried there, where Moses had deposited them. His hearers, viewing this tale as plausible, appeared in arms. They posted themselves in a certain village named Tirathana, and, as they planned to climb the mountain in a great multitude, they welcomed to their ranks the new arrivals who kept coming. But before they could ascend, Pilate blocked their projected route up the mountain with a detachment of cavalry and heavy infantry, who in an encounter with the firstcomers in the village slew some in a pitched battle and put the others to flight. Many prisoners were taken, of whom Pilate put to death the principal leaders and those who were most influential among the fugitives.

When the uprising had been quelled, the council of the Samaritans went to Vitellius, a man of consular rank who was governor of Syria, and charged Pilate with the slaughter of the victims. For, they said, it was not as rebels against the Romans but as refugees from the persecution of Pilate that they had met in Tirathana. Vitellius thereupon dispatched Marcellus, one of his friends, to take charge of the administration of Judaea, and ordered Pilate to return to Rome to give the emperor his account of the matters with which he was charged by the Samaritans. And so Pilate, after having spent ten years in Judaea, hurried to Rome in obedience to the orders of Vitellius, since he could not refuse. But before he reached Rome Tiberius had already passed away.

— Flavius Josephus, *Jewish Antiquities* 18.85–89.

In the year 36 CE, a violent and armed clash between the Samaritans and Roman soldiers took place in a village near the Samaritan Holy Mountain, Mount Gerizim (Figure 2.1). It was the first such clash between the two groups recorded by the Jewish historian Flavius Josephus. Another calamitous confrontation between the two parties occurred thirty years later in the summer of 67 CE on top of Mount Gerizim. Both encounters ended with a defeat of the Samaritans and, in the year 67, the death of a great number of their people—11,600 according to Josephus.

What makes the first incident special is the oblique reference to one of the Samaritans' basic beliefs. Josephus claims that a con man promised the Samaritans that he would show them where Moses had buried the sacred vessels on Mount Gerizim if they followed him to the top of the mountain. Although the Samaritans must have known from the Bible that Moses never entered the Holy Land and could therefore not have deposited the sacred vessels on Mount Gerizim, they viewed this tale as plausible and a great multitude gathered in a nearby village in preparation for climbing the mountain. The question arises: if the Samaritans knew that Moses had never entered the Holy Land, why then did they view the words of the deceiver as credible? The most likely answer is that such a prospect corresponded to a belief and a hope in the community, namely the expectation that at the end of time a figure will come and bring back the Tabernacle. The sacred vessels promised by the imposter represent this larger belief. This figure of the end times is later called Taheb from Aramaic תוב, meaning "to return." However, in addressing non-Samaritans, the Samaritans often called, and still call, the *Taheb* "Messiah" as did already the Samaritan woman at the well in John 4:25, even though the Samaritan concept of th eschatological prophet is different from the Jewish and Christian ideas of the Messiah.

THE ONLY LEGITIMATE SANCTUARY

For the Samaritans, the Tabernacle was and is the only legitimate sanctuary. For them, there never was a lawful temple on Mount Gerizim or anywhere else. This is despite the literary, epigraphic, and archeological evidence marshaled by scholars. This includes mention of the temple on Mount Gerizim in 2 Maccabees 6:2; two second century BCE Greek inscriptions from the island of Delos that refer to a sanctuary on Mount Gerizim; Josephus's account of the founding of a temple on the mountain in the fourth century BCE and its destruction in the second century BCE; and the remains of a sacred precinct or *temenos* recently excavated on Mount

2.1   Nablus and Mt. Gerizim, from Mt. Ebal (Yair Dov, Wikimedia Commons).

Gerizim. Although all this data points to a temple that stood on the highest peak of the mountain from the fifth to the second century BCE, for the Samaritans they are not proof of the existence of such a sanctuary. They explain the impressive traces unearthed by archeology since 1982 as remains of administrative buildings needed for the large city on top of the mountain, or perhaps as a "sacrificial compound." With one possible exception, none of their chronicles that recount the ancient history of the community as seen by the Samaritans mention a legitimate temple on Mount Gerizim. The one possible exception is found in only one source and is not mentioned in other Samaritan writings, and today the building alluded to in this one text is explained as being without any religious significance.

In the Samaritan tradition, the figure of the *Taheb* has receded into the background and hardly plays any role in contemporary Samaritan theology. On their website, *israelite-samaritans.com*, they simply state: "The next prophet after Moses, of a similarly illustrious standing, will be 'A Prophet Like Moses.' In our tradition we call such a one *Taheb* (meaning *Returner*). He will bring tranquility to the People of Israel. And he will make other peoples believe in the true faith of the Almighty of Israel." The memory of the Tabernacle, on the other hand, remains present to this day.

THE TABERNACLE IN THE BIBLE AND IN SAMARITAN TRADITION

The Pentateuch, the common scripture of Samaritans and Jews, devotes a large amount of its narrative to the Israelite tent sanctuary or the Tabernacle, which is also called the "tent of meeting" or "tent of testimony." It contained the Ark of the Covenant, an incense altar, the eternal light, Aaron's staff, a table, a candelabra with seven lights, a container with manna, and the vessels used by the priests (Exodus 25–28 and 35–40). According to the Jewish Bible, the Tabernacle was erected in Shilo after the conquest of the land under Joshua (Joshua 18:1; 19:51). It was the center of worship and the symbol of God's presence. According to 1 Samuel (1:9; 2:11), the priest who served in the Tabernacle was Eli, who was possibly descended from Ithamar, one of Aaron's sons, or, alternatively, from Eleazar, another of the sons of Aaron. Eli's sons abused their position by eating from the sacrificial meat that people brought to the Tabernacle. When the Israelites were beaten in a battle with the Philistines, they, in their consternation, thought the presence of the Ark among them would protect them in the future. They therefore fetched it from Shilo into their camp; with it came the two sons of Eli. When the Philistines learned of it, they were afraid that the Israelite God would help them. They therefore attacked the Israelites again, defeated them, and captured the Ark, and the two sons of Eli, Hophni and Pinḥas, died in the battle. When the news was brought to Eli in Shilo, who then was ninety-eight years old, he fell over backwards and broke his neck. While the Ark later came again into the possession of the Israelites, it is not clear what happened to the Tabernacle. According to the Book of Chronicles, the Tabernacle was eventually put into Solomon's Temple.[1] Nothing more is said about it in the other narrative books of the Bible. Only Psalm 74:7 and Lamentations 2:6–7 refer to the destruction of the Temple and, with it, of the Tabernacle.

This is in essence the account of the Tabernacle in the Hebrew Bible revered by Jews and Christians. The Samaritan account differs considerably. This story, though, is found in the Samaritan chronicles, which obviously borrowed from the Jewish scriptures. It was altered to suit Samaritan concerns. Moreover, the legend of the hiding of the Tabernacle vessels seems to have been part of late antique folklore. The most detailed Samaritan account is to be found in Abu l-Fatḥ's *Kitub al-Tarikh*, which was written in the second half of the fourteenth century CE but incorporates what are most likely older sources. Similar narratives are found also in other Samaritan chronicles, such as the *Tulidah* (also called *Chronicle Neubauer,* the earliest parts going back to the middle of the twelfth century CE), the Samaritan (Arabic) *Book of Joshua* (going back to the thirteenth century CE), and the *New Chronicle* (also called *Chronicle Adler*)—which continues to the modern period.

According to these chronicles, the priest Eli son of Yefani, a descendant of Aaron's son Ithamar, quarreled with the sons of Pinḥas, the son of Aaron's son Eleazar, because he wanted to seize the high priesthood from Uzzi who, as descendant of Pinḥas, was the rightful priest (Numbers 25:12–13). Eli was fifty years old at that time, rich, and in charge of the treasury of the Israelites. He did not want to serve under the much younger Uzzi and gathered a group of like-minded people who swore to do whatever he asked them to do. One day, Eli offered a sacrifice deliberately without the salt prescribed in Leviticus 2:13. When Uzzi learned of this, he chided Eli. In response, Eli and his sympathizers revolted and left for Shilo, taking with them their animals and all their possessions. In Shilo, Eli built a sanctuary on the model of the shrine on Mount Gerizim. In it, he erected an altar on which he offered sacrifices. Whereas the Bible relates that his two sons, Hophni and Pinḥas, ate from the sacrifices, the Samaritan accounts state that they brought young attractive women into the sanctuary; not only did they have them eat from the food of the sacrifices, but they also slept with them in the shrine.

Eli's actions caused the Israelites to split into factions: a (loyal) faction on Mount Gerizim; a heretical faction worshipping false gods; and the faction around Eli in Shilo. In the words of Abu l-Fatḥ: "When the people had become indifferent to rectifying excesses, pretending not to notice; when their eye-sight had become dimmed, and they were reluctant to show disapproval," God became angry and withdrew from them. The fire in the Tabernacle went out and a day of calamity like the one when Adam left the garden arose. When Uzzi the high priest entered the sanctuary to conduct the service, it was dark. He realized that God had taken away his grace from them. Suddenly, he saw the opening of a cave that he had never seen

before. He took all the sacred vestments and vessels, and deposited them in the cave. When he left the cave, he sealed its entrance. Although he marked the place where the entrance was located, he could not find it anymore when he returned on the next day. He wept and lamented the fate that had befallen the Israelites. When their leaders heard him and asked what the reason for his weeping was, he told them that God's anger had come over them and that the time of favor (called by the Samaritans *Rehuta,* pronounced *Roota*) had ended and the time of disfavor, of God's turning away from the Israelites (*Panuta,* pronounced *Fanuta*) had begun.

Although this account tells only of the hiding of the *implements* of the Tabernacle, both the *Tulidah* and the *New Chronicle* make clear that what is intended is the explanation for why the Tabernacle had disappeared. Interestingly, Pseudo-Philo, a first-century Jewish text, and the fourth-century Church Father Epiphanius of Salamis claimed that Jacob had buried the foreign gods (Genesis 35:4) on Mount Gerizim. Later, rabbinic writings, discussed by Shana Strauch Schick and Steven Fine in this volume, also identified the place where Jacob had buried the idols with the peak of Mount Gerizim. It may be that these sources reflect a polemic against the Samaritan belief that the vessels of the Mosaic Tabernacle are hidden on the mountain.[2]

THE DISAPPEARANCE OF THE TABERNACLE IN EARLY SOURCES

This account of the events that led to the disappearance of the Tabernacle is based on relatively late sources, all written in the Middle Ages and later. However, non-Samaritan sources allow us to reach further back in time, namely to the first century CE. As noted at the beginning of this article, Josephus in his *Jewish Antiquities* (18.85–89) recounts a hostile encounter between the Samaritans and the Romans in the year 36 CE, and in the course of his narration he gives us a hint about the Samaritan beliefs about the Tabernacle in the first century CE. He reports that, like the Jews under the Roman governor Pontius Pilate (26–36 CE), the Samaritans too had their share of calamities. A certain deceiver told them that they should go with him to Mount Gerizim because there he would show them the holy vessels that Moses had buried there. They believed him, appeared in arms, and got ready to ascend the mountain. But before they could do so, Pilate's cavalry and heavy infantry barred their way. The Roman troops engaged them in a ferocious battle in which many were killed, others were taken prisoners, and still others fled. The Samaritans reported Pilate to his superior, Vitellius, the Governor of Syria, claiming that they were not revolting against the Romans but were fleeing from the persecution enacted by Pilate. Pilate was then summoned to Rome.

Everything in this narrative fits the picture of messianic claimants known among Jews of that time. As pointed out above, in Samaritan terms the swindler was seen as the prophet who was to come at the end of times, the *Taheb*. The promised restoration of the hidden vessels refers to the *Taheb's* legitimating miracle of bringing back the Tabernacle when he comes.

The legend of the hiding of the Tabernacle and its implements was shared by Samaritans, Jews, and Christians alike. It is found in

2.2 Torah Shrine Curtain, *Masakh*. Damascus, 1509/10. Red silk with silver threads. Gift of Jacob son of Abraham son of Isaac of Damascus to the Nablus synagogue. Artisan: Joseph son of Tsedakah the Priest. Synagogue, Kiryat Luza, Mount Gerizim. (Courtesy of the Center for Jewish Art, Hebrew University of Jerusalem).

cally fashioned metal Torah scroll cases and drawings on parchment and paper in modern times (from the early sixteenth to the twentieth century). Thus, synagogues with mosaics depicting the Holy Ark were found in el-Khirbe near Samaria-Sebaste and in Khirbet Samara southwest of Jenin (Figure 7.7). The mosaic of the el-Khirbe synagogue shows the showbread table with loaves, cups, jars, and libation bowls (Exodus 25:28–29); a seven-branched candelabra; the façade of a shrine with a curtain that some suggest may represent the Ark of the Covenant (Exodus 26:31–34); trumpets on each side of the candelabra; an incense shovel; and the upper part of a jug. The mosaic of the Khirbet Samara synagogue depicts twice the façade of a shrine with a curtain and four pillars that seems to represent the Holy Ark. Unfortunately, the mosaic is only partially preserved, and we do not know whether the other items depicted in the el-Khirbe synagogue were included in Khirbet Samara. In addition, cult symbols appear also on oil lamps (Figure 0.13), particularly on one found in Umm Khalid near Netanya on which can be seen the Holy Ark, the menorah, an incense shovel, and various vessels.

Almost one thousand years lie between these visual expressions of the importance of the Tabernacle for the Samaritans, on the one hand, and the designs on Torah scroll cases, silk, parchment, and paper, on the other. The oldest extant specimen is a red silk curtain, embroidered with silver thread, in the synagogue of Nablus. It dates from the Islamic year 915, that is, 1509/10 (Figure 2.2). The second oldest is a Torah scroll case that once was kept in the Nablus synagogue but was moved to the synagogue on Mount Gerizim when the community relocated and built Kiryat Luza (the place of Jacob's dream in Genesis 28) during the 1990s. It is called al-Tur in Arabic, simply "The Mountain." The Torah case is made of brass and inlaid with silver and gold, and dates to the Islamic year 928, that is, 1522 (Figure 2.3). This case is called by the Samaritans the "Scroll Case of the Images" and contains the most revered Torah scroll, the Abisha Scroll, which is believed to have been written by Abisha, the great grandson of Aaron, in the thirteenth year of the conquest of Canaan.

The designs on the silk curtain and on this scroll case reappear with minor modifications on all known subsequent drawings (Figures 0.8, 2.4, 13.2). Some are entitled "Depiction of the Holy Tabernacle which Our Lord Moses Made in the Desert," while others are entitled "This Is a Depiction of the Holy Tabernacle on Mount Gerizim." In the Holy of Holies are shown the Ark, the Mercy Seat, two winged creatures (cherubs), and the rods of Aaron and Moses.[3] Outside the Holy of Holies are represented the menorah,[4] showbread table,[5] the altar of incense or the golden altar,[6] a jar for the manna,[7] tongs,[8] fire pans, and the entrance to the tent of meeting. In the court, the following implements are seen: the laver[9] and the garments of the high priest,[10] including the headdress.[11] Additionally, the two trumpets,[12] basins,[13] two pairs of knives, the bronze altar,[14] two hooks, and two oblong objects that look like poles are shown.[15] On the curtain between the two sections of the Holy of Holies an inscription lists, on some of the drawings, the names of the high priests who were "the keepers of the holy sanctuary": Moses and Aaron and Eleazar and Pinḥas and Abisha and Shishi and Beḥqi and Uzzi; and in the days of this Uzzi, the Lord concealed the Tabernacle.

several Jewish sources from the time around the turn of the eras. The most important are 2 Maccabees 2:4–8 (late second century BCE), 2 Baruch (*Syriac Apocalypse of Baruch*) 6.7–9 (early second century CE), 4 Baruch (*Parelipomena Jeremiae*) 3.7–8, 14 (early second century CE), and *Vita Jeremiae* 11–19 (probably first century CE). The Samaritans took part in this transposition of motifs and adapted the details to their own theology. The Jewish prophet Jeremiah was replaced by the only Samaritan prophet, Moses, although later the priest Uzzi is connected with the Tabernacle tradition.

THE TABERNACLE IN SAMARITAN ART

The continued importance of the Tabernacle for the Samaritans becomes clear from various visual expressions ranging from mosaic floors and decorations on lamps in the Byzantine period to artisti-

REINHARD PUMMER

2.3   The "Ark [*Aron*] of the Images," Torah Case, Egypt, 1522. Gift of Jacob son of Abraham of the Puqa family. Artisan: Isaac son of Tsedaka of the Yatrina. Brass, silver and gold. Synagogue, Kiryat Luza, Mount Gerizim (Photograph by Moshe Alafi).

The purpose of the Tabernacle drawings may have been to teach the community members about the Tabernacle. They are not manuscript illustrations as they exist in Judaism. Their very size precludes such a use. Instead, they are items of religious art in their own right to be hung on the wall. Eventually, a number of them were sold, often created as tourist items, and are now in various Western collections. In addition to the drawings on parchment and paper, there is also a scroll, written circa 1930, in which the scribe, the priest Jacob son of Uzzi (1900–1987; high priest 1984–1987), created spare ground calligrams to depict within the text of Exodus 25–26 the Ark of the Covenant, the menorah, the showbread table, and the Tabernacle itself (Figure 2.5). The very same creative priest, discussed further by Haseeb Shehadeh in this volume, drew several Tabernacle drawings on paper (Figure 13.2). Up to recently, these drawings of the Tabernacle were the only pieces of representational art to be found among the Samaritans since the Byzantine period. Only dec-

orations of manuscripts and marriage contracts existed (Figures 2.6, 2.7). In the last several years, however, drawings of other Samaritan ceremonies were produced. A completely new phenomenon is the work of the award-winning painter Miriam Tsedaka, who produces colorful paintings of various aspects of the religious life of the Samaritans (Figure 2.8).

Benyamim Tsedaka, the Samaritan scholar, journalist, and community leader, has asked in an article published in April 2019 in *A.B. – The Samaritan News*, "What Happened to the Tabernacle Utensils Made by Eelee (עלי, Eli) the Priest?" After outlining the story of the Tabernacle and its implements as it is found in the Samaritan chronicles, he compares it with the fate of the utensils according to the Jewish scripture. Their final destiny was to be taken to Rome after Emperor Titus had destroyed the temple in 70 CE. Rumors that they are in the Vatican or in Ethiopia are, in Tsedaka's words, "fake traditions." In sum, the pivotal role played by the Tabernacle in the

ⵯⵎⵆⵞⵥⵯⵯⵆ

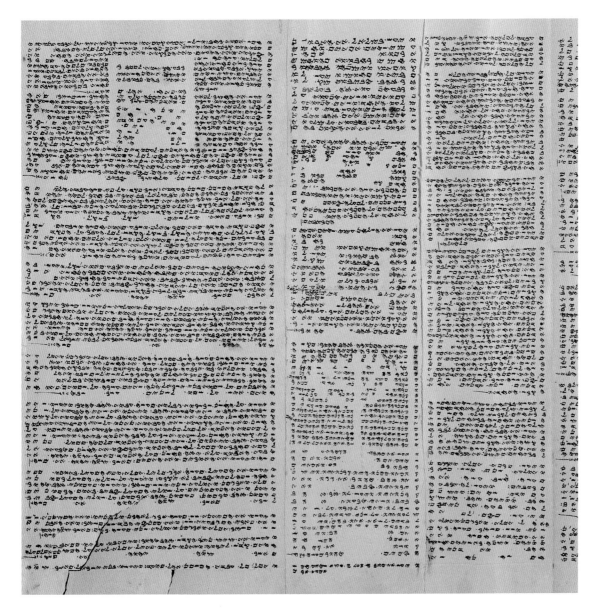

2.5 Samaritan Torah Scroll, Exodus, Scribe: Uzzi son of Jacob (reigned 1984–1987, Rare Books and Special Collections, the University of Sydney Library, MS Add. 390).

2.6 Miriam Tsedaka, "Pilgrimage to Mount Gerizim," 2000 (Courtesy of Benyamim and Miriam Tsedaka, photograph by Steven Fine).

Marriage Contract (*mikhtav zivug*) of Tamim son of Israel son of Ishmael Danafi and Pu'ah daughter of Abraham son of Marḥiv, Marḥiv Tsafr, Nablus, 1901. Scribe: Jacob son of Aaron, Levite [high priest] (Library of Congress, Hebraic Section).

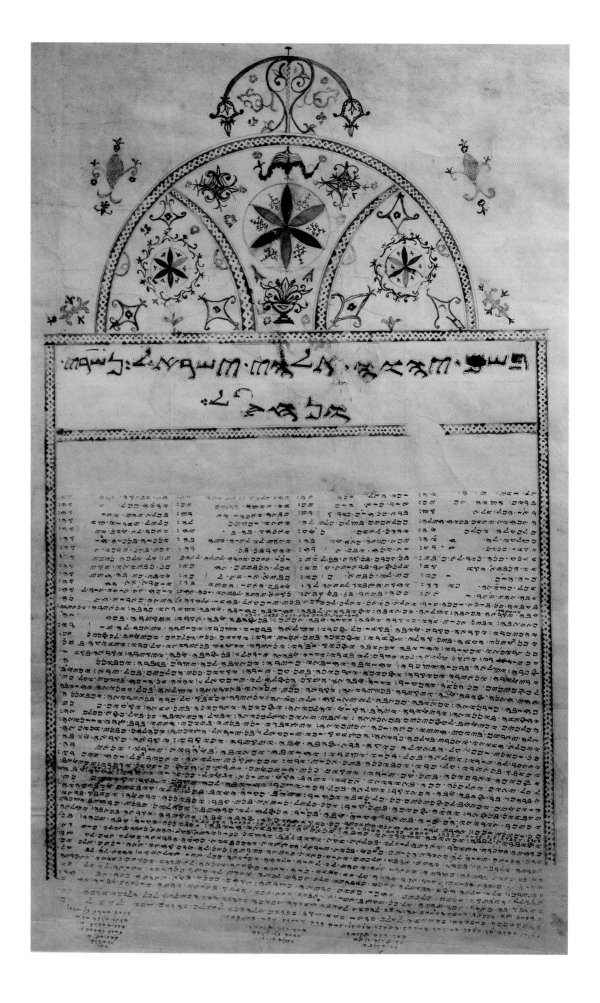

2.8 Public Reading of the Marriage Contract by the High Priest Joseph son of Ab-Ḥisda son of Jacob son of Aaron (reigned 1987-1998) at a wedding in Kiryat Luza, Mount Gerizim. Kiryat Luza, Mount Gerizim (Photograph by Ori Orhoff).

Samaritan tradition can be documented from the first century CE to the present, albeit with a gap of almost a thousand years in the documentation from the Byzantine period to the early sixteenth century. Today, the Samaritans steadfastly claim that Mount Gerizim has been the only sacred place ever since the Tabernacle with all its contents was hidden in a cave on the mountain; it will be revealed only in the end times by the Prophet Like Moses. The Samaritans are convinced that there never was a "temple" on Mount Gerizim in the meantime, no matter what non-Samaritan scholars say. It is the mountain itself that is sacred.

For Further Reading

James D. Purvis, "The Sanctuary and Holy Vessels in Samaritan Art." In *Samaritan Researches*, edited by Vittorio Morabito, Alan D. Crown, and Lucy Davey. Sydney: Mandelbaum Publishing, 2000, 4.27–38.

Reinhard Pummer. "Samaritan Tabernacle Drawings." *Numen* 45 (1998): 30–68.

——. "The Mosaic Tabernacle as the Only Legitimate Sanctuary: The Biblical Tabernacle in Samaritanism." In *The Temple of Jerusalem: From Moses to the Messiah: Studies in Honor of Professor Louis H. Feldman*, edited by Steven Fine. Leiden: Brill, 2011, 125–150.

1   1 Chronicles 6:16–17; 23:32; 24:6; 2 Chronicles 29:5–7.
2   Jerusalem Talmud, Avodah Zarah 5:3 and parallels.
3   See Exodus 25:10–22; 37:1–9; and Numbers 17:16–26. Only Aaron's rod is mentioned in the Bible.
4   Exodus 25:31–40; 37:17–24.
5   Exodus 25:23–30; 37:10–16.
6   Exodus 30:1, 27; 39:38, etc.
7   Exodus 16:32–33.
8   Numbers 4:9.
9   Exodus 30:17–21; 38:8.
10   Exodus 28:1–43.
11   Exodus 28:4 and 39.
12   Numbers 10:1–10.
13   Exodus 27:3; 38:3; Numbers 4:14.
14   Exodus 38:30; 39:39; on the altar of burnt offering, see Exodus 27:1–8; and 38:1–7.
15   See Exodus 27:3; 38:3; and Numbers 4:14.

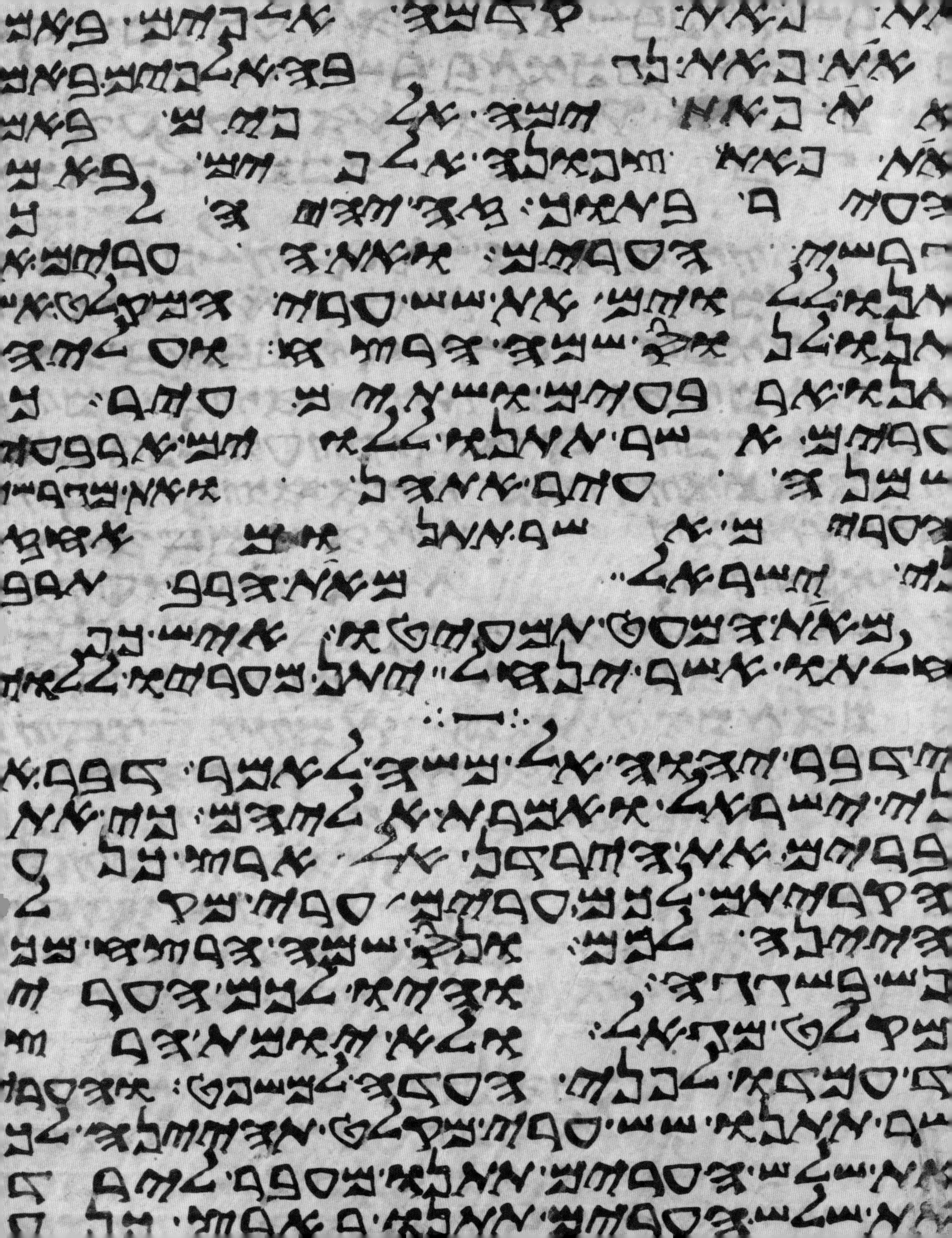

3

"Woe to Those Who Exchanged the Truth for a Lie, When They Choose for Themselves a Different Place": Samaritan Perspectives on the Samaritan–Jewish Split

STEFAN SCHORCH

Happy are the committed who prostrate themselves to You,

In perfect faithfulness,

He who is committed to You in faithfulness will flourish,

For You are with him in every place,

Provide him as You see fit,

Guard him by day and by night,

And he will sleep and not fear.

And he will flourish, for You watch over and do not sleep.

And no king can stand before You,

And no war can frighten You,

There is no victory other than yours.

All mouths will say to You:

Who is like you among the gods (Exodus 15:11)?

Your name strikes fear in the universe,

And what is this before your great might?

There is no God but one,

There is no prophet like Moses,

And there is no writ like the Holy Torah,

And there is no worship but to the Lord,

Facing Mount Gerizim, the House of God,

the chosen, the holy, the finest on earth.

— *A Liturgical Poem by Amram Dare*, 4:14–33[1]

From antiquity to the present, Samaritans and Jews have lived as close neighbors in the Land of Israel and in nearby diaspora communities. The descendants of Judah and Israel share a deep and profound biblical and cultural heritage. It is difficult to imagine Judaism without Samaritanism, or Samaritanism without Judaism—the two are intertwined in profound ways. This very closeness, however, has often been the source of intense friction. It is already present in the prayer by the famous Samaritan poet Amram Dare (fourth century CE) that is cited at the top of this article. This poem exemplifies the fundamental similarity between Judaism and Samaritanism in terms of strict monotheism, the central role of Moses's prophecy, the Torah as sacred scripture, and regarding God's one central

sanctuary. However, it also highlights the most important and most contentious difference between the two rival groups—the localization of Israel's one Holy Mountain. For the Samaritans, the sacred mountain is Mount Gerizim (Figures 3.1-4), whereas for Jews it is Mount Zion, the "Temple Mount" in Jerusalem.

According to the current scholarly view, Samaritans and Jews had been sliding apart for centuries. This interpretation is based on a wide array of textual and archeological sources, some discovered only recently (Figure 3.5, 4.2, 3). The final split between the Samaritans and Jews occurred in the late second century BCE, when the troops of the Hasmonean leader in Judah and high priest at the Jerusalem Temple John Hyrcanus (164–104 BCE) destroyed the Samaritan sanctuary on Mount Gerizim in the course of their campaign in Samaria in 111–110 BCE (Josephus, *Antiquities* 13). Apparently, John Hyrcanus even stationed a garrison on the mountain in order to prevent the return of the Samaritans and to force their recognition of the Jerusalem Temple. The importance of this event was felt so immensely by Jews that *Megillat Taanit*, a list of minor feast days celebrated by Jews, marks the twenty-first of Kislev (in December) as "Mount Gerizim Day," *Yom Har Gerizim.*[2] It was mainly these drastic military and political events, so it seems, that caused the irreparable break between Samaritans and Jews.

Traditional Jewish views of the split, on the other hand, propose a very different history. 2 Kings 17 describes the destruction of Samaria and the exile of the people of Israel by Shalmaneser V king of Assyria (ruled 727–722 BCE), and suggests that they were replaced with subject peoples from beyond the Euphrates:

> So Israel was exiled from their own land to Assyria until this day. And the king of Assyria brought people from Babylon, Kuthah, Avva, Hamath, and Sepharvaim, and placed them in the cities of Samaria instead of the people of Israel; and they took possession of Samaria, and dwelt in its cities. And at the beginning of their dwelling there, they did not fear the LORD; therefore the LORD sent lions among them, which killed some of them. So the king of Assyria was told, "The nations which you have carried away and placed in the cities of Samaria do not know the law of

3.4 Samaritan Pentateuch Codex, Latin Kingdom of Jerusalem (Yavneh?), 1232, folio 458r, Numbers 35. The circle set off within the text represents Mount Gerizim. (Dorot Jewish Division, The New York Public Library). The *Tasqil* (colophon) reads:

I, Abraham son of Israel son of Ephraim son of Joseph the Prince [*Nasi*], King of Israel, wrote this copy of the Holy Torah myself for my children in the six hundred and twenty ninth year of the Islamic ascendancy, corresponding to the three thousand, two hundredth year of Israelite settlement in the land of Canaan, *anno mundi* 5993. It is the seventy-fourth Torah that I have written and I am now sixty years old. I give thanks to the Lord and entreat him to prolong their life, so that they can teach from it [their] children and grandchildren. Amen, amen, amen.

ꙮꙮ

the God of the land; therefore he has sent lions among them, and behold, they are killing them, because they do not know the law of the God of the land." Then the king of Assyria commanded, "Send there one of the priests whom you carried away thence; and let him go and dwell there, and teach them the law of the God of the land. (2 Kings 17:23–30)

In the end, these foreigners revert to their pagan ways. This polemic reflects sustained biblical animosity toward the northern tribes by the Jerusalem authorities, which appears prominently once again in Ezra 4. There, Israelites from Samaria are barred from participating in the rebuilding of the Jerusalem Temple. As a result, they worked to convince the Persian authorities of Jewish nefariousness in order to stop the work. Their mischief was of no avail, we are told, and the work of rebuilding went on. In his retelling of 2 Kings 17, Josephus calls the Samaritans *Kutheans*, highlighting that they are not trustworthy Israelites, but of foreign descent (*Antiquities* 9.14). In Josephus's time, this was not the only perspective on the Samaritans, for in another passage in the *Antiquities* Josephus speaks of the Samaritans as "compatriots." In rabbinic literature, however, *Kutim* became the general identification of the Samaritans, underscoring the view that the Israelite identity of Samaritans was problematic from the outset.

The Samaritan view on the split differs radically from the Jewish perspective. According to the Samaritan-Arabic chronicle assembled by Abu l-Fath in 1355 CE, after upon entering the Land of Israel, Joshua had established the sanctuary on Mount Gerizim:

> Joshua built an altar of stones on Mount Gerizim, as Almighty God had told him (to do); and offered sacrifices upon it. Half the people stood facing Mount Gerizim, while the other half faced Mount Ebal. Joshua read out the Torah in its entirety in the hearing of all Israel. (*The Chronicle of Abu l-Fath*, Chapter 4)[3]

One year later, the Tabernacle was transported up the mountain, and Joshua built a temple there:

> We declare that tradition has it that the sons of Israel entered Canaan in the first month, corresponding to the month of Nisan; and that they set up the stones (from the Jordan) on Mount Gerizim; that Eleazar the high priest wrote down all the prescriptions of the Law on them in metric verse; and that they set about repairing the road for transporting the Tabernacle up to the Holy Mountain—for the Tabernacle had stood, according to what is said—in the Plain for the space of a year: from Passover to Passover. In the second year Joshua built the Temple on Mount Gerizim and put the Tabernacle in it. (*The Chronicle of Abu l-Fath*, Chapter 7)[4]

However, Eli son of Yefani, of the priestly line of Ithamar, revolted against the descendents of Pinhas, who held the legitimate high priesthood, and, after being rebuked, set off with his followers for Shilo, where he built a temple for himself, with a copy of the altar, causing the split of Israel:

> At this time, the Children of Israel became three factions: a (loyal) faction on Mount Gerizim; a heretical faction that followed false Gods; and the faction that followed Eli son of Yefani in Shilo.... God became angry at them, his indignation fell upon them, and he took his patronage from them. The fire which was manifest by his divine power in the Tabernacle went out. (*The Chronicle of Abu l-Fath*, Chapter 9)[5]

Most obviously, the chronicle presents a counter-history of the erection of the Tabernacle at Shilo as told in the Jewish Book of Joshua (18:1), including a reference to Eli's priesthood at Shilo (1 Samuel 1–4). Since the Ark is ultimately moved from Shilo to Jerusalem, according to 1–2 Samuel and 1 Kings, the main presupposition of this counter-narrative is exactly the main point of contention between Samaritans and Jews—namely that Mount Gerizim and not Jerusalem is the only true sanctuary of Israel. Thus, according to the Samaritans, the Jews left the legitimate holy place, namely Mount Gerizim, for an illegitimate one.

The background for the Samaritan claim emerges from the text of the Torah. According to Deuteronomy 12:11, the central sanctuary of the Israelites was chosen by God "to establish his name there." While the identification of this holy center with Jerusalem is one of the basic tenets of Judaism, Samaritans recognize it as Mount Gerizim.

From a textual perspective, there is an obvious difference between these two identifications. Jerusalem is never mentioned in the Torah, at least not explicitly. The Jewish connection of Jerusalem with the divinely chosen place as established in Deuteronomy is created only through texts outside the Pentateuch, most prominently in 2 Chronicles 6:5–6:

> Since the day that I brought my people out of the land of Egypt, I have not chosen a city from any of the tribes of Israel in which to build a house, so that my name might be there, and I chose no one as ruler over my people Israel; but I have chosen Jerusalem in order that my name may be there, and I have chosen David to be over my people Israel.

Therefore, the Jewish identification of Jerusalem as the holy center of Israel is achieved through paratexts elsewhere in the Jewish Bible. The Samaritan identification of the chosen place with Mount Gerizim, on the other hand, is indeed explicitly present in the Torah, most prominently in the Samaritan version: according to the Samaritan text of Deuteronomy 27:4–5, the altar to be erected by the Israelites immediately after their crossing the Jordan into the promised land is to be built on Mount Gerizim, and not on Mount Ebal:

> So when you have crossed over the Jordan, you shall set up these stones, about which I am commanding you today, on Mount Gerizim, and you shall cover them with plaster. And you shall build an altar there to the Lord your God, an altar of stones on which you have not used an iron tool.

The localization of the altar on Mount Gerizim in the Samaritan text of the Pentateuch notably differs from the Jewish Masoretic text. It instead reads "Mount Ebal." The Old Greek translation of this passage, attested in a Latin manuscript of the *Vetus Latina*, also reads "Mount Gerizim," likely the original version. Within the Samaritan Pentateuch, this same passage is repeated in Exodus 20 and Deuteronomy 5, inscribing the veneration of Mount Gerizim at the end of the Ten Commandments. Thus, in the Samaritan tradition, the election of Mount Gerizim and the divine order to establish the center of Israel's worship there is part and parcel of the laws revealed on Mount Sinai, as opposed to the Jewish Torah.

Another textual variant of the Samaritan Pentateuch relating to Mount Gerizim is more complex. In the centralization formula occurring first in Deuteronomy 12:5, and repeated no less than twenty-one times in this book, the Samaritan Pentateuch reads "the place which the Lord your God chose" (בחר), instead of the Masoretic "will choose" (יבחר). The exact reference point for the Samaritan past tense (which is found in other ancient textual witnesses as well and preserves an original reading) is unclear, and therefore also which event the text has in mind. Samaritan midrashic exegesis aims to fill this gap. The results can be observed already in the earliest layers of Samaritan liturgical poetry, as well as in the Samaritan midrashic collection *Tebat Marqe*.

According to *Tebat Marqe*, Mount Gerizim had been prepared by God to house the sanctuary of Israel since the creation of the world:

> Four caves were prepared on the third day (of creation): Machpelah for the righteous, Mount Gerizim for the Tabernacle, Mount Hor for the priesthood, and Mount Nebo for the prophecy. (*Tebat Marqe* 2:57)

This statement not only links four pillars of Samaritan-Israelite identity and four different places, but additionally claims that these connections were predetermined by God on the third day of the creation account, that is, the day when God created the surface of the earth (Genesis 1:9–13). Three of the sites are explicitly mentioned in the Torah. Machpelah served as a burial place for Abraham (Genesis 23; 25:9–10), at Mount Hor the prototypical priest Aaron died (Numbers 20:28), and at Mount Nebo the prophet Moses died as well (Deuteronomy 34). The fourth case, a cave at Mount Gerizim serving as the hiding place for the Tabernacle, is obviously without reference in the Torah, even if the Samaritan Pentateuch identifies Mount Gerizim as the place of the sanctuary. The tradition is not unique to *Tebat Marqe*, but is known from earlier sources as well. The earliest parallel appears in Josephus's description of an event that happened during the governorship of Pontius Pilate (26–36 CE), which is also discussed by Reinhard Pummer in this volume:

> The Samaritan nation too was not exempt from disturbance. For a man who made light of mendacity and in all his designs catered to the mob, rallied them, bidding them go in a body with him to Mount Gerizim, which in their belief is the most sacred of mountains. He assured them that on their arrival he would show them the sacred vessels which were buried there, where Moses had deposited them. (Josephus, *Antiquities* 18.85)

Here, Josephus seems to report a tradition known among the Samaritans in the first century CE, according to which the sacred vessels were buried on Mount Gerizim. This tradition recurs in *Tebat Marqe*,

which postdates Josephus by at least three centuries. The core motif that the sacred vessels were buried in a cave can even be traced back to the middle of the second century BCE. New in *Tebat Marqe* is the claim that this cave had already been prepared and determined for its ultimate purpose at the creation of the world. Most obviously, this modification of the motif relies on the Samaritan concept that Mount Gerizim itself was chosen from the outset as Holy Mountain, a view commonly acknowledged in the early Samaritan prayers as well as in *Tebat Marqe*. Thus, according to *Tebat Marqe* 2:45, Mount Gerizim is among the "choicest things" created by God:

> Seven choicest (creations) exist in the world, which the True one chose and set them apart for his divinity: the Light, the Sabbath, Mount Gerizim, Adam, the two stone tablets (of the Ten Commandments), the great prophet Moses, and Israel. ... Mount Gerizim is the choicest sanctuary, which God had chosen as dwelling for His Glory.

And thus, Mount Gerizim was holy from the outset:

> The Good mountain is the holiest of all mountains, and its holiness began from the beginning of the act of creation. (*Tebat Marqe* 2:44)

The concept that Mount Gerizim was chosen and holy from the very beginning of the world connects closely to another association that contributes to the special rank of Mount Gerizim, the creation of humans from dust taken from there:

> Adam, whom God created from the dust of the Good mountain, is the choicest creature, and the Good mountain is the choicest elevated land. (*Tebat Marqe* 2:44)

The motif of Adam created from dust taken from the place of the sanctuary is also found in Jewish midrashim from late antique Palestine, for example in *Genesis Rabba* 14:8:

> He [i.e., Adam] was created from the place of his atonement, as you read *An altar of earth (adama) you will make for me*. (Exodus 20:24)[6]

While the basic claim of the Samaritan *Tebat Marqe* and the Jewish *Genesis Rabba* may seem the same, namely that Adam was created from earth taken from the place of the sanctuary, the underlying exegetical arguments are quite different. The Jewish version of the motif rests on the keyword אדמה "earth." Thus, Adam was created "of dust from the earth," linking him from the outset to the cultic service at the "altar of earth" in the Temple in Jerusalem. The Jewish adaptation of the motive, therefore, stresses that ever since his creation Adam's existence has depended on the cult in order to endure.

Samaritan sources from late antiquity also create a connection between Adam and the cult, but in a very different way:

> Form from dust
> everything was created on their behalf,
> every descendant of Adam needs
> to be subservient to You (*Tebat Marqe* 10:69–72).

STEFAN SCHORCH

Marqe's prayer substantiates cultic service with the view that God created the world on man's behalf, even though the first man was formed from dust himself. Thus, the cultic service depends on the existence of men, and not *vice versa*. In the same vein, Adam's creation from the dust of Mount Gerizim does not express the predetermination of the cultic service, but rather Adam's endowment as one of the seven choicest creations (*Tebat Marqe* 2:45; see above): he was created from dust taken from the choicest part of the earth, that is, Mount Gerizim:

> *The Lord God formed man from the dust of the earth* [Genesis 2:7], from the good dust of the Good Mountain. The House of Adam is exalted by The True One, for he is the choicest of all the creatures. And like all the choicest things appointed for the holy, imperfection has no share in it. Every offering that is offered by men for the sake of the holy name is empowered and glorified. Such is the body of Adam, the choicest of all creature(s), since he was only taken from what preceded him: "the Good Mountain," the choicest of all the mountains. And like every chosen thing offered to Holiness, there is no flaw in it. Every chosen thing offered by men to the holy name becomes exalted and glorified. Similarly, the body of Adam, the choicest of all creature(s), was only taken from what preceded him: the Good Mountain, the choicest of all the mountains. At the beginning of "In the beginning" [i.e., in the seven days of creation, Genesis 1], the Creator raised it up. (*Tebat Marqe* 2:44)

Thus, according to this passage from *Tebat Marqe*, just as an offering has to be flawless to be appropriate as a gift for the deity, so also Adam's body was necessarily flawless to be exalted and glorified by God. This flawlessness was guaranteed, since Adam was formed from dust taken from Mount Gerizim, that is, from the best part of the world. The closest parallel to this view from Jewish sources seems to be the first-century philosopher Philo of Alexandrias interpretation of the creation of Adam's body as most excellent because the purest and utmost refined part was separated out from pure matter (Philo, *On the Creation*, 136–137). As in the Samaritan sources, God's choice of the best material is the reason for Adam's elevation as opposed to the other living creatures. But while in Philo's case the best material is selected by God from the different parts of the earth, Samaritan sources state that the best material is only to be found at Mount Gerizim, due to its antecedent appointment by the divine.

In connection with the aboriginal election of Mount Gerizim, and as its consequence, the Samaritan tradition postulates that Mount Gerizim has been the holy center of worship since the days of Adam:

> Adam worshipped towards it [i.e., Mount Gerizim], and Enosh *called the name of the Lord* [Genesis 4:26] at it, and Enoch knew it and rushed toward it, and Noah built an altar and stood on it and praised the Lord of the world. (*Tebat Marqe* 2:47).

Most prominently, the very first proper sacrifice according to the Torah, the one offered by Abel (Genesis 4), took place on Mount Gerizim (*Tebat Marqe* 2:48). A roughly contemporary Jewish midrash stresses that Abel offered a sacrifice at the site of the future Jewish Temple:

> *Cain rose up against his brother Abel* etc. [Genesis 4:8] Rabbi Joshua of Siknin said in Rabbi Levi's name: Both took land and both took movables, but about what did they quarrel? One said, "The Temple must be built in my area," while the other claimed, "It must be built in mine." For thus it is written, *And it came to pass, when they were in the field* [ibid.]: now *field* refers to to none other than the Temple, as you read, *Zion* [i.e., the Jerusalem Temple] *shall be plowed as a field* [Micah 3:12]. (*Genesis Rabba* 22:7)[7]

Both the Samaritan and the Jewish texts share the same motif—Abel offers a sacrifice at the place of the sanctuary—but the rationale provided by each for this localization is different. According to the Jewish midrash, the site is expected to house the future Temple. In other words, the place is not yet a special cultic site. According to the Samaritan source, on the other hand, God's presence already dwells in this place.

Another feature of Mount Gerizim in Samaritan theology is its elevation, towering as it does over Shechem and the neighboring valley at 881 meters. This elevation was not just symbolic but is also taken to be a geological reality (in fact, Mount Ebal is slightly taller at 940 meters). Samaritan traditions claim that, due to its height, Mount Gerizim was the only mountain not covered by the waters of the flood. It was therefore the only part of the earth that did not become ritually impure after the flood from the dead bodies found in the water: "The water of the flood did not reach it, and no men died there and made it impure" (*Tebat Marqe* 12:33).

Confirmation of both the specifically Samaritan context of this story and its antiquity comes from a Jewish source preserved in *Genesis Rabba* 32:10:[8]

> *And the waters prevailed [and all the high mountains were covered*— Genesis 7:19]. Rabbi Jonathan was going up to pray in Jerusalem, and he passed by the *palatinus* [that is, Mount Gerizim].
> A Samaritan [*shamrai*] saw him and said, "Where are you going?"
> [Rabbi Jonathan] said to him, "To pray in Jerusalem."
> [The Samaritan] said, "Is it not preferable for you to pray at this blessed mountain rather than at that refuse dump?"
> [Rabbi Jonathan] said to him, "Why is [Mount Gerizim] blessed?"
> [The Samaritan] said to him, "Because it was not inundated by the waters of the Flood!"
> Rabbi Jonathan was momentarily at a loss to reply,
> So his donkey-driver said, "Rabbi, permit me and I will answer him."
> [Rabbi Jonathan] said, "Do so."
> [The donkey-driver] said [to the Samaritan], "If [you claim that Mount Gerizim] is one of the high mountains then scripture says, '*All the high mountains … were covered*' (Genesis 7:19), but [if you claim that Mount Gerizim] is one of the low ones, then scripture ignored it completely.

This passage shows that Jews in late antiquity were not only aware of the motif that the dead bodies in the water of the flood had polluted the earth, but also of its Samaritan application as proof of the sanctity and purity of Mount Gerizim. Moreover, the story also seems to imply that the motif was not known to have been applied with regard to Jerusalem, since *Genesis Rabba* presents the motif as distinctively Samaritan.

As a consequence of this tradition, Samaritan sources claim that the altar that Noah built immediately after the flood, according to Genesis 8, was found on Mount Gerizim:

> And since this place was perfect in every respect, Noah came and was seeking his holiness and performed a ritual which was perfectly holy without any blemish. And he took from all the pure animals, and he would not have been able to act in purity in an impure place, since he knew that all places were impure from the death of all living beings. (*Tebat Marqe* 12:34)

Samaritan tradition localizes Noah's altar (Genesis 8:20) at Mount Gerizim. In light of the extensive tradition described so far treating Mount Gerizim as God's holy place since the creation, it will hardly come as a surprise that the Samaritan tradition also locates every legitimate holy place, altar, or offering in the account of the pre-Sinaitic period at Mount Gerizim. This is particularly true of places related to Abraham and Jacob. With respect to Abraham, two biblical traditions have to be mentioned: the altar built at Shechem (Genesis 12) and the altar on Mount Moriah built on the occasion of the binding of Isaac (Genesis 22). For the former, *Tebat Marqe* 2:44 reads as follows:

> As he did say in the beginning to the first of the righteous: *To your offspring I will give this land, and he built an altar there* (Genesis 12:7). And where did he build the altar, if not toward Mount Gerizim.

Similarly, the altar of Isaac's supposed sacrifice at Mount Moriah is in fact built on Mount Gerizim (Figure 3.5):

> Therefore, it is said about Noah just in the same way as about Abraham: *And Noah built an altar* (Genesis 8:20)—*And Abraham built there the altar* (Genesis 22:9). As Noah did it in a truthful way, Abraham did it in a truthful way (*Tebat Marqe* 2:47).

The place at which Jacob saw a ladder leading toward heaven and set up a pillar, according to Genesis 28, is identified with Mount Gerizim. Consequently, several names appearing in this story became designations for Mount Gerizim, especially Beit-El, Luza, and "Gate of Heaven,"

> The second [name of Mount Gerizim] is Beit-El, since the mighty and awesome God is a shield and a support for those who trust him. He made it a shelter for refuge for all who return to God, the Lord. (*Tebat Marqe* 2:50)

As can be observed in this last case, the identification of a place from the biblical tradition with Mount Gerizim is not unidirectional but involves a complex intertextual dynamic. On the one hand, the biblical site receives a geographical setting familiar to the reader within

3.5 Pilgrimage to the site of the Binding of Isaac, Passover morning, Mount Gerizim, 2020 (Photograph by Ori Orhof).

the sacred geography of the Samaritan community. On the other hand, however, Mount Gerizim is qualified theologically. In this case, the role of Beit-El for Jacob (Genesis 28) is conferred on Mount Gerizim, which is thus a place of refuge and divine revelation.

Samaritan tradition emphasizes Mount Gerizim as the only holy place of Israel. This mountain is associated with all the attributes found in the biblical stories about holy places:

> (Mount Gerizim) is the house of God and the dwelling place for his glory. There is no divine presence but on it, as is said *Unto his habitation shall you seek* [Deuteronomy 12:5], and there is no sacrifice but toward it, and there is no offering but on it, and there is no gift but at it, and there is no willing offering, and no tithe, and no first fruits, and no ransom. And blessing is never received except from it. Because it is the place of the divine presence of the True one, and the encampment of the Great glory. (*Tebat Marqe* 2:48)

Mount Gerizim plays a pivotal role in the Samaritan concept of history, discerning three different periods: history began with the period of divine favor. This extended from the time of the creation up to the entrance into the promised land. During that period, all Israel had focused on Mount Gerizim, which bestowed blessing and divine favor. This was followed by the period of divine disfavor (*Fanuta*), which began with the split between those Israelites who left Mount Gerizim and, under the leadership of the priest Eli, inaugurated a schismatic cultic site in Shilo (and later in Jerusalem), and the remainder of the people, who truthfully remained at the true sanctuary under increased pressure. The *Fanuta* continues to the present. Finally, the period of renewed divine favor will be inaugurated by the *Taheb*, a future "Prophet Like Moses." He will restore the sacrificial cult on Mount Gerizim and at the same time turn the sanctuary into the center of political power. This is expressed in a liturgical poem by Amram Dare:

> Happy is the *Taheb*,
> and happy are his disciples which are like him.
> Happy is the world when he comes,
> who brings with him the peace,
> and reveals the period of divine favor,
> and expurgates Mount Gerizim, the House of God,
> and removes the wrath from Israel.
> God gives him a great victory,
> and fights through him against the whole world.
> (*A Liturgical Poem by Amram Dare*, 16:33–41)

Thus, the importance of Mount Gerizim as the one and only holy place is not restricted to the past and the present. It also has an imminent future and eschatological dimension.

Within Samaritan tradition, the centrality of Mount Gerizim has textual and conceptual significance. It is the *axis mundi*, the center of the world. This can be observed at numerous excavated Samaritan synagogues from late antiquity, which are generally aligned toward Mount Gerizim and demonstrate the direction of prayer (Figure 3.6). Samaritan written sources express the same idea based on midrashic exegesis of texts from the Torah. Here is one example:

> (Abraham) went for the place which God had chosen, and when he saw it from afar, he turned his face toward it and prayed, and when he finished his prayer, *he lifted up his eyes* [Genesis 22:4] and he did not lift up his eyes but from prayer, because it was in the morning, and he was standing and prayed. And to where was the direction of his prayer, if not toward Mount Gerizim? (*Tebat Marqe* 2:46)

The direction of prayer toward Mount Gerizim is also present in the liturgy, as in this prayer composed by the Samaritan poet Marqe (fourth century CE):

> Look upon us, Lord,
> We have nothing to turn our face to
> but to you, the merciful. (*Tebat Marqe* 1:1–3)

Turning the face toward Mount Gerizim is a literary *topos* in this prayer, aiming at the reciprocity of a face-to-face connection with God. A new stage was reached in the eleventh century, with the introduction of a prayer at the beginning of the liturgy, which accompanies the act of turning the face toward Mount Gerizim. The direction of prayer, therefore, which used to be a habit that followed the orientation of Samaritan synagogue buildings, developed into an explicit performative act.

The Samaritan concentration of traditions of holy space in Mount Gerizim parallels directly the development of Jewish traditions, which associate everything from the burial of Adam to the altar of Abel to the binding of Isaac with the Temple Mount in Jerusalem—toward which all prayer is directed. While Samaritans and Jews share the concept of one holy center, their differing cultural approaches lead to very different mountains. This rupture was in-tensified by an element inherent in the concept of one single holy center, as required by the Torah: there cannot be two! This is expressed polemically in a passage from *Tebat Marqe*:

> [Mount Gerizim] is the place of the divine presence of the True one, and the encampment of the Great glory. Woe to those who exchanged the truth for a lie, when they choose for themselves a different place. (*Tebat Marqe* 2:48)

Jews could not have agreed more. *Tractate Kutim* 2:8, a late rabbinic text, disqualifies Samaritans from becoming Jews until "they renounce Mount Gerizim and acknowledge Jerusalem."[9]

For Further Reading

Ze'ev Ben-Ḥayyim. תיבת מרקה [*Tibât Mârqe*]. *A Collection of Samaritan Midrashim, Edited, Translated and Annotated*. Jerusalem: Israel Academy of Sciences, 1988. [Hebrew].

——-. *The Literary and Oral Tradition of Hebrew and Aramaic amongst the Samaritans. Volume III, Part 2: The Recitation of Prayers and Hymns*. Jerusalem: The Academy of the Hebrew Language, 1967. [Hebrew].

Stefan Schorch. "Is a Qibla a Qibla? Samaritan Traditions About Mount Garizim in Contact and Contention." *Near and Middle Eastern Studies at the Institute for Advanced Studies, Princeton: 1935-1918*, edited by Sabine Schmidtke. Piscataway, NJ: Gorgias Press, 1918, 95-100.

Abraham Tal. *Tibât Mârqe The Ark of Marqe Edition, Translation, Commentary*. Berlin: De Gruyter, 2019.

---

1   Ed. Ben-Ḥayyim, 49–50.
2   Ed. Noam, 46.
3   Ed. Stenhouse, 14.
4   Ibid., 28.
5   Ibid., 42.
6   Ed. Theodor-Albeck, 132.
7   Ibid., 213.
8   Ibid., 296–297.
9   Ed. Goldstein and Katzman, 191–192.

4

"Kinsmen" or an "Alien Race?": Jews and Samaritans from the Hasmoneans to the Mishnah

JOSEPH L. ANGEL

In former times they would light signal fires lifted on staves [to signal that the new month had been decreed]. When the *Kutim* corrupted this, they decreed that messengers should go out. How did they light the torches? They used to bring long poles of cedar and reeds and olive wood and flax fluff and they tied them all together with a string. And someone used to go up to the top of a mountain and light them with fire and wave them back and forth and up and down until he saw the next one doing the same thing on the top of the second mountain; and so on the top of the third mountain. At what places did they light the torches? From the Mount of Olives [in Jerusalem] to Sartaba, and from Sartaba to Gripina, and from Gripina to Hauran, and from Hauran to Beit Biltin. From Beit Biltin they did not move, but rather waved [the torch] back and forth and up and down until he saw the whole of the diaspora before him lit up like one bonfire.

— Mishnah Rosh Hashanah, 2:2–4

In this anonymous passage of the Mishnah (redacted circa 200 CE), rabbis remember an episode that occurred decades earlier, presumably some time before the destruction of Jerusalem in 70 CE. This text recalls how certain activities of the Samaritans (referred to with the pejorative term *Kutim*) brought about the need for a change in the Jewish system of announcing the arrival of a new lunar month. In former times (*ba-rishonah*), the tradition states, Jewish communities as far away as Babylonia (modern Iraq) were alerted that the new moon had been spotted and verified by the court in Jerusalem through a chain of signal torches kindled on a succession of mountain tops—beginning from the Mount of Olives east of Jerusalem and continuing up the Jordan Rift valley toward the north. The second station was Sarbata (also called Alexandrion), a Hasmonean Fortress overlooking the Jordan River. The route then passed close to the Samaritan heartland and northward to Gripina, making its way across the Syrian desert to the important Jewish communities of the Euphrates–Tigris River valley. According to our text, the *Kutim* collectively "corrupted" this system of torches apparently by lighting their own competing ones. In their supposed debasement,

they disrupted Jewish communication of news of the new moon, and thus the entire calendar and holiday structure. A more reliable—if slower—system involving messengers was then instituted.

While the historical circumstances behind this incident remain unclear, this text reflects a larger pattern of religious competition between Jews and Samaritans during this period. It is unlikely that the Samaritans would have taken such actions if they had shared identical calendrical practices with the Jews of our Mishnah. This mischief would have come at the unacceptable cost of violating the festivals themselves. In fact, later Samaritan tradition preserves a lunisolar calendar similar but not identical to the one employed by Jews—one of the main differences being that the new moon is determined in this system not by direct observation but rather by the calculation of the conjunction of the moon with the sun (as has been the case for Jews since late antiquity as well). The Samaritan chronicle known as the *Tulidah* (twelfth century CE) refers to this system as the "True Reckoning" (*Ḥeshban Qishtah*). According to this tradition, the tools of accurate calendar calculation were passed down "from Pinḥas son of Eleazar son of Aaron the priest … who was taught by Moses the prophet. … For he [Moses] is descended from the three fathers, Jacob, Isaac and Abraham. … This [knowledge] was made known to them by Ever [who received it] from Shem [who received it] from Noah [who received it] from Seth [who received it] from Adam [who received it] from the angels of *Shemaa* [literally 'The Name,' God]. Pinḥas applied this computation to the latitude of the holy Mount Gerizim."[1] While this source is preserved in a twelfth-century chronicle, and one cannot simply assume that this system was in place in ancient times, some substantial distinction between Samaritan and Jewish calendrical practices surely existed in antiquity. Rabbinic sources assume that the Samaritans might celebrate Passover earlier or later or on the same day that Jews do (Tosefta Pesaḥim 2:2). The fifth-century Christian historian Socrates Scholasticus testifies to Jewish–Samaritan disagreement over this very same matter (even as his understanding is incomplete): "The Jews observe no exact rule either in time or manner of celebrating the paschal [festival] solemnly: and the Samaritans, who are an offshoot from the Jews, always celebrate the festival after the equinox."[2] Josephus suggests that the issue reaches back all the way to the Second Temple period. He relates that the following happened on a certain Passover during the prefecture of Coponius (6–9 CE):

> Some Samaritans, who had secretly entered Jerusalem, began to scatter human bones in the porticoes and throughout the Temple. As a result, the priests, although they had previously observed no such custom, excluded everyone from the Temple, in addition to taking other measures for the greater protection of the temple. (*Antiquities* 18.29–30)

Had this day been considered Passover also by the Samaritans, they would effectively have been making themselves impure and unfit for their own celebration of the holiday. In any case, given the tensions between the two communities and the Samaritan loyalty to Mount Gerizim and its leadership, it seems unlikely that they would have heeded calendrical decisions made by Jewish authorities in Jerusalem or elsewhere.

Debate over the determination of the correct calendar—the very construction of sacred time, so essential to the correct celebration of Passover and all the other festivals ordained in the Torah of Moses—was not unique to ancient Jewish–Samaritan relations. Indeed, different Jewish groups in Greco-Roman Palestine fought bitterly over this issue. An important example is found in the polemical calendrical works of the Dead Sea Scrolls community, who adopted a strictly solar calendar. The disagreement between the Pharisees and the Samaritans, however, was not as profound, as it apparently was rooted in the details of their respective lunisolar calculations. Often, though, what seem to us to be small issues among similar groups were of world-changing significance for our subjects—prime examples of "the narcissism of small differences."

The Mishnaic tradition introduced above speaks to Jewish suspicions of hostility and subversive behavior on the part of the Samaritans, at least in one localized case. At the same time, it also implies a certain shift in the rabbinic perception of the nature of the relationship, namely, that in former times (*ba-rishonah*) the relationship with Samaritans was less contentious, and thus that closer and more cordial relations were the norm. Such a shift is asserted in numerous later Amoraic sources, which offer broader and more developed perspectives on what some rabbis call Samaritan "corruption." This is well illustrated by an expanded version of Tosefta Pesaḥim that appears in the Jerusalem Talmud:

> Rabban Shimon son of Gamaliel says: Any commandment practiced by the Samaritans is observed more meticulously than by Israel.
>
> Rabbi Shimon says: That was true originally when they were still dwelling in their villages. But now that they do not have even a single commandment nor the remnant of a commandment, they are suspect and they are corrupted. (Tosefta Pesaḥim 1:1, 27b)

Here, the "corruption" of the Samaritans relates to a perceived abandonment of Torah observance in the period after the Bar Kokhba Revolt (132–135 CE). Moreover, this development is explicitly connected with a demographic shift—the expansion of the Samaritan population beyond Samaria proper, which resulted in increased contacts with pagans in Romanized cities and led to cultural assimilation. Later Amoraic explanations would paint Samaritans in an even worse light, accusing them of engaging in outright idolatrous behaviors.

Of course, accusations of corruption and mistrust can swing both ways. It is no surprise that the notion of Jewish religious deviance and ill will is prominent in Samaritan sources. According to *The Chronicle of Abu l-Fath* (fourteenth century), the very origins of Judaism were marred by a number of dubious acts such as King David's rejection of Mount Gerizim, Solomon's building of the Temple in Jerusalem, and Ezra's tampering with the Torah. Interestingly, we also find a parallel accusation of idolatry in Roman times. Abu l-Fath recounts how the emperor Hadrian (who actually ruled 117–138 CE), upon entering the Holy of Holies of the Jerusalem Temple, observed the statue that the Jews had been worshipping.

A reflection of the Samaritan view of Jewish religious corruption appears in a story in *Genesis Rabba* about one Rabbi Jonathan. Traveling from the Galilee in order to pray in Jerusalem, he comes to the region of Shechem, where he is approached by a *Shamrai*, a Samaritan. He is not a *Kuti* but a Samaritan on his home turf! Pointing toward Mount Gerizim, the Samaritan taunts the rabbi: "Is it not preferable for you to pray at *this* blessed mountain rather than at that dunghill [lit. 'corrupted house']?" (*Genesis Rabba* 32:10).[3] By placing the phrase "corrupted house" in the mouth of the Samaritan, this story suggests that the concept of religious "corruption" that the Sages applied to them so frequently could also flow in the opposite direction.

The developing rabbinic notion of Samaritan "corruption" dovetails with the findings of diachronic surveys of rabbinic tradition concerning the status of Samaritans in Jewish law. While later Amoraic sources tend to increasingly exclude Samaritans, ultimately rejecting them completely within the framework of a binary contrast between Jew and non-Jew, earlier Tannaitic sources essentially understand them as Jews, even as they commonly criticize them for improper practices and disparagingly refer to them as *Kutim*. A poignant illustration of both ambiguity and a developing exclusionary attitude is the disagreement between Rabban Shimon son of Gamaliel, who taught that "a *Kuti* is like a Jew in all respects," and his son Rabbi Judah the Patriarch, who taught that "a *Kuti* is like a non-Jew" (Tosefta Terumot 4:12, 14). While this debate originally was limited to a specific case concerning the separation of priestly dues, the two Talmuds would eventually understand it as pertaining to the general, overall status of the Samaritan.[4] In a similar vein, according to an enigmatic Mishnaic tradition, it was declared before Rabbi Aqiva that

> Rabbi Eliezer used to say, "He that eats the bread of the Samaritans is like one that eats pig's flesh." He [Rabbi Aqiva] replied: "Be quiet! I will not tell you what Rabbi Eliezer taught concerning this." (Mishnah Shevi'it 8:10)

The bold rhetorical move to compare Samaritan bread, a questionable category, with pork, which is categorically forbidden, belies the uncertainty of the claim. Moreover, the fact that Rabbi Aqiva silences his interlocutors implies that he disagrees with this statement and would permit the eating of Samaritan bread. Although he refuses to explain further, he implies that Rabbi Eliezer's teaching differs from or contradicts what was reported. Again, the ambiguity stands in contrast to later rabbinic sources, discussed in detail by Shana Strauch Schick and Steven Fine later in this volume, which assume unambiguously and without challenge that Samaritan bread is forbidden.

In Tannaitic sources, the legal status of Samaritans is not determined by broad pronouncements; rather, it is established on a case-by-case basis in relation to their specific behaviors and particular legal issues. Most often, the *Tannaim* equate Samaritans with "Israelites," over against gentiles, in a variety of legal arenas ranging from tort law to ritual purity. For example, after a long discussion of the *Kutim* and their trustworthiness in regard to Passover law, the Tosefta discusses matzah baked by *Kutim* for Passover use by Jews:

> The unleavened bread of the *Kutim* is permitted, and a person may fulfill his obligation [of eating unleavened bread] with it on Passover.

> R. Eleazar [ca. 150 CE] prohibits it, for they are not expert in the specific regulations regarding unleavened bread.

> Rabban Shimon son of Gamaliel [ca. 150 CE] says: Any commandment which the Samaritans have taken hold of, they are much more meticulous about than Israel. (Shimon son of Pesaḥim 2:3)

Here we see that, despite some clear reservations, the distance between Jews and Samaritans could appear quite small in the second century CE. A similar sense of closeness (both religious and physical) emerges from Mishnah Berakhot 7:1, which rules that when three individuals have eaten together, a *Kuti* may be included in the requisite ritual invitation (*zimmun*) to make the blessing after meals.

In most cases, though, serious reservations about the inclusion of Samaritans are evident. For example, in determining the trustworthiness of those who were not followers of the rabbis in dealing with issues of agricultural tithing, Samaritans are categorized together with *ammei ha-arets*, Jews who are ignorant or otherwise have no interest in rabbis. They are not, however, treated as gentiles:

> If one takes [already tithed] wheat to a *Kuti* miller or to an *am ha-arets* miller, it retains its previous status regarding tithes and sabbatical produce. (If one takes wheat) to a gentile miller, it is considered *demai* [i.e., produce about which there is a doubt whether or not it has been appropriately tithed]. (Mishnah Demai 3:4)

In another instructive case concerning who may pay the temple tax, we find that Samaritans are grouped together with gentiles: "If a non-Jew or a Samaritan paid the *sheqel* they do not accept it from them … as it is said: 'You have nothing to do with us to build a house unto our God'" (Ezra 4:3). This is a rare exception that may in fact prove the rule. The Samaritan's exclusion in this particular case is directly linked to his divergent religious views. Since he denies the

sanctity of the Jerusalem Temple, instead preferring Gerizim, he has "nothing to do with us to build a house unto our God." The biblical reference implicitly links the Samaritans, at least in this limited matter, to "the adversaries of Judah and Benjamin" and "the people of the land" who harassed the returnees from Babylon and obstructed the building of the Temple in the times of Zerubbabel. While the picture emerging from all of these sources together is mixed, it is clear that the *Tannaim* tended to relate to Samaritans as Jews, albeit of inferior status with suspect religious practices and views.

The mixed and evolving rabbinic attitudes regarding the legal status and "corruption" of the Samaritans represent just one piece of a much larger picture of a complex developing relationship between two groups bound together not only by their geographical, linguistic, and cultural proximity, but also by their intertwined scriptural and religious heritage and similar traumatic political experiences under Greek and Roman rule. Consideration of other types of evidence such as non-legal narratives and folktales, material culture, and earlier Second Temple period sources illuminate just how varied and multifaceted the patterns of relations between Jews and Samaritans in antiquity could be. Indeed, even as they disagreed as groups about core religious tenets, expressing hostility and accusing one another of religious corruption, such views did not govern every single daily interaction between individuals. A Jewish person could simultaneously oppose the religious views of his or her Samaritan neighbor and engage them in friendly conversation. Likewise, a Samaritan might reject Jewish scriptures and the notion of Jerusalem's sanctity but still engage in business dealings with Jews. In turn, such individual interactions and social choices would inevitably impact the overall shape of collective relations.

Samaritan sources suggest some intriguing examples of close friendships between Samaritan and Jewish individuals. Abu l-Fath recounts how before his death in Constantinople the famed Samaritan leader and religious reformer Baba Rabba (third or fourth century CE) sought out a Jewish friend and entrusted the care of his son Levi to him. Baba makes his Jewish companion swear that he will guard him from "anything that could make him unclean" and to "look after him as if he were your son." Beyond the intimate expression of trust, it is remarkable that the Jew and the Samaritan are assumed to share a similar core understanding of what causes one to be "unclean." In a sense, this is reminiscent of the Tannaitic sources that tend to treat Samaritans and Jews as "Israel" over against gentiles, a contrast that would have been particularly apparent to Baba while on his deathbed in Constantinople.

Another revealing episode narrated by Abu l-Fath concerns the devious attempt of certain Jews to assassinate Baba Rabba at the synagogue of Namara at the behest of the Roman authorities. Before the Jews' plot could be executed though, a Jewish woman with knowledge of the plan became concerned for the well-being of "a very close friend who was a Samaritan woman" and warned her to stay away from the synagogue.[5] Ultimately, the plot is divulged and Baba is able to escape and imprison, kill, and burn his Jewish opponents. Particularly against the backdrop of such distrustful and explosively violent intercommunal relations, it is striking that a

Monumental Staircase
Leading to the Sacred
Precinct of the Samaritan
Temple, Mount Gerizim,
eastern slope, early second
century BCE (Courtesy of
www.HolyLandPhotos.org).

commitment to a close personal relationship between a Samaritan and a Jew is portrayed as outweighing ethnic allegiances.

Personal interactions between Samaritans and Jews must have occurred commonly in earlier times as well, although they are less frequently attested in the sources. One significant example is the extensive exchange between Jesus and a Samaritan woman at a well in the region of Shechem depicted in the Gospel of John (4:4–42), discussed in depth by Steven Notley and Jeffrey García later in this volume. Most Second Temple period sources, however, tend to express more generalized views of group dynamics, focusing on political or religious enmity, and hence obscure the existence of different kinds of social relations. For example, Josephus, our most abundant source, discusses in detail numerous intercommunal disputes and political and military clashes between Samaritans and Jews, Greeks, and Romans. At the same time, he displays little interest in or knowledge of Samaritan beliefs or practices, and there is no evidence that he maintained a personal acquaintance with the Samaritan community or with individual Samaritans. Even so, Josephus is often antagonistic toward them as a group and accuses them of duplicity. For instance, he makes the following reflection:

> When the Samaritans see the Jews prospering, they call them their kinsmen, on the ground that they are descended from Joseph and thus are related to them through their common origin, but that when they see that the Jews are in trouble, they say that they have nothing in common with them and declare that they are aliens of another race. (*Antiquities* 9.291)

As an example of this kind of behavior, he notes that when the Samaritans witnessed the Jews suffering under the persecutions of Antiochus IV (167–164 BCE), they attempted to distance themselves from the trouble and "no longer admitted that they were kin" (*Antiquities* 12.257). It seems that Josephus's negative portrayals do not so much reflect his own personal views as they do his use of the Samaritans as a foil against which to make the Jews look more loyal and sensible in the eyes of the Romans.

An earlier Jewish perspective concerning the Samaritans is expressed by the Jerusalem sage Joshua son Elazar son of Sira. Writing around 190 BCE, he remarks: "Two nations my soul detests, and the third is not even a people: those who live in Seir, and the Philistines, and the foolish people that live in Shechem" (Sira 50:25–26).[6] The third group clearly refers to the Samaritans, who are not only classified with two traditional biblical enemies, but are also portrayed as fulfilling the words of Deuteronomy 32:21: "I will make them jealous with what is no people, provoke them with a foolish nation." Ben Sira's peculiar understanding of the verse, underscoring a derogatory attitude toward the Samaritans and probably the "jealousy" caused by their alternate cult site at Mount Gerizim, represents the beginning of a long history in Jewish biblical interpretation. A Hasmonean-era manuscript from the Dead Sea Scrolls employs the same verse when it refers to the descendants of Joseph (= Samaritans) as "fools" who "make for themselves a high place upon a high mountain to provoke Israel to jealousy … reviling the tent of Zion and speaking the word of falsehood."[7] A related understanding of this verse underlies the labeling of Shechem as "a city of fools" in the Greek *Testament of Levi* (7:2). Rabbinic interpretation makes a similar equation: "'I will stir them to jealousy with a non-people' (Deuteronomy 32:21): These are the Samaritans."[8] In the light of this long-standing Jewish exegetical tradition, it is interesting to note

𐤉𐤌𐤒𐤔𐤅𐤓𐤀

that a Samaritan midrash in *Tibat Marqe* understands the beginning of Deuteronomy 32:21, "They made me jealous with a no-god," as a specific reference to Jewish worship in Jerusalem.[9]

To an extent, the attitudes expressed in this exegetical debate are mirrored in historical sources pertaining to the Hellenistic era. According to Josephus, the Jewish and Samaritan communities of Alexandria already quarreled in the time of Ptolemy VI Philometor (180–145 BCE) about the proper location of the Temple, each side asserting that its sanctuary had been built "in accordance with the laws of Moses" (*Antiquities* 13.74–79). Echoes of an early conflict centered on the competing holy sites are recorded in a scholion, an addendum, to *Megillat Taanit*. Commenting on the "Day of Mount Gerizim" (21 Kislev), this source narrates a legendary account of a bitter dispute between Jews and Samaritans in the days of the Jewish high priest Simon the Righteous, a contemporary of Ben Sira. According to the

narrative, an assault on Jerusalem and its temple by the Samaritans is stymied by Simon when he dresses himself in the high priestly vestments and goes out to greet Alexander the Great at Antipatris at the source of the Yarkon River in the Coastal Plain.[10] Upon beholding Simon, Alexander dismounts and bows down before him, explaining to his companions that the image of this very man had appeared to him in a vision just prior to his riding out to victory in battle. As a result of acquiring Alexander's favor, not only is the Samaritan plot nullified, but Mount Gerizim is plowed over and sowed with undesirable plants, "just as they had plotted to do to the Temple (of Jerusalem)." While this story of jubilant reversal is historically problematic on a number of levels—Simon and Alexander were not contemporary, a parallel legend is told by Josephus about Alexander and the high priest Jaddua (*Antiquities* 11.326–329), and there is no historical basis for Alexander having made such a visit to Jerusalem—it at least

4.2 Dedicatory Inscription, Delos, 150-50 BCE. (© Ephorate of Antiquities of the Cyclades, Ministry of Culture and Sports Archaeological Receipts Fund): "The Israelites on Delos who make offerings to the temple (on) [or, to sacred] Argarizein, crown with a golden wreath Sarapion, son of Jason of Knossos, for his beneficence toward them."

4.3 Dedicatory Inscriptions in Samaritan Script from the Peak of Mount Gerizim, third to second century BCE. Left: Tetragrammaton. Right: …] priest[… p]riests… (*kohanim*) …]r bḥ[… (Magen, 2004, nos. 383–384, Museum of the Good Samaritan, photograph by Steven Fine).

ꗉꗙ꘍ꗙꘅ꘍ꗏ THE SAMARITANS

reflects a Jewish view of what could have happened, and some scholars maintain that it preserves the kernel of a memory of a historical Jewish–Samaritan dispute that took place in the time of Simon. Historians generally understand it as preserving echoes of John Hyrcanus's later destruction of the Samaritan Temple on Mount Gerizim and the surrounding city in 111–110 BCE, an attack that was clearly part of a larger Hasmonean project to Judaize the Holy Land.[11]

On the Samaritan side, archeological discoveries have affirmed the religious attachment to Mount Gerizim during the Hellenistic era in a spectacular way (Figure 4.1). Two Greek inscriptions discovered on the island of Delos in the Aegean Sea express support for the "Israelites who send their temple tax to *Argarizein* (Mount Gerizim, Figure 4.2)," confirming the existence of a community bound by its reverence for this holy place, even at a great distance. In addition, hundreds of Hebrew and Aramaic (and some Greek) votive inscriptions left by pilgrims have been unearthed at the summit of Mount Gerizim itself (Figure 4.3). One of these, an inscription in Aramaic, reads: "This is [the stone] that Delayah, son of Shimon, dedicated for himself and his children, [this] ston[e for] good remembrance before God in this place."[12] Such inscriptions serve not only to affirm active worship at the site but also the existence of a community dedicated to its own place of worship there, and not in Jerusalem. This evidence may be dated to the first half of the second century BCE, close to the time of Ben Sira and well before the destruction of the Mount Gerizim Temple and the surrounding city by John Hyrcanus in 111–110 BCE (Figure 4.4).

In conclusion, while Second Temple period Jewish sources tend to emphasize poor intergroup relations and even episodes of severe animosity and violent conflict between Samaritans and Jews, this is only part of a far more complex story. Poor relations are still relations nonetheless, and the separation between the groups was never total. In fact, the harsh viewpoints expressed by authors such as Ben Sira and Josephus belie a certain intimacy—the very sources of tension between the groups are related inextricably to their intertwined scriptural and religious heritage and their status as neighbors in competition within a small land occupied by the same Greek and Roman authorities. The fraught and mixed nature of Jewish–Samaritan relations peeks through the Tannaitic sources even more clearly.

To the *Tannaim*, Samaritans are essentially Jews/Israelites, but they are also *Kutim*, neighbors of inferior status with suspect religious practices and beliefs. Again, however, the case-by-case consideration of Samaritan legal status implies intimate knowledge of Samaritan practices and beliefs by the rabbis as well as sustained social contacts. Despite the widening separation between the two communities in later generations, parallel developments in material culture brought to light by archeology, such as synagogues, synagogue mosaics (Figures 0.7, 3.2, 6.2, 7.2-4, 7), and ritual baths, betray a level of continued social engagement, mutual familiarity, and cultural exchange throughout the Roman and early Byzantine eras.

For Further Reading

Louis H. Feldman. "Josephus' Attitude Toward the Samaritans: A Study in Ambivalence." *Studies in Jewish Civilization* 3 (1992): 23–45, reproduced in Louis H. Feldman, *Studies in Hellenistic Judaism*. Leiden: Brill, 1996, 114–146.

Gary Knoppers. *Jews and Samaritans: The Origins and History of Their Early Relations*. Oxford: Oxford University Press, 2013.

Reinhard Pummer. *The Samaritans in Flavius Josephus*. Tübingen: Mohr Siebeck, 2009.

Lawrence Schiffman. "The Samaritans in Tannaitic Halakhah." *Jewish Quarterly Review* 75 (1985): 323–350.

---

1   Ed. Florentin, 49–52.

2   *Historia Ecclesiastica* 5.22; Pummer, 2002, 216.

3   Ed. Theodor-Albeck, 296.

4   Jerusalem Talmud Berakhot 7:1, 11a; Demai 3:4, 23c; Babylonian Talmud Ḥullin 6a.

5   Ed. Stenhouse, chapter 43, pp. 190-192.

6   Purvis, 1965.

7   Schuller, 1990, 4Q372 1 11–14.

8   *Midrash Tannaim to Deuteronomy*, ed. D.Z. Hoffmann, ad. loc. [Hebrew].

9   Ed. Ben-Ḥayyim, 288, 294–297.

10 Cf. Bablyonian Talmud Yoma 69a.

11 *War* 1.62–66, *Antiquities* 13.254–256.

12 Kartveit, 2014, 455.

4.4 The Destruction of the Samaritan Temple by John Hyrcanus I, *Keter Kehunah, hu Sefer Yossipon be-Lashon Ashkenaz*, Yossipon in Yiddish, attributed to Joseph ben Gurion the Priest. Amsterdam: Kosman son of Yosef Barukh, 1770/71 (Yeshiva University, Mendel Gottesman Library, Strauss Collection).

5

"But a Samaritan … Had Compassion": Jesus, Early Christianity, and the Samaritans

R. STEVEN NOTLEY AND JEFFREY P. GARCÍA

And behold, a lawyer stood up to put him to the test, saying: "Teacher, what shall I do to inherit eternal life?" He said to him: "What is written in the law? How do you read?" And he answered: "You shall love the Lord your God with all your heart, and with all your soul, and with all your strength, and with all your mind; and your neighbor as yourself." And he said to him: "You have answered right; do this, and you will live." But he, desiring to justify himself, said to Jesus: "And who is my neighbor?"

Jesus replied: "A man was going down from Jerusalem to Jericho, and he fell among robbers, who stripped him and beat him, and departed, leaving him half-dead. Now by chance a priest was going down that road; and when he saw him, he passed by on the other side. So likewise a Levite, when he came to the place and saw him, passed by on the other side. But a Samaritan, as he journeyed, came to where he was; and when he saw him, he had compassion, and went to him and bound up his wounds, pouring on oil and wine; then he set him on his own beast and brought him to an inn, and took care of him. And the next day he took out two *denarii* and gave them to the innkeeper, saying: 'Take care of him; and whatever more you spend, I will repay you when I come back.' Which of these three, do you think, proved neighbor to the man who fell among the robbers?" He said: "The one who showed mercy on him." And Jesus said to him: "Go and do likewise."

— Luke 10:26–37

Few nameless New Testament characters are better known than "the Good Samaritan." The subject of exegesis, art, and emulation throughout Christian history, the Story of the Good Samaritan has motivated acts of kindness and "love" for two millennia—from the numerous hospitals named for him to the "Good Samaritan laws" passed by American legislators to protect and celebrate those who perform acts of uncommon kindness. Throughout the history of Christianity, artists have depicted the pathos of the "Story of the Good Samaritan" and of the "Story of Jesus's Encounter with the Samaritan Woman at the Well" (Figures 5.1-8). Christian visitors to the Holy Land visited—and continue to visit—Nablus and Mount Gerizim to see the people of the "Good Samaritan." Stereoscope slides and some of the earliest silent films staged the "Story of the Good Samaritan" and the "Story of the Samaritan Woman at the Well," sometimes with real Samaritans as props (Figures 5.1, 5.5). The proprietor of the Samaritan Museum on Mount Gerizim regularly identifies himself to tourists as "the Good Samaritan." The tale of the "Good Samaritan" is so embedded in our culture that hospitals, service organizations, and products ranging from healing balms to elixirs have been named for him. Ironically, this man without a name is so embedded in our culture that the popular, yet fictional, comic/ movie character Hellboy named his favorite sidearm after him, the "Samaritan" revolver.[1] Samaria and Samaritans are also featured in the texts of nascent Christianity. Situated between Galilee and the Roman province of Judea, Samaria appears in the Gospels as a place of rest for travelers making their way from Galilee to Jerusalem. These accounts reflect rites of pilgrimage to Jerusalem that were practiced in the Second Temple period.[2] The reason for choosing to travel in Samaria was the historic route that follows the central ridge through the hill country of Samaria and Judah, which was used by the Patriarchs already in the biblical period. The route makes its way through or near several important biblical cities: Samaria, Shechem, Bethel, Jerusalem, Bethlehem, and Hebron.

In the Book of Acts, the region of Samaria is envisioned as an integral part of the Land of Israel and a place of growth for the early church. One of Jesus's final instructions to his followers is reported in Acts 1:8b: "And you shall be my witnesses in Jerusalem, in all Judea and Samaria and to the ends of the land."[3] Yet, there is an apprehensive attitude toward the people of Samaria exhibited in the Gospels[4] that corresponds to the contemporary ancient Jewish debate regarding them. Even so, the New Testament stories of encounters of Jesus with Samaritans suggest a more nuanced relationship between Jews and Samaritans in Roman antiquity than is sometimes acknowledged.

5.1 *On the Road to Jericho. The Parable of the Good Samaritan*, Stereoscope slide, Washington, DC: Underwood and Underwood, 1899 (Collection of Leah and Steven Fine, New York).

5.2 Jost Amman, "The Good Samaritan," from *Bibel. Band II: Das Neuwe Testament Teutsch* (The Bible in German) translated by Martin Luther, Frankfurt am Main: Johann Feyerabend, 1580 (Archives of the Evangelische Regionalverband Frank, permanent loan to the Bibelhaus Erlebnis Museum/ Frankfurt Bible Society).

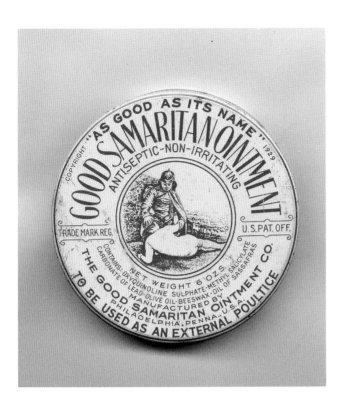

5.3 *Good Samaritan Ointment, "As Good As Its Name,"* Philadelphia, 1929 (Collection of Leah and Steven Fine, New York).

5.4 Victor Gillam, "The Good Samaritan," *Judge Magazine,* 1897, responding to the protective tariffs enacted under the Dingley Act, supported by President William McKinley (Collection of Leah and Steven Fine, New York).

THE GOOD SAMARITAN.

And the free-silverites, and likewise the free-traders, passed by.   But a certain Samaritan, as he journeyed, came where he was; and when he saw him he had compassion on him, and went to him, and set him on his own beast and brought him to an inn, and took care of him

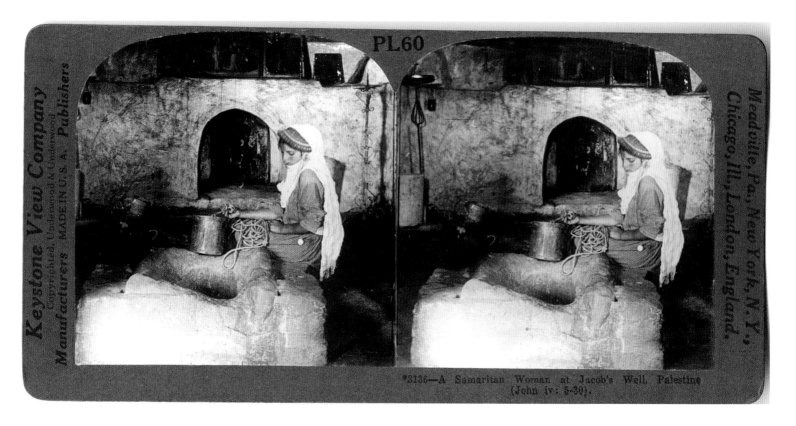

5.5 *Samaritan Woman at Jacob's Well, Palestine (John iv:5–30),* Stereoscope slide, Keystone View Company, Underwood and Underwood Publishers, ca. 1900 (Courtesy California Museum of Photography, University of California, Riverside. Gift of Mr. and Mrs. Arnold M. Gilbert).

5.6 *Samaritan Woman at the Well,* Armenian Gospel Book, folio 221v, Constantinople, c. 1620-1640 (Museum of the Bible, The Green Collection).

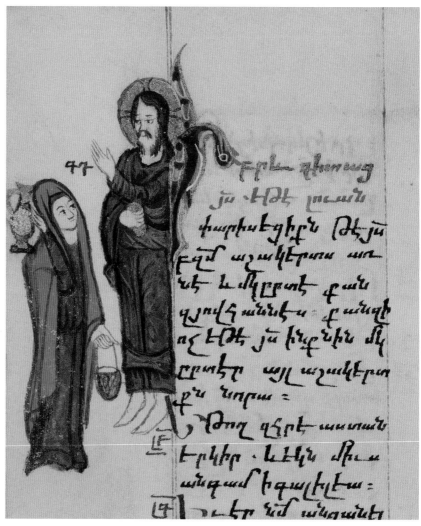

ꗁꗏꗦꗏꗦ

5.7 Laura James, *Samaritan Woman at the Well*, 2000 (Courtesy of Laura James).

5.8 Willy Wiedmann, *Samaritan Woman at the Well*, from *The Wiedmann Bible: The World's Longest Painted Bible* (Lachen, Switzerland: Wiedmann Media, 2015, *Jesus Christus*, 54, Courtesy of Martin Wiedmann).

THE CLEANSING OF THE TEN LEPERS

In the "Story of the Cleansing of the Ten Lepers" in the Gospel of Luke (17:11–19), Jesus passes between Galilee and Samaria on his way to Jerusalem to celebrate the Passover (Luke 19:28). He enters a village and is greeted by ten lepers. Seeking mercy from him on their behalf, he directs them to go to the priests to be examined.[5] As they depart, they are cleansed. One of the cleansed lepers, a Samaritan, turns back to express thanks:

> Then one of them, when he saw that he was healed, turned back, praising God with a loud voice; and he fell on his face at Jesus' feet, giving him thanks. Now he was a Samaritan. Then said Jesus: "Were not ten cleansed? Where are the nine? Was no one found to return and give praise to God except this foreigner?" And he said to him: "Rise and go your way; your faith has made you well." (Luke 17:15–19)

This account shares aspects with an earlier story in Luke's Gospel in which an unidentified person is cleansed of leprosy. Jesus also tells him to go to the priests (Luke 5:12–14). However, unlike the earlier story, the "Story of the Cleansing of the Ten Lepers" interjects the issue of national identity. Jesus refers to the Samaritan with the term "foreigner" (*allogenes*). This is the only occasion that *allogenes* occurs in the New Testament. In the Greek Bible, the term most commonly renders *nekar* ("foreign/er") to describe foreign people, foreign lands, foreign gods, or just about anything else that is considered "wholly other," generally with a negative connotation.[6]

More pertinent for our discussion, the Greek term appears in the so-called "Temple Warning" inscription, a large square stone that stood, according to Josephus, in the barrier that surrounded the inner courts of the Temple in Jerusalem. The warning was intended to prevent "foreigners," that is, non-Jews, from entering the inner precincts of the Temple:[7]

> No foreigner (*allogene*) may enter within the balustrade that surrounds the sanctuary and the enclosure. Whoever is caught will be himself responsible for his ensuing death.

A complete inscription was discovered by Charles Clermont-Ganneau in 1871 near the Temple Mount. It is now housed at the Istanbul Archaeology Museum. In 1935, a second partial inscription was also discovered near the Lion's Gate in Jerusalem and is now exhibited at the Israel Museum.

Jesus's designation of the Samaritan as an *allogenes* betrays his opinion about the ethnic status of the Samaritans. Although we have episodes of social engagement with the Samaritans, for legal purposes he considered them "the other." In other words, Jesus held the view that the Samaritan leper was not Jewish. Ethnic differences between Jews and Samaritans sometimes spilled over into tensions between the two communities. For example, a Samaritan village along the route to Jerusalem refused to allow Jesus to use their village as a throughway to affirm the Temple in Jerusalem as the rightful place where God chose to reveal his name (Luke 9:52).

These differences of opinion notwithstanding, in the "Story of the Samaritan Leper" he is not turned away. He is healed just as the other nine lepers, who we assume were Jewish. Jesus seems to have balanced the question of the legal status of the Samaritans and their traditional claims to Mount Gerizim with the fact that the Samaritans were nonetheless human beings and thus worthy of being healed. The Samaritan leper does not hesitate to follow Jesus's directive to go to the priests. We are not told whether he intended to go to the priests in Jerusalem or to the priests on Mount Gerizim. In any event, Jesus commends the faith of the Samaritan and the praise that he alone renders to God.

Jesus's attitude concerning the ethnic status of the Samaritan is part of a larger debate in ancient Judaism. His designation of the Samaritan leper as *allogenes* should be read in the same vein as the comments that Ben Sira expressed nearly two hundred years earlier:

> With two nations my soul is vexed, and the third is no nation: Those who live on Mount Seir, and the Philistines, and the foolish people that dwell in Shechem [i.e., Samaritans]. (Ben Sira 50:25–26)

Both the Hebrew and Greek versions of Ben Sira suggest that the sage disdains the three peoples. More importantly, in Ben Sira's estimation the Samaritans should not even be considered a "nation" (Greek, *ethnos*; Hebrew, *'am*). This may be due to Ben Sira's priestly emphasis.

The remark in Ben Sira about the Samaritans follows on the heels of a praise-filled elegy for Simon, the high priest of Jerusalem (ca. 219–199 BCE). In fact, Ben Sira's opinion is distinctly connected to the early Jewish exegesis of Deuteronomy 23:21 that seems to adapt the biblical passage as a critique against the creation of the competing Temple at Mount Gerizim.

Josephus also presents the Samaritans with a separate ethnic identity, distinguishing the Israelites from the Samaritans, in that the latter originated as "Cutheans." Different points of view existed in antiquity among the variety of Jewish estimations about the Samaritans. In 4 Baruch, they are considered Israelite exilic returnees. Ultimately rejected from Jerusalem because of their intermarriage with Babylonian women and not allowed to return to Babylonia because of their animosity toward that city's inhabitants, they made their way north of Jerusalem and rebuilt the city of Samaria (Josephus, *Antiquities* 8.11–12). For the author of 2 Maccabees, Samaritans and Jews suffered together as a single people during the Antiochian persecution:

> So Antiochus carried off eighteen hundred talents from the Temple, and hurried away to Antioch, thinking in his arrogance that he could sail on the land and walk on the sea, because his mind was elated. And he left governors to afflict the people [sg., *genos*]: at Jerusalem, Philip, by birth a Phrygian and in character more barbarous than the man who appointed him; and at Gerizim, Andronicus; and besides these Menelaus, who lorded it over his fellow citizens worse than the others did. (2 Maccabees 5:21–23)[8]

Nevertheless, even with a shared Israelite origin and shared suffering with the Jewish people during times of persecution, most texts distinguish the Samaritans from the Jewish people. They are not considered gentiles (*ethne*) but seem to hold an intermediate identity, being neither fully gentile nor Jewish. This in-between status may be reflected in the following Matthean statement: "These twelve Jesus sent out, charging them, 'Go nowhere among the gentiles, and enter no town of the Samaritans, but go rather to the lost sheep of the house of Israel'" (Matthew 10:5–6). As Joseph Angel shows in this volume, the opinions of the *Tannaim* regarding the Samaritans differed. A good deal of Tannaitic law associates them with Israelites (i.e., Jews; Mishnah Nedarim 3:10), and as being distinct from gentiles.[9] The Samaritans are assumed participants in the Jewish halakhic system; and even though they are perceived to observe aspects of the Torah incorrectly, they are largely still considered to be Israelites.

DISCOURSE WITH THE WOMAN OF SAMARIA

The relationship between Jews and Samaritans appears again in the New Testament in the "Discourse with the Woman of Samaria" in the Fourth Gospel (John 4:4–30). Jesus and his disciples are once again on the pilgrimage route to Jerusalem. Jesus stops at Sychar, a nearby suburb of the city of Shechem (see John 4:8). Weary from his journey, he sits at Jacob's Well and encounters a Samaritan woman. The ensuing conversation serves to exhibit the intersections and sensitivities between Jews and Samaritans in the Second Temple period.

According to this story, the disciples have gone away to the city in order to purchase food. The underlying assumption is that Jesus's disciples, and perhaps also Jesus himself, had little problem with Samaritan food purity laws. Rabbis also present a broad range of approaches, from general acceptance to complete rejection—positions that change over time. The interaction with the woman at the well involves issues of ritual purity: "The Samaritan woman says to him, 'How is it that you, a Jew, ask a drink of me, a woman of Samaria? For Jews have no dealings with Samaritans'" (John 4:9). This hesitation has little to do with the tensions between the communities but rather with concerns about ritual purity and the sharing of vessels. The woman is initially hesitant because she seems aware of certain

Jewish opinions regarding Samaritan women and their supposed impurities.[10]

The conversation then transitions from well water to living water as a metaphor for what Jesus offers, namely, God's gift, which will spring forth to eternal life. Underlying this conversation are contemporaneous traditions that utilize a "well of living water" (*mibe'er mayim ha-chayyim*) known from the Dead Sea Scrolls.[11] This "living water" is sometimes envisioned as an eternal fountain that represents God's instruction and his covenantal faithfulness to Israel.[12] The Samaritan woman is presented in the story as being familiar with this metaphor, because she requests to be given this water, despite her acknowledgment of the religious differences between the communities: "Our fathers worshipped on this mountain; and you say that in Jerusalem is the place where men ought to worship" (John 4:20). The Evangelist describes Jesus as redirecting the conversation. His reply to the woman about a time when God will not be limited to a single location, neither in Jerusalem nor on Mount Gerizim, is more fitting to Jewish sentiments heard after the destruction of the Temple:

> Woman, believe me, the hour is coming when neither on this mountain nor in Jerusalem will you worship the Father. You worship what you do not know; we worship what we know, for salvation is from the Jews. (John 4:21–22)

Josephus wrote *War* in the decade after the Roman desecration of the Temple. He places a similar expression on the lips of those who were defending Jerusalem. The Jews in the besieged city rebuffed the Roman general Titus saying: "They were unconcerned for their native place (i.e., the Temple), and that *the world was a better temple for God than this one*" (*War* 5.458). This attitude is heard in another work composed around the same time in the apocryphal Baruch (3:24): "O Israel, how great is the house of God! And how vast the territory that he possesses!" According to the parallelism of the author's declaration, the dwelling place of God is now understood to encompass a vast area in the world.

What is most critical in Jesus's response to the woman is his unvarnished statement that the Jews, and not the Samaritans, are the beneficiaries of God's covenantal salvation. Together, the discussion regarding living water and Jesus's statement about salvation assumes God's covenantal faithfulness to the people of Israel. Although, notably, the Samaritan's perception that Jesus is a prophet and the later-voiced expectations of a coming Messiah suggest some shared traditions.

THE STORY OF THE GOOD SAMARITAN

Perhaps the most enduring image of a Samaritan in religious history and popular culture is the "Story of the Good Samaritan," which is cited at the start of this article (Luke 10:25–37). The anecdote is prefaced by an encounter with a legal expert (*nomikos*), who pointedly asked Jesus: "What shall I do to inherit eternal life"?[13] In good Jewish legal discourse, Jesus responds with a question: "What is written in the law? How do you read?" Elsewhere, eternal life, or life in the world to come (*ḥayei haolam habba*), is associated with aspects of Torah observance.[14]

The legal expert's understanding of the law is encapsulated in the well-known double commandment to love: "You shall love the Lord your God with all your heart, and with all your soul, and with all your strength, and with all your mind; and your neighbor as yourself" (Luke 10:27). The commonly attested pairing of Deuteronomy 6:5 and Leviticus 19:18[15] is based on the unique wording "and you shall love" (*ve'ahavta*), which occurs in the Hebrew Bible four times.[16] Jesus affirms the inquirer's scriptural answer that life is attained through loving God and one's neighbor. "Do this and you will live!" (Luke 10:28). The expert continues to probe as expected in halakhic discussions; he seeks to define who is to be considered his neighbor. Jesus's narrative answer to the legal expert's question in the "Story of the Good Samaritan" is unique to Luke's Gospel.

The setting for the story is the well-known route from Jericho to Jerusalem through Wadi Qelt. Strabo notes that when the Roman general Pompey conquered Judea in 63 BCE, one of his first initiatives was to cleanse the area of Wadi Qelt of robbers and tyrants (Pliny, *Geography* 16:40). It appears that by the first century little had changed. On that route, the anonymous victim is left to the side half-dead (*hemithanes*). The Greek term *hemithanes* describes one somewhere between life and death. As such, the injured party fell under the legal designation of the Hebrew equivalent *goses*, which describes an individual who is in the process of dying. Contact with a dead person proved to be the most rigorous form of ritual impurity for the Levitical priesthood. In particular, priests could only defile themselves tending to their closest relatives (Leviticus 21:1–3). The imminence of death and the issue of ritual purity would have been reason enough to explain why the priest and the Levite passed the victim.

Yet, the injured man in the story is still alive. The *Tannaim* taught: "A person does not convey impurity until the person's soul departs, or even when he/she has severe lacerations, or he/she is dying (*goses*)" (Mishnah Ohalot 1:6). As long as the victim is alive, anyone who assists him or her does not contract ritual impurity. Later deliberations suggest that priests are an exception and can contract ritual impurity from someone in the grips of death (Babylonian Talmud Nazir 43a). The description of the priest and Levite passing by the victim hints that this discussion in Amoraic sources may have roots in an earlier period.

While the issue of ritual impurity may lie behind the actions of the priest and the Levite, the introduction of the Samaritan turns the story upside down. Typically, when a series of characters are introduced and begin with priests and Levites, they are followed by Israelites.[17] Jesus's substitution of the Samaritan for the Israelite is intentionally provocative. If there is a cultural imprint behind the story, then the appearance of the priest and Levite may only be coincidental, and the issue of their purity is secondary.

The Samaritan is the only one to aid the man left for dead. Moved by compassion, he attends to the victim's wounds and brings him to an inn. Going one step further, the Samaritan pays the innkeeper and offers to compensate him should he incur any more debt. The provocation of the Samaritan's presence in the story is not solely

𐎕𐎘𐎖𐎌𐎛𐎗

because his care and concern seem to exceed expectations. Behind the story lies the third verse in the Hebrew Bible that preserves the command *ve'ahavta*: "the stranger who sojourns with you shall be to you as the native among you, and you shall love (*ve'ahavta*) him as yourself" (Leviticus 19:34). This is the only occasion in recorded biblical interpretation where the double commandment to love is expanded with a third decree.

Yet, it is the Samaritan, not an Israelite, who observes this biblical commandment, which appears in both Jewish and Samaritan traditions. For a community that is routinely regarded as not observing the commandments with exactness, the Samaritan's mercy on behalf of one who is likely an ethnic foreigner to him is intended to be particularly acute in a Jewish setting. Perhaps this is why Jesus's final question: "Which of these three, do you think, proved neighbor to the man who fell among the robbers," is met with the terse answer: "The one who had mercy on him."

Our story seeks to define who is the neighbor for whom one is responsible to love. According to the "Story of the Good Samaritan," in instances of human need and acts of mercy ethnic/national distinctions are of little importance. As Leviticus 19:34 instructs, even the foreigner is to be loved because of a shared humanity: "for you were (also) foreigners in the land of Egypt." Our story is an effect of the innovations brought by Jewish humanism in the days of the Second Temple and the inherent value awarded to human life, regardless of the national identity of the individual.

It seems that Jesus considered the Samaritans with a nuanced approach. In legal matters, he, like other Jews of his time, distinguished between the Jews and the Samaritans. In cases of human need, his attitude was one that recognized their shared humanity as Israelites—again, much like the rabbis. The presentation of the protagonist in the "Story of the Good Samaritan" is among the few explicitly positive images of Samaritans that appear in early Jewish and Christian texts. The willingness of Jesus to interact with the Samaritans, liminally set between Jews and gentiles, may have influenced the early church to introduce its newfound faith first in Samaria before turning to the gentile world (Acts 8:5–25).

SAMARITAN TRADITION AND CHRISTIANITY

Samaritan tradition remembers little of these early relationships. In fact, the Samaritan chronicles maintain but small nuggets of memory of Jesus the man. In the twelfth-century *Tulidah*, it goes like this: "In the time of this Jonathan (Yehonatan) Jesus the son of Mary, the son of Joseph . . . was killed in Jerusalem during the days of Tiberius the Roman king by Pilate its governor."[18] Interesting in itself, the main purpose of this text is to remind readers that Jesus—a known person—was not killed by the Samaritans! Abu l-Fath blames the Romans explicitly, and a more recent version, called the *New Chronicle*, blames "the Jews." This deflection is no wonder in light of Jewish–Samaritan disdain through most of re-

corded history, and the persecutions inflicted upon the Samaritans under Rome and Christian Rome—including the Christian appropriation of Mount Gerizim and the building of a church to the Theotokos, the "Mother of God," by the emperor Zeno in 484 CE (Figure 8.1). Abu l-Fath has much to say about those difficult times, and early Christian sources even more. It is indeed unfortunate that, in the long history of interactions between the Samaritans and the Church, the relationship has usually not been positive—until small groups of Bible-reading British and American Protestants took up their cause during the nineteenth and early twentieth centuries. The Christian community too often has forgotten the pioneering humanistic approach of Jesus and the sympathy with which he treated the Samaritans, even as "the Good Samaritan" has become a cultural icon of universal import.

For Further Reading

David Daube. "Jesus and the Samaritan Woman: The Meaning of συγχράομαι." *Journal of Biblical Literature* 69, no. 2 (1950): 137–147.

Stanley Isser. "Jesus in the Samaritan Chronicles." *Journal of Jewish Studies* 32, no. 2 (1981): 166–194.

R. Steven Notley, and Jeffrey P. García. "Hebrew-Only Exegesis: A Philological Approach to Jesus' Use of the Hebrew Bible," *The Language Environment of First-Century Judaea: Jerusalem Studies in the Synoptic Gospels Volume 2*, edited by Randall Buth and R. Steven Notley, Leiden: Brill, 2014, 362–366.

Brad H. Young. "The Samaritan: Love Your Enemies." In *The Parables: Jewish Tradition and Christian Interpretation*. Peabody, MA: Hendrickson Publishers, 1998, 101–118.

---

1   *Hellboy*, directed by Guillermo del Toro (Columbia Pictures, 2004).

2   For example, Luke 17:11; and John 4:4–5.

3   See Acts 8:25; 9:31.

4   For example, John 8:48.

5   Leviticus 13:49; 14:2–4.

6   For example, Genesis 17:27; Exodus 12:43, etc.

7   Cf. Josephus, *War* 5.193–194.

8   Cf. 2 Maccabees 6:1–2.

9   For example, Mishnah Berakhot 7:1.

10 Mishnah Niddah 4:1; see also Mishnah Kelim 1:1–3.

11 Damascus Document 19:34; see also 1Q*Serekh haYahad*[b] 1:6.

12 4QWords of the Luminaries A 1 2 R v 2–9.

13 Matthew 19:16; Mark 10:17; Luke 18:18.

14 Mishnah Avot 2:7; Mishnah Peah 2:1; Tosefta Peah 1:1–3.

15 For example, Jubilees 20:2, 7; 36:4–8; and Didache 1:2.

16 Leviticus 19:18; 34; Deuteronomy 6:5; 11:1.

17 Mishnah Peah 8:6; Mishnah Taanit 4:2; 1 Esdras 1:21; Damascus Document 14:5.

18 MacDonald and Higgins, 1971, 72; Isser, 1981.

6
"Do You Have an Onion?": Rabbis and Samaritans in Late Antiquity

SHANA STRAUCH SCHICK AND STEVEN FINE

Rabbi Shimon son of Yoḥai taught:

The Israelites are prominent because they know how to
    please their Creator.

Rabbi Yudan said: Like the *Kutaei*.

The *Kutaei* are clever in business.

One of them went to a woman.

He said to her: "Do you have an onion? Give it to me."

When she brought it to him, he said to her:
    "What's an onion without bread?"

When she brought it to him, he said to her:
    "What's a meal [*maakhil*] without drink?"

Out of this he ate and drank.

— *Leviticus Rabba* 5:8[1]

Folklorist Galit Hasan-Rokem categorizes this story among the "tales of the neighborhood," as a story that reflects the lives of real people, of the Jewish "folk" in late antique Galilee. Embedded in a fifth-century CE collection of homilies, *midrashim*, called *Leviticus Rabba*, this is a humorous tale told by the rabbis about daily life in their time and place.

Imagine the situation. With a knowing glance, the storyteller looks out and reminds his audience that "the *Kutaei* are clever in business." This is not the usual "theoretical" *Kutim* of legal discussions or the straw man of theological polemics in rabbinic literature, but perhaps a peddler. This is a profession well known in Roman Palestine, including in the cities and towns that bordered Samaria—from Beit Shean to the northeast to Caesarea Maritima on the Mediterranean shore and even Lod and Emmaus in the Judean Shephelah. Jews and Samaritans were in regular contact, living and working in close proximity in places large and small. In Caesarea, Samaritans seem to have outnumbered Jews and pagans combined! Contacts were often close. Part of the mosaic floor of the Samaritan synagogue at Beit Shean was laid by the same craftsmen who also created the mosaic of the Beit Alpha synagogue. We usually assume that the mosaicists "Marianos and his son Haninah"

were Jews, but perhaps they were Samaritans. Uniquely, a legal text found on the floor of the nearby Reḥov synagogue, just south of Beit Shean, details exactly what parts of nearby Samaria were subject to rabbinic agricultural law. This could be important information for a pious woman buying produce from an itinerant Samaritan peddler. Each member of the audience, we imagine, might have had his or her own stories.

Our *Kuti*, "wise in business," passed from woman to woman selling his wares—and in this case teasing a good meal out of a gullible or perhaps kindly client. A later version of this tradition makes that explicit: "These *Kutim* [sure do] know how to go from door to door!" The peddler of *Leviticus Rabba*, with his quick tongue, does pretty well for himself—collecting an onion, bread, and even a drink, all from the same person! The "Samaritan peddler" fills a liminal role in this story. He is a laughable character, a trickster—a social position inhabited by Jewish peddlers in both ancient and many modern settings—a role that Jews also filled along the tortuously multicultural byways of late antique Palestine.

Tellingly, our Samaritan is not referred to as a *Shumra*, an Aramaic term used occasionally by the rabbis. Gedaliah Alon suggests that *Shumra* was used by the folk, while rabbis preferred the pejorative *Kuti*. *Shumra* too was used in a neutral way by both Christian Aramaic speakers and the Samaritans themselves.[2] The Samaritan of our story is a *Kuti*, a pejorative term referencing the purportedly forced conversion of the *Kutim* described in 2 Kings 17, which distances him from Jewish society even as he is part of the "neighborhood." He is inside as he is outside, "clever" because of his unstable localness. Hasan-Rokem is right that "the Samaritan's ability to obtain food with some humorous cunning is, like the folklore scoundrel's tricks, regarded with a loving smile and admiration, yet mixed with some anger and bitterness."[3]

The editor of *Leviticus Rabba* categorized our *Kuti*, together with other low status "Israelites"—smooth-talking Jewish women and Jewish field laborers, building up to the relationship in which Israel knows "how to please their creator." Unlike the others, though, *Kutim* are not Jews, but members of the people of Israel. This status was not disputed by the early rabbis. A story in *Genesis Rabba* (94:7) has it that Rabbi Meir once disputed the lineage of the Samaritans—arguing that they were descendants of Issachar rather than Joseph. Insulted as Samaritans might have been by these comments, Rabbi Meir did not question their very Israelite identity.[4]

THE *AMORAIM* ON SAMARITANS

Samaritans were of particular interest to the small group of late antique rabbinic literati who we call the *Amoraim* (third to fifth centuries CE)—as they have been to a large and multigenerational group of modern scholars who have studied rabbinic deployment of the *Kuti*. Some, like our story in *Leviticus Rabba*, describe what feel like actual social interactions. Others are more theoretical or formulaic. Some are both. With the development of the rabbis as a leadership group and self-contained academic collegium in late Roman Palestine, the flexibility that existed in Tannaitic sources of the late first and second centuries hardened in subsequent centuries, and the Israelite status of Samaritans (as well as Jews who disregarded the rabbis, heretics, and Jewish Christians) was much discussed. The Palestinian *Amoraim* did not entirely exclude Samaritans from the Israelite polity. Moshe Lavee is correct that the Jerusalem Talmud, edited in Tiberias around 400 CE, focuses upon specific sins perpetrated by *Kutim* and their legal ramifications. Even when mocked and sidelined, the essential membership of the *Kutim* in the Israelite polity was not questioned. Unlike Christians, they could not be excluded as pig-eating, Sabbath-breaking, uncircumcised gentiles. Who, then, were they?

Jerusalem Talmud Gittin 1:4, 43c is a fine place to start. This text narrates various reasons why it is forbidden for a Jew to marry a Samaritan. Rabbi Yoḥanan son of Napha, leader of the rabbinic academy in Tiberias during the mid-third century, expresses a distinct distaste for *Kutim*:

> As to the Samaritans, why are they considered unfit [marriage partners]? Said Rabbi Yoḥanan: "Because they are lion converts."
>
> But there is a question: what about one who converted but not for the sake of Heaven and then converted again for the sake of Heaven, do we not accept him? [If so, should we not consider the Samaritans full-fledged Jews?]
>
> R. Yoḥanan in the name of Rabbi Eleazar: "Because [of the law that states] 'If a non-Jew or slave had sexual relations with a Jewish woman, the child is a *mamzer* [Samaritans thus intermarried with Jewish women and their children have the status of *mamzerim*, 'bastards']."
>
> But has not Rabbi Aqiva stated: "They are sincere converts"?
>
> Because they require betrothed women [the event of the death of their betrothed] to enter levirate marriages and exempt married women [and so, violating Israelite practice in this regard, they are deemed to be *mamzerim*].
>
> But do rabbis not maintain: There is no [problem of] *mamzer* in a case of a levirate wife [who marries without either levirate marriage or release from such a marriage, *ḥalitsah*]?[5]
>
> It is because they are not experts in the laws of preparing divorce documents.
>
> But Rabban Gamaliel validates their divorce documents.
>
> R. Yaakov bar Idi said in the name of Rabbi Yoḥanan: Since they were mixed

among them the priests of high places, [as it says,] "They made priests of some of the people (*miqtsat ha-am*, approximately 2 Kings 17:32, *miqtsotam*)." Said Rabbi Ila: [They made priests] from the thorns that were among the people and from the unfit that were among the people.

The question of marriageability discussed by this complex text strikes at the core of the relationship and had serious repercussions for future Jewish–Samaritan relations. This is the earliest rabbinic text to explicitly refer to *Kutim* as "lion converts," which as noted above, references 2 Kings 17, the purportedly forced conversion of the *Kutim*. It is especially important because this uncomplimentary designation is attributed to the profoundly influential Rabbi Yoḥanan. In light of this negative assessment, the Jerusalem Talmud then struggles to mitigate earlier far more accepting positions, notably that of the towering second-century sage Rabbi Aqiva, who held that Samaritans are true converts. Yet, at the same time that this passage bars Jewish–Samaritan marriages, it does not question their status as Israelites—indeed, the editors of the Talmud argue that, while they may have initially been lion converts, for Rabbi Yoḥanan they ultimately became sincere ones. Furthermore, the rabbis did not conclude that marriage between Samaritans and Jews is forbidden because they are not Israelites. When all else fails, Rabbi Yoḥanan and two of his students distance the *Kutim* through derision. They assert that Samaritan priests are "thorns" and "unfit." This status of the priestly leadership somehow disqualifies marriage between Jews and *Kutim*.

This tacit acceptance, coupled with derogatory attitudes, was apparently widespread among the students of Rabbi Yoḥanan as documented in other *Yerushalmi* passages. In its most famous formulation, the late-third-century sage from Caesarea Maritima, Rabbi Abbahu, claimed that the *Kutim* had once been acceptable, but had "corrupted" themselves. This is the *leitmotif* of Jerusalem Talmud Avodah Zarah 5:3, 44d, which is a rather long rabbinic essay on the Israelite status of *Kutim*. Early on, this essay presents peers and students of both Rabbi Yoḥanan and his prominent student, Rabbi Abbahu, who were far more positive toward *Kutim*, maintaining earlier relationship patterns. The early-third-century Rabbi Ammi, the successor of Rabbi Yoḥanan as head of the academy in Tiberias, permitted eggs roasted by Samaritans, and Rabbi Eleazar ben Pedat, a Babylonian contemporary of Rabbi Yoḥanan who lived in Tiberias, expansively permitted Samaritan cooked food. Such foods would certainly be prohibited were Samaritans idolaters. Fourth-century sages, including Rabbi Aha, as well as Rabbi Jeremiah and Rabbi Hezekiah, latter students of Rabbi Abbahu, are each reported to have eaten foods prepared by Samaritans. Rabbi Aha ate dumplings, Rabbi Jeremiah ate leavened bread, and Rabbi Hezekiah ate locusts.

This accepting approach was vehemently rejected later in this passage. We cite the most poignant section:

> Rabbi Abbahu forbade their [*Kuti*] wine according to the testimony of Rabbi Ḥiyya, Rabbi Asi and Ami.
>
> They were going up to *Har ha-Melekh* [literally "the Mountain of the King," areas of the Judaean hill country confiscated by Rome as a result

of the Jewish War] and saw a *Kuti* who was suspect regarding their wine [idolatrous wine produced by gentiles].

They came and they related this to him (to Rabbi Abbahu).

He said to them: "Can we not [forbid Samaritan wine] for this reason [alone]?"

There are some who would say: One Sabbath eve no wine was found in all of Samaria.

At the end of the Sabbath it was found to be full [of wine] that the non-Jews had brought and that the Samaritans had accepted from them.

There are some who would say: When Diocletian the king came here (to the Levant) he decreed and said that all the nations must pour out libations [to the emperor], except for the Jews.

Therefore, the Samaritans poured out libations.

Thus, their wine was considered forbidden [since they were involved in idolatrous worship].

There are some who would say: They have a kind of dove and they pour out libations to it.

The Samaritans of Caesarea asked Rabbi Abbahu: "Your fathers would make use of our [wine]. Why don't you use our [wine]?" He said to them: "Your fathers did not corrupt their deeds; you have corrupted your deeds." (Jerusalem Talmud Avodah Zarah 5:3, 44d).

Rabbi Ḥiyya here informs Rabbi Abbahu that his peers had seen a Samaritan drinking gentile wine. For Rabbi Abbahu, this is sufficient rationale to distrust the ritual observance of all *Kutim* and thus forbid Jews from drinking wine produced by them. In rabbinic thought, wine and its consumption is an important boundary marker, one that is intimately bound up with religious significance. Wine made by gentiles was forbidden to Jews on the assumption that it would inevitably be used in idolatrous ways. Banning Samaritan wine thus had larger implications for their treatment as "kosher" Israelites.

The anonymous editor of the Jerusalem Talmud follows with three hypothetical events that may have sparked Rabbi Abbahu's ire. In the first, the *Kutim* in Samaria obtained wine from gentiles—on the Sabbath no less! In the second, Samaritans offered wine libations, apparently to the imperial cult, by order of Diocletian. This emperor did, in fact, visit Palestine two times—in 286 CE and 297–298 CE. In the judgment of the *Yerushalmi*, these *Kutim* should have availed themselves of the exemption from the imperial cult enjoyed by Jews. Beginning under the Severan Emperors (193–235 CE), Roman law distinguished Samaritans from Jews, and did not allow Samaritans the privileges enjoyed by Jews. Most starkly, Samaritans were forbidden to circumcise their sons, a decision noted by the Church Father Origen of Caesarea (a contemporary of Rabbi Yoḥanan) and remembered with sadness by Abu l-Fatḥ.[6] Samaritans were thus caught between the expectations of rabbis, who assumed that they were covered by the Jewish exemption, and Roman law, whose punishments included the death penalty. Over time, this Roman distinction between Jews and Samaritans came to frame this process of differentiation between these communities.

The last explanation offered is also the most severe. Samaritans are idolaters because they voluntarily offer libations to a certain dove.

6.1 City Coin of Neapolis, 251–253 CE, bronze. Left: Bust of Emperor Trebonianus Gallus. Right: The Goddess Tyche (Fortuna) flanked on each side a dove in a gabled dovecote, Mount Gerizim above (Courtesy of Classical Numismatic Group).

A source preserved in the Babylonian Talmud (Ḥullin 6a) amplifies this point in the name of the Babylonian Rav Nahman son of Isaac (mid-fourth century). This text claims that "they found the image of a dove at the peak of Mount Gerizim and they served it." Significantly, the *Kutim* "found" the pagan sculpture—they did not originate it! A rare coin of Neapolis shows the image of two doves, each within a cage, flanking a sculpture of the goddess Tyche (Latin: Fortuna, Figure 6.1). Below is the she-wolf, the *lupa*, suckling Romulus and Remus, above the image of a Roman temple atop Mount Gerizim. Some scholars have associated this coin with alleged Samaritan "dove worship."[7] In fact, such coins were not unique to Neapolis. A similar coin was minted in Damascus, circa 244–249 CE. Still, perhaps knowledge of these coins (and the cult that they illustrate), together with intentional melding of pagan Neapolis (a city founded by Vespasian in the heart of Samaria for retired military personnel) with the indigenous Samaritans provided raw materials from which this notion took flight. As with wine in our text, it might only take one Samaritan to "worship a dove" to tar all with the charge of idolatry. Significantly, a fifth-century mosaic from the Khirbet Samara synagogue shows an empty bird cage (Figure 6.2), whereas in parallel Jewish and Christian mosaics the cage contains a bird. Samaritan art was particularly fastidious in applying the Torah's strictures against illicit images. The smear of dove worship has followed the Samaritans into modern times (Figure 6.3).

We raised the issue of idolatrous behavior by *Kutim* above:

Rabbi Ishmael son of Rabbi Yose went to Neapolis.

Kutim came up to him.

He said to them: "I see that you do not prostrate yourselves before that mountain. Rather, [you bow] to the idols that Jacob our father buried beneath it, for it is written: "'And Jacob hid them under the oak which was near Shechem.'" (Genesis 35:3)

This late-second-century rabbi enters the Roman city adjacent to Mount Gerizim and taunts local Samaritans. He claims that *Kuti* idolatry is not merely a matter of contemporary corruption, but is historic. It reaches back to the "foreign gods" that the Patriarch Jacob confiscated from his household in Shechem immediately after

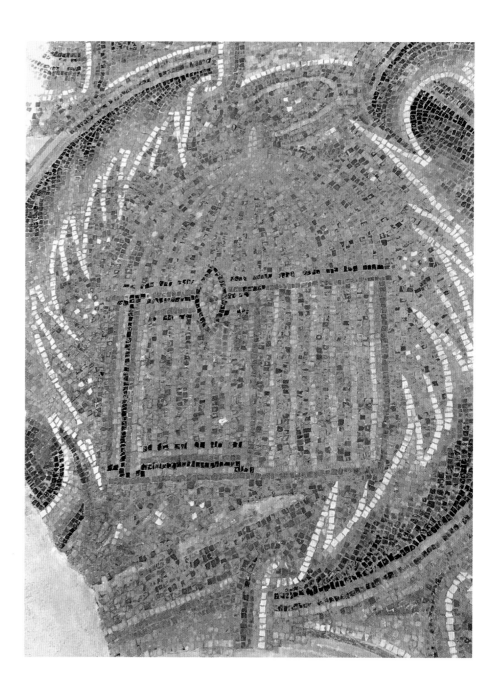

the Dina incident. He even questions the Samaritan allegiance to Mount Gerizim! Rabbis took note that Samaritans were no slouches in this competition. An anecdote in *Genesis Rabba* 32, discussed by Stefan Schorch in this volume, has a certain Rabbi Yonatan pass near Mount Gerizim en route to Jerusalem, where a Samaritan taunts him with the following question: "Wouldn't you rather pray at this Holy Mountain, and not in that refuse dump [Jerusalem]?"

Our excerpt from Jerusalem Talmud, Avodah Zarah 5:3, 44d closes with a second anecdote involving Rabbi Abbahu. *Kutim*, we are told, addressed the sage directly to find out for themselves why he had stopped buying their wine. This once again illustrates the close proximity that existed between Jews and Samaritans. His unapologetic response was that *Kuti* behavior had changed for the worse, requiring Jews to distance themselves from them.

Rabbi Abbahu's claim that *Kuti* behavior had actually changed,

requiring a rabbinic response, has some roots in Tannaitic literature. Mishnah Rosh Hashanah's claim that originally—*be-rishonah*—torches were lit heralding the new moon, until the *Kutim* sabotaged the system points to an early change in *Kuti* behavior—or at least can be read that way. Rabbi Eliezer son of Hurqanos's characteristically harsh assertion in Mishnah Shevi'it 8:10 that "whoever eats *Kuti* bread is as if he ate pig meat" was kept under wraps by his student, Rabbi Aqiva. Still, the Mishnah (ca. 200 CE) did preserve this statement, and the editor of the Mishnah, Rabbi Judah the Prince, did declare regarding priestly gifts that "a *Kuti* is like a gentile" (Tosefta Terumah 4:14). Indicative of this change of attitude, in Jerusalem Talmud Pesaḥim 1:1, 27b Rabbi Shimon ben Gamaliel's determination that sometimes Samaritans were more meticulous in observing certain commandments than Jews is contextualized and overturned: "Rabbi Shimon said: … 'That was true originally when they

6.3 *Several False Gods Worshipped by the Samaritans.* From Augustin Calmet *An Historical, Critical, Geographical, Chronological, and Etymological Dictionary of the Holy Bible...* London, 1732 (Yeshiva University, Mendel Gottesman Library).

were still dwelling in their villages. But now that they do not have even a single commandment nor the remnant of a commandment, they are suspect and they are corrupted.'" Concluding this rabbinic essay, Rabbi Abbahu went even further, proclaiming that he would have gone so far as to prohibit their water were that possible! The anonymous Talmud concludes by allowing Jews in Caesarea to lend money to *Kutim* with interest—something that would be forbidden were they Jews.

The Samaritan population that spread from Samaria into the southern Coastal Plain, the Beit Shean region and especially into Caesarea and southern Carmel during the late Roman period could well have caused some Jews, and especially rabbis, to feel squeezed by the *other* Israel—and act to distinguish themselves. On a larger scale, the efforts surrounding the great leader and reformer Baba Rabba must certainly have raised Samaritan confidence, perhaps cowing some Jewish observers. The relationship could be quite tense. Rabbis remember with apparent rage Samaritan responses to the death of Rabbi Abbahu: "When Rabbi Abbahu died, the

columns of Caesarea cried. Said the *Kutayya* [Aramaic for *Kutim*]: 'They are sweating [not crying]! Israel [that is, Jews] responded: 'Do those who are distant know how much those who are close cry'?'" (Jerusalem Talmud Avodah Zarah 3:1, 42c).[8]

Hovering above these scholastic deliberations was the change in Roman attitudes toward the Samaritans under the Severan emperors. From the third century onward, Roman law ceased to categorize Samaritans under the rubric of Jews/Judeans. This change had long-term deleterious implications for the Samaritans. Jewish attitudes hostile to the Israelite identity of Samaritans gained force, especially among *Amoraim* associated with Rabbi Yoḥanan. These Rabbinic attitudes could conceivably have even strengthened Roman attitudes, as relations between the Jewish Patriarch and the Severans, beginning with Rabbi Judah the Prince, were particularly warm. Yitzhak Magen associates the fourth-century Samaritan renaissance under Baba Rabba to a growing internal sense of Samaritan distinction, owing to the pressures placed upon them by Romans, Jews, and then the Christian empire. Samaritans had none of the legal protections that partially shielded Jews. As a result of their difficult situation, the Samaritans rebelled in 495 CE and 529 CE, in both cases to disastrous effect.

Still, who really changed? This rabbinic differentiation from Samaritans was part of a larger process. Samaritans were not the sole target of hostility; Rabbi Abbahu likewise denounced Christians, other sectarian groups, and romanizing Jews. This construction of the Samaritan "other" is analogous to the rabbinic construction of *ammei ha-arets*, literally "people of the land" but actually Israelites—often disliked—who had less of a connection to the rabbis. *Song of Songs Rabba* 1:39, a Byzantine period source, amplifies Rabbi Abbahu's scorn. This text reports that Abbahu assailed the Jewish community of Caesarea as "blasphemous and shameful." This harshness did not go unnoticed by his colleagues. Rabbi Shimon ben Lakish, we are told, responded by putting sand in his mouth and admonishing him: "God is not pleased with one who speaks badly of Israel." As such, Rabbi Abbahu may not have been singling out Samaritans so much as reacting broadly to the complex cosmopolitan mores of Roman Palestine, and particularly of Caesarea, the Roman provincial capital. Indeed, Rabbi Abbahu ultimately did not—perhaps could not—ban the use of water drawn by *Kutim*, much as he may have wanted to. This deployment of water is in jarring contrast to the story told in John (4:4-26), which was written two centuries earlier. John describes a Samaritan woman who did not expect Jesus, as a Jew passing through Samaria, to drink water that she had drawn from a well.

The rabbis in Sasanian Babylonia (modern Iraq) had little engagement with actual Samaritans. Babylonia Talmud Gittin 45a presents the two interactions preserved in this literature. Rav Ḥisda, who lived in the city of Sura (third century), is reported to have contacted a *Kuti*, requesting that he return a slave who had run away to the Samaritan's house (*bei Kuti*). The *Kuti* did not return the slave, in accordance with a strict reading Deuteronomy 22:3. He had no interest in the more expansive rabbinic interpretation, which would have required the return of the slave. In a parallel case, Abaye, who lived in Pumpedita (late third to fourth century), contacted a *Kuti* and requested that he return his donkey, who had run away to the "house of the *Kuti*" (*bei Kuti*). Abaye could not present adequate proof of ownership, and so the *Kuti* was under no legal obligation to return the donkey. The *Kuti* nonetheless did so, in deference to Abaye's known piety and truthfulness. Both anecdotes present the *Kuti* as a knowledgeable nearby "other" who had no interest in rabbinic law. The first *Kuti* behaved according to his own Pentateuch-based legal understanding. The second went beyond his Torah-mandated responsibility in deference to Abaye's piety, and returned the donkey. Abaye's *Kuti* well expresses the complexity for the Sages of Samaritans as Torah-keeping Israelites who have no interest in rabbinic law and yet can honor Abaye as a holy man for his piety. No extra-Talmudic evidence exists for the presence of Samaritans in Sasanian Babylonia. In general, the Babylonian Talmud deploys *Kutim* as a useful "generative" and liminal category of not-quite-gentiles who are not-quite-Israelites either.

FROM CHRISTIAN ROME TO EARLY ISLAM

During the age of transition from Christian Rome to Islam, boundaries hardened, as Jews, Christians, and Samaritans looked for coherence and paths forward under the new and very different Islamic umbrella civilization. As Aramaic waned, all moved toward Arabic as both their spoken and religious language. Jews and later Samaritans each developed a literary Hebrew for some genres of literature, Hebrew being the "holy language" of both groups. Both were responding, no doubt, to Muslim identification of Arabic as the holy tongue. Storytelling on the model of Islamic literature took hold, replacing the homiletical, *midrashic*, mode of earlier centuries. That the Quran, Sura 20, scornfully called the makers of the Golden Calf *Samiri*—clearly refracting Jewish attitudes toward the golden calves of the Exodus (Exodus 32) and Jeroboam the Israelite king in Samaria (1 Kings 12:26–30; Hosea 8:5)—must certainly have magnified the significance of negative proclivities inherent in earlier rabbinic sources. In addition, the status of the Samaritans as a protected (if lower caste) "People of the Book," as *dhimmis*, has always been tenuous. Beyond the theological, then, Jews had every practical reason to distinguish themselves from the *Kutim*. A short treatise, *Tractate Kutim*, organized mostly Tannaitic determinations regarding the Samaritans, and leans toward the position that *Kutim* were gentiles and not Israelites. Still, the treatise *Kutim* leaves open the possibility of reunification: "When do we accept them? When they deny Mount Gerizim and admit [the truth of] Jerusalem."

Not so a tradition preserved in two well-known midrashic works of this period, *Pirqe de-Rabbi Eliezer* and *Midrash Tanḥuma* (*va-Yashev* 3, Figure 6.4).[9] This tradition imagines a rabbinic attempt to convert the lion-fearing *Kutim* brought to Samaria by the Assyrians. Named rabbis, "Rabbi Dostai and Rabbi Zechariah," were even sent to teach and circumcise these potential converts. While the *Kutim* are called *Shomronim*, we are told, this is because they live in Samaria and by implication are not descendants of the northern tribes. Our tradition imagines an attempt to assassinate Nehemiah by the *Kutim*, followed by a grand battle against Ezra and Nehemiah. For their sins, they are definitively excommunicated at "the Temple of the Lord" in Jerusalem:

> They [Ezra, Nehemiah, and others] brought three hundred priests and three hundred children and three hundred shofars with three hundred Torah scrolls in their hands and they sounded [the shofars]. The Levites melodized and sang and excluded the *Kutim* with the secret of the ineffable Name, both in writing on tablets, including the excommunication of the heavenly court and the excommunication of the earthly high court [decreeing] that no person of Israel may eat *Kuti* bread, ever. From here they said. "Whoever eats *Kuti* bread is as if he ate pig meat" (Mishnah Shevi'it 8:10). You may not convert a *Kuti*, and they have no part in the resurrection of the dead. (*Pirqe de-Rabbi Eliezer* 38)

This amazing text amplifies the exclusion of Samaritans from the building of the Second Temple in Ezra 4, even claiming that the Babylonian Jews added their own excommunication and "Cyrus the King put them under the ban, eternally." This is a rather final sound-

ꚗꛃꚒꛀꚚꚒꚛ

6.4 *Midrash Tanḥuma to Genesis and Exodus*. Yemen, 15th century. *va-Yashev* 3 (Yeshiva University, Mendel Gottesman Library, on loan from Richard and Debra Parkoff).

secure imperial permission to rebuild the Jerusalem Temple. This almost worked. Reworking Ezra 4 to the benefit of the Samaritans, Abu l-Fatḥ has it that "Sanballat and his assembly wrote a letter to 'Anusharwan the king ... and said to him: 'Al-Quds [Jerusalem] is a city which has provoked a number of kings [in the past]. Should you give them permission to rebuild the city they will rebel against you, and no more tribute will come from the [Jordan] River, nor from within [from Jewish Palestine].'" The Persian king subsequently "forbade the rebuilding of Jerusalem and they demolished what had already been erected in it." Our author laments that "[consequently] bad feeling worsened between the Samaritans and the Jews, and their mutual loathing intensified." As a result, Ezra and Zerubbabel set about "making up an alphabet of their own"—referring to the Jewish square script, which actually was adopted by Jews during the Persian period (and hence the rabbis called it *ketav Ashurit*, "Assyrian script"). Unforgivably, we are told, Jews "tampered with the Torah," removing explicitly Samaritan elements from it (Chapter 20).[10]

Beneath the surface of academic and narrative exclusion, ranging from trust to "bad feeling" and even "loathing," relations on the ground seem to have been variegated during the many centuries that we call late antiquity. This is exemplified by the Samaritan peddler with whom we opened this article and in the sometimes tortured attempts by rabbinic scholastics to disconnect from *Kutim* and to engage with them—sometimes all at once! The complexities of the relationships between Jews and Samaritans—both real and theoretical—continued to develop in fascinating and twisting ways into the medieval and modern worlds.

For Further Reading

Izhak Hamutovski. "Rabbi Meir and the Samaritans: The Differences between the Accounts in the Yerushalmi and the Bavli." *Jewish Studies, an Internet Journal* 8 (2009): 34–39. [Hebrew].

Joseph Heinemann. "Anti-Samaritan Polemics in the Aggadah." *Proceedings of the World Congress of Jewish Studies 1973* (1977): 57–69.

Moshe Lavee. "The Samaritan May Be Included: Another Look at the Samaritan in Talmudic Literature." In *Samaritans: Past and Present*, edited by Menachem Mor and Friedrich V. Reiterer. Berlin: De Gruyter, 2010, 147–173.

Lawrence H. Schiffman. "The Samaritans in Amoraic Halakha." In *Shoshanat Yaaqov: Jewish and Iranian Studies in Honor of Yaakov Elman*, edited by Shai Secunda and Steven Fine. Leiden: Brill, 2012, 371–389.

1 Ed. M. Margoliot 1:123–124.

2 Alon, 1977, 1, note 5.

3 Hasan-Rokem, 2003, 42–43.

4 Ed.Theodor-Albeck, 1178.

5 Mishnah Yevamot 4:13; Tosefta Qiddushin 4:16.

6 Commentary on Matthew 17:29 (Pummer, 2002, 62); Ed. Stenhouse, chapter 38, pp. 171- 172. For additional sources, Pummer, 2002, 46.

7 Meshorer, 1985, 52, no. 148.

8 Lieberman, 1991, 375-378.

9 Venice, 1545.

10 Ed. Stenhouse, 96–98.

ing statement of a relationship millennia old, a clear attempt to differentiate Jews from Samaritans in the early Islamic world—and to distance Jews from Samaritans by means of imperial support.

The ultimate sin a Jew can commit with a *Kuti*, *Pirqe de-Rabbi Eliezer* claims, is eating his bread, or perhaps in our lingo, "breaking bread" with him. We have come quite a distance since the late-first-century sage Rabbi Eliezer son of Hurqanos's assertion "Whoever eats *Kuti* bread is as if he ate pig meat" was silenced by Rabbi Aqiva (Mishnah Shevi'it 8:10). In *Pirqe de-Rabbi Eliezer*, this statement is cited anonymously as established, apodictic law, and as exemplary of the way good Jews *should* avoid *Kutim*. The kind of fraternization that *Leviticus Rabba* images is clearly beyond the pale.

Samaritans, clearly at a disadvantage under both Christianity and Islam, moved in similar directions. A tradition preserved by Abu l-Fatḥ, admittedly later, responded to the Jewish Book of Ezra with its own counter-history. This text reverberates with the harshness of our *Pirqe de-Rabbi Eliezer* passage, though here the Samaritans are the aggrieved, well-connected, and powerful party. "Zerubbabel and Ezra, leaders of the Jews," we are told, attempted to

7
"A Place in which to Read, to Interpret, and to Hear Petitions": Samaritan Synagogues

STEVEN FINE

On the periphery of the Holy Mountain, Baba Rabba built a water pool for purification at prayer times, that is, before the rising of the sun, and its setting. And he erected a prayer house for the people to pray in, opposite the Holy Mountain; and these still existed up to the time the Franks ruled, may God curse them, as did the prayer house which Baba Rabba built according to the specifications of the house of prayer which had been built in the days of the *Radwan* in Basra. He copied it, and gave it an earthen floor just as he had seen in Basra. Then he took seven stones from the Temple that Saul's men had demolished, and made them into tier-like seats for the seven *Ḥukama*. He took a large(er) stone and placed it for himself to sit upon.

Baba Rabba built eight synagogues, with no timber in any of them, in small(er) villages. These were the synagogue of Awarta and the synagogue of Salem, the synagogue of Nmara and the synagogue of Qaryat Haja, and the synagogue of Qarawa and the synagogue of Tira Luza the synagogue of Dabarin and the synagogue of Beit Gan. He built in them a place in which to read, and to interpret and to hear petitions, in the southern part of the house of prayer, so that anyone with a personal problem could ask the *Hukama* about it, and be given a sound answer.

Whoever aspired to the title of *Ḥakim* ["Sage"] had to present himself at the time of the Feasts and the New Moons before the great high priest and the *Ḥukama* [the Sages] and if they considered him suitable he was granted the title of *Ḥakim*. Baba Rabba said that the reason for building (such) a house of prayer and place of learning was so that the kings of the world would not think that he bothered himself with what concerned kings and their realms, which had forsaken the worship of God and the carrying out of his injunctions; or that (he bothered himself) with anything that was superficial.

— *The Chronicle of Abu l-Fath,* Chapter 41[1]

Synagogues are an important theme in Abu l-Fath's chronicle. They are distinctly Samaritan spaces, places of both rejuvenation and loss. Baba Rabba (literally, "Baba the Great") is recorded across the Samaritan chronicles as the leader of a Samaritan renaissance and revolt against Rome. According to Abu l-Fath and the other chroniclers, this legendary hero set about establishing the instruments of Samaritan self-governance, including the apportioning of land, the appointment of a civil administration of "sages," and the building of numerous synagogues—sometimes called "prayer places"—in Samaria. Abu l-Fath describes these "places of assembly" as "places of prayer and learning." In fact, Baba Rabba uses this construction to distinguish himself from human kings. He is a royal sage, a leader of sages. We do not know exactly when the historical Baba Rabba lived—perhaps during the reign of Commodus (180–193 CE) or as late as the fourth century. Whenever it was, though, he is remembered for his great leadership, which included the construction of synagogues. This construction parallels the first monumental Jewish synagogues built after the destruction of Jerusalem in 70 CE, including the third-century structure at Nabratein and Dura Europos in Syria (245 CE), as well as the spread of churches in Roman Palestine (the earliest known at Legio, just north of Samaria). It fits comfortably with the great building boom of Samaritan and Jewish synagogues and churches that took place during the fourth, fifth, and sixth centuries. The projects of Baba Rabba thus reflect the larger prosperity experienced in Christian imperial Palestine.

SAMARITAN DIASPORA SYNAGOGUES

Abu l-Fath writes of a synagogue in Nablus that was modeled on an even older one at Basra in Syria.[2] The presence of important synagogues in Samaritan diaspora communities—at least in Syria—is assumed in this passage, a reality expressed in Roman law, patristic texts, and early modern sources. A dedicatory inscription discovered in Thessaloniki in Greece, which dates to the fourth to sixth century, for example, derives from a now-lost synagogue there (Figure 7.1). It is bilingual, the main text containing the priestly blessing (Numbers 6) and a dedicatory formula in Greek, which is framed by a seeming liturgical refrain. The upper inscription reads "Blessed is our God eternally" and the lower inscription reads "Blessed is his name eternally" in Samaritan Hebrew: the inscriptions are carved by a less sure hand than the Greek one:

© STEVEN FINE, 2022 | DOI:10.1163/9789004466913_009

ᚑᛗᛞᚤᚠ

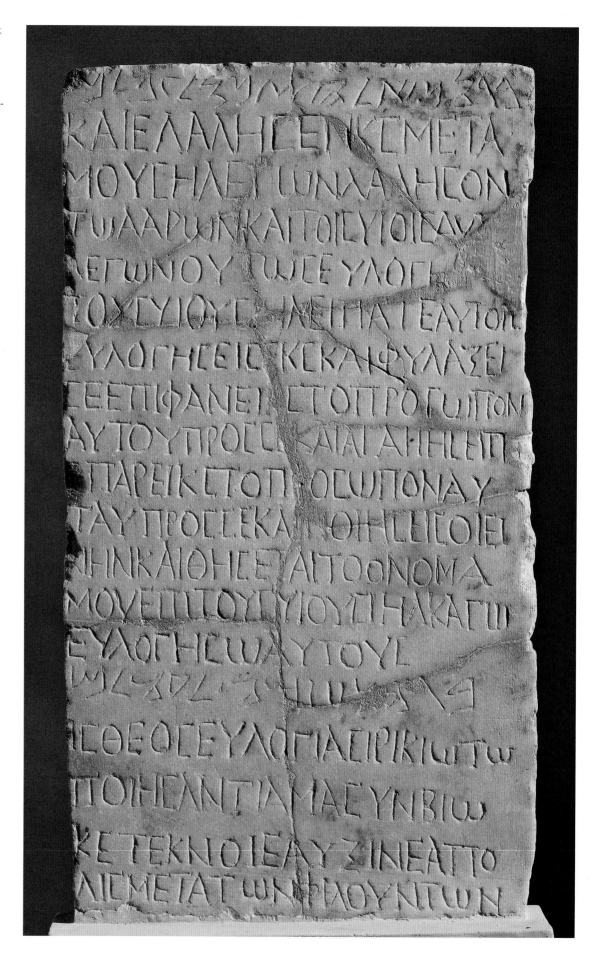

7.1 Dedicatory Inscription in Greek and Samaritan Hebrew, Thessaloniki, Greece, fifth century CE (© Archaeological Museum of Thessaloniki, Ministry of Culture and Sports, Archaeological Receipts Fund. Photograph by Orestis Kourakis).

Blessed be our God forever!

"And the Lord spoke to Moses saying:

'So you will bless the sons of Israel.

Tell them: The Lord will bless you and protect you. The Lord will reveal his face to you and favor you. The Lord will lift up his face to you and make peace for you.

And my name will be placed upon the sons of Israel and I will bless them'" (Numbers 6:22–27).

Blessed be His name forever!

God (is) one. A blessing to Siricius who has made this with his wife and children. Prosper, Neapolis, with those who love you!

A column inscribed with Numbers 10:35—"Arise, O Lord, let your enemies be scattered"—from Syracuse in Sicily may well derive from a synagogue.[3] Cassiodorus Senator (485/490 – ca. 580 CE), an official of the Ostrogoth kings in Ravenna, mentions a synagogue in Rome that had been "acquired" by Pope Simplicius at the beginning of the sixth Christian century.[4] Earlier still are two dedicatory inscriptions from Delos that date to the first century BCE and praise donors who adorned the "Samaritan prayer place (*proseuche*) on Delos" (Figure 4.2).

Abu l-Fath dates the Basra synagogue to before the split between Israel and Judah, during the idyllic *Radwan*. The Basra synagogue, and hence its Nablus successor, thus had particular significance as bridges to the ideal past. While no late antique Palestinian Jewish synagogue was ascribed such antiquity, the Jewish pilgrimage synagogue of *Shaf ve-Yativ* in Nehardea in Sasanian Babylonia was described in medieval sources as having been built at a similarly traumatic moment, the exile of Jehoiachin, the last king of Judah, to Babylonia in 586 BCE (e.g. Rashi on Babylonian Talmud Megillah 29a). The Basra and Nablus synagogues serve a similar function for Samaritans as the Abisha Scroll and its later copies, attaching the present to an idealized past and thus to the messianic future. Even with this pedigree (or perhaps because of it), the Nablus synagogue, we are told, was destroyed by the "Franks," the Crusaders.

LATE ANTIQUE SYNAGOGUES: LITERARY SOURCES

Baba Rabba is described as having built eight synagogues in "smaller villages" across Samaria. These, we hear, were impressive stone buildings, with "no timber in any of them." The interior arrangements described by the sources are not clear. Each house of prayer contained "a place in which to read, and to interpret and to hear petitions . . . in the southern part . . . so that anyone with a personal problem could ask the *Ḥukama* [the 'Sages'] about it, and be given a sound answer." Abu l-Fath describes the synagogue as a "place of prayer." Though no prayers attributed to Baba Rabba exist, a vast collection of liturgical poetry in Aramaic attributed to Amram Dara, Marqe, and Nina son of Marqe are extant from the Byzantine period. These are integral to Samaritan liturgy to this day.[5]

The construction at the southern side of each synagogue is reminiscent of study houses of the rabbis or, perhaps more pointedly for Abu l-Fath, an Islamic *madrassa*. "Reading, interpretation and petitions to sages" are central to all three environments. The Arabic

term used for Samaritan authorities, *Ḥukama*, parallels the Samaritan Aramaic *Ḥakim* and the language used for Jewish "Sages," who are called *Ḥakhamim*. We do not know what kinds of "interpretation" are imagined by Abu l-Fath's chronicle, though considerable Samaritan biblical interpretation from late antiquity survives in *Tebat Marqe*, an assembly of homiletical texts, and the legal literature of the Samaritans in Arabic is quite rich. The "school" plays a major part in *Tebat Marqe* and in early liturgical poetry. Marqe's projection of a Samaritan "school" as a place for instruction and prayer into the Exodus epic is particularly poignant:

> And on that very day the leaders of the people heard and told the congregation, and like them, believed [that God had sent Moses and Aaron]. Immediately, all of them, as on the day that the king Pharaoh died, sighed and cried aloud. On that day they believed in the signs that they had seen and heard, for God truly remembers and forgets nothing. "They bowed and prostrated" (Exodus 4:31), all of them, and said praises and prostration to the God of their fathers. After the people left their schoolhouse [*me-bisfaron*] the prophets "went to Pharaoh" (Exodus 5:1) the king. (*Tebat Marqe* 1:19)

The term "synagogue" must be used with caution in describing late antique Samaritan institutions, as it does not appear in late antique Samaritan literary sources or in synagogue inscriptions; it appears in later texts.[6]

Near the close of his chronicle, Abu l-Fath describes a third synagogue. This one was built by a high priest named Aqbun (there were a few of this name). The chronicle affords this synagogue special status, writing that "from the end of the *Radwan* up until the above-mentioned high priest, the people did not have (such) a synagogue." Abu l-Fath relates that the synagogue had particularly large "doors that the people of Hadrian had carried away from the hated Temple in Jerusalem for the Temple which he had erected on the Holy Mountain [Mount Gerizim] and which had been hidden when the Temple was destroyed. Their dimensions and their hiding place had been handed down from high priest to high priest."[7] Such *spolia* and reuse were not rare in antiquity. Christian traditions correctly held that spoils of Herod's Temple were used by Hadrian to build the Temple of Aphrodite on the site of the current Holy Sepulcher,[8] and late antique twisted columns believed to come from Solomon's Temple stood in Old Saint Peter's in Rome. The huge bronze doors of the Roman Curia Julia, created under Domitian (94 CE), were transferred to St. John Lateran during the mid-seventeenth century.[9] Our author describes the synagogue doors as made of "Andulusian bronze." Perhaps this is a garbled memory of the famed Corinthian bronze doors donated by Nicanor of Alexandria to the Jerusalem Temple,[10] though the emperor Vespasian is identified as Hadrian—whom Samaritans believed favored them owing to his imagined wife, whom they believed to have been a Samaritan. This synagogue is said to have been built on a grand scale, and that it was supported by Rome itself. This shrine housed a trophy brought from the hated Jerusalem Temple and preserved over generations by heroic Samaritan priests. Alas, our author reports that this syn-

On the northeastern side of Samaria, at Beit Shean / Scythopolis, a third synagogue carpet mosaic was discovered by Nehemiah Zuri in 1962. The apse is aligned southward, either toward Jerusalem, or, more likely, toward Mount Gerizim. Before the apse of this basilical structure was laid the image of a Torah shrine flanked by two menorahs. Each menorah is flanked by an incense shovel and a shofar. This sixth-century mosaic is similar to floor mosaics in the Jewish synagogues at Ḥammath Tiberias, Sepphoris, Naaran, and nearby Beit Alpha. An inscription in a side room proclaims that the flooring was laid by Ḥaninah and his son Marianos—the same artisans who created the Jewish synagogue mosaic at Beit Alpha. A Greek inscription written in Samaritan script in another room reads "O Lord, help Ephrai[m] and Anan," suggesting again a complex linguistic environment where the appearance of Samaritan script, even for a Greek text, was valued. Ephraim was not a common Jewish name during this period, perhaps owing to the association of the biblical Ephraim with Shechem. Ḥanan (Anan) was used by both Jews and Samaritans. When first discovered, this building was identified as a Jewish synagogue. This identification was made more complex by the discovery of the Samaritan inscriptions. Zuri posited that this was a space shared by Jews and Samaritans. Only in recent years has this building been interpreted as a Samaritan synagogue, written into the enlarged corpus of Samaritan buildings discovered since the 1980s. Archeologist Ruth Jacoby strengthened this connection, noting that the Torah shrine panel of this mosaic lacks a marker common to all the Jewish mosaics: a *lulav* bundle and an *etrog*.[16] This image, common to specifically Jewish contexts since the coins of the First and Second Jewish Revolts, appears in no Samaritan context. This is because Samaritans interpret Leviticus 23:40 differently from Jews, and do not use the *lulav* bundle and *etrog* in their liturgy. This distinction between Jewish and Samaritan biblical exegesis is discussed by Laura Lieber in this volume. In addition, the inscription discovered in this building uses Samaritan script, and the telltale Jewish script does not appear. Similarly, no images of animals or people appear in the admittedly fragmentary mosaic. All of this together points to a Samaritan synagogue.

The discovery of an incense burner by Zuri further parallels the glowing embers of the intense shovel of the mosaic, and points to the liturgical experience of this synagogue. So close in iconography and construction to Jewish synagogues of the Beit Shean valley, this floor points to a closeness between the two Israelite peoples as well as a real attempt to distinguish a Samaritan synagogue from Jewish ones. Vastly similar to the modern viewer, the indicators of Samaritan culture identified in the mosaic were likely the tip of a "distinguishing iceberg" in antiquity. An ancient visitor would hear very different liturgies in each of these contexts that would have been unmistakable and perhaps intolerably similar.

Synagogue discoveries during the last decade of the twentieth century, at Tsur Nathan, east of Netanya, el-Khirbe, and Khirbet Samara in the Samaritan highlands and elsewhere have transformed our knowledge of ancient Samaritan synagogues. The synagogue at el-Khirbe was excavated by Yitzhak Magen in 1990. This stone structure was built in the fourth century, and it was used until the

7.5a   Amulet Pendant, Israel (?), Bronze, fifth to sixth century (Bible Lands Museum, Jerusalem). Abbreviated biblical verses in Samaritan Hebrew on both sides:

     1. There is none like G[od] (Deuteronomy 33:26).
     2. Mighty (Exodus 15:3).
     3. Rise up, Lord! (Numbers 10:35).
     4. Lord [is One] (Deuteronomy 6:4).
     5. His name (Exodus 15:3).

7.5b   Amulet Capsule. Gold, Samaria (?), ca. fourth-sixth century CE. Inscribed in Greek, *Theos Boethos,* "God, help [me, us]," and in mirror Samaritan script, "Rise up, Lord!" (Numbers 10:35). Unopened amulet inside (David and Jemima Jeselsohn Collection, Zurich, Switzerland).

sixth. It was restored during the seventh century and continued to be used during the early Islamic period. Reinhard Pummer connects this sixth-century lapse with punitive measures taken by the imperial regime against the Samaritans after their failed revolts in the late fifth and early sixth centuries, which were codified in Justinian's decree that "Samaritan synagogues must be destroyed." The vaulted central hall of the synagogue measures 14 x 12 meters, and the interior is lined with benches. An *exedra* on the northern side leads one into the sanctuary. The hall is paved with a partially preserved carpet mosaic. Near the entrance is an exquisite mosaic panel showing a large, gabled shrine covered with a curtain to the far right, almost certainly a Torah shrine (Figure 0.7, 13). To the far left is a seven-branched menorah topped with oil lamps, which is flanked by horns, tongs, and an incense shovel—but no *lulav* bundle as one would expect in Jewish contexts. In the center of this composition is a round table, topped with a gray plate, upon which is arrayed serving vessels and loaves of bread.[17] The plate bears a strong resemblance to the one discovered at Na'anah (Kibbutz Na'an) in the Shephelah. The rim of the Na'anah plate, now at the Louvre, is decorated with the image of a Torah shrine and a menorah—but no *lulav*. This table has been identified as a representation of the biblical "table of the showbread," which I might reject out of hand, since the biblical table was arrayed with twelve unleavened loaves, and not with a meal. A fish meal appears, for example, in a Jewish gold glass from Rome, now in the collection of the Metropolitan Museum of Art. I would not be surprised if our mosaic were to represent dining practices within the synagogue. The 1509/10 Torah curtain and the 1522 case of the Abisha Scroll, followed by many of the nineteenth-century Tabernacle drawings, show an array of

7.6 Diadem of Mariam the Priestess. Gold (detail), Samaria (?), ca. fourth to sixth century CE, inscription in Samaritan Hebrew: *Bli Adi Mariam Kahanta,* "Without [likely a defensive formula], Ornament of Mariam the Priestess" (David and Jemima Jeselsohn Collection, Zurich, Switzerland, photograph by West Semitic Research).

goblets atop the table (Figures 0.7, 2.2–4, 13.2). It may well be that the artists in both cases—separated by a thousand years—were at a loss to illustrate the showbread table and its breads in a distinctive manner (as were Jewish artisans in the Sepphoris synagogue). They presented this biblical appurtenance as a standard table with food arrayed upon it.

The synagogue of Khirbet Samara was excavated by Magen in 1991/1992 in one of the largest towns in Samaria. The central hall measured 16.4 by 12.7 meters, with two tiers of benches along the northern and southern walls. A large apse on the eastern side, an addition to the structure, is aligned with Mount Gerizim. Before this edifice was a large atrium. An exquisite rendition of a tetrapylon, likely a Torah shrine, appears on the floor mosaic within the hall. Built during the fourth century, the synagogue was destroyed during the sixth, perhaps owing to the Samaritan revolts (Figure 7.7). Ash from this destruction was discovered in the apse. The hall was later partially rebuilt, benches added on the other walls, and the Torah shrine mosaic covered with flagstones. Immediately to the east of the apse, a relief depicting a Torah shrine was discovered above a stepped pool, called by Jews a *miqveh*. Ritual baths used for purification purposes are common in Samaritan contexts, as they are in contemporary Jewish areas, though no similar baths were

used by Christians. Tannaitic literature of the second and early third centuries (Tosefta Miqvaot 6:1) mention the efficacy of *Kuti* pools, and even the Jerusalem Talmud (Avodah Zarah 5:3, 44d) grudgingly acknowledges that Samaritan *miqvaot* are "kosher" even when constructed in less than a rabbinically ideal manner.

The *miqveh* at Khirbet Samara reflects a different approach to purity in the synagogue among Samaritans than among contemporaneous Jews. In Jewish practice, *miqvaot* were closely associated with synagogues during the first century. This changed after 70 CE. Not a single *miqveh* was built in proximity to a Jewish synagogue during late antiquity. The pool at Khirbet Samara fits well with Abu l-Fatḥ's concern with the construction of "water pools for purification." Ritual purity continues to be important to Samaritans, though ritual baths have been replaced for menstrual purification with bathtubs in which the drain is kept open to create running, "living," water.

SAMARITAN SYNAGOGUES: EARLY MODERN AND MODERN

Few remains of medieval and early modern synagogues are preserved. In 1708, the Samaritan synagogue at Fustat, ancient Cairo, was transferred to the Rabbanite community with the end of the Samaritan community there. An apparent house synagogue from sixteenth-century Damascus was adorned with an exquisite niche, a Mameluke *mihrab* formed, it seems, as a Torah shrine (Figure 7.8). The niche, 3.02 meters tall, is constructed of colored marble, ceramic tiles, and mosaics. Samaritan inscriptions were set within the red spandrels of the arch and within rosettes that flank it on either side, and rectangular inscriptions lined the walls of the room.

An Italian visitor to Damascus, Pietro Della Valle, describes a remarkably similar use of inscriptions that he encountered in June 1616, noting their polychromy:

> Here I had the pleasure of visiting the gardens and the houses (though of mean appearance externally) very fine inside, being all set out with paintings in gold with their Samaritan characters cut in and in many places also painted, as is also their Synagogue.[18]

Similar to the Samaritan *mezuzah*, placed near the entrances of private homes, the inscriptions contain abbreviated Torah verses.

The *Tulidah*, followed by a late-nineteenth-century work, the so-called *New Chronicle*, describes a synagogue built in Gaza by a beneficent "good man." Ab Galuga "built houses of holiness [*batei miqdash*, that is, "synagogues"] and built the synagogue of Shechem on the model of the house of the Ark (*beit arona*)," the place where the Torah case (the *aron*) was stored. The phrase *batei miqdash* refers to Exodus 25:8, according to the Samaritan version of the Torah—"Make Me a *miqdash* and I will dwell in *your* midst (*be-tokhekhem*)." The Samaritan synagogue is conceived in terms of the biblical Tabernacle as a holy place. This is not unlike Jewish synagogues, which also take up Tabernacle and Jerusalem Temple metaphors.

The furnishings of Samaritan synagogues are referred to in terms derived from the Tabernacle. Thus, the area containing the Torah shrine is called a *muzbah*, after the sacrificial altar. The Torah case is an *aron*, after the Ark of the Covenant, and the curtain before the Torah shrine is called a *masakh*, after the curtain at the entrance to the Tabernacle: "And you shall make a screen for the entrance

7.8   Niche (*mihrab*), Samaritan home (house-synagogue?), Damascus, eighteenth century (Museum für Islamische Kunst, Berlin, Wikimedia Commons).

7.11 Synagogue, Holon, 2018. Large inscription: Deuteronomy 28:6, "Blessed shall you be when you come in, and blessed shall you be when you go out"; Inner arch: Exodus 25:8, "Make me a sanctuary, that I may dwell in *your* midst (Samaritan version). Menorah base, Deuteronomy 6:4, "Hear O Israel" (Photograph by Steven Fine).

7.12 Street Sign, Holon (Photograph by Steven Fine).

7.13 *Mezuzah* Plaque affixed to the home of Issachar and Dror, the sons of Abraham Marḥiv, Holon, 2017. The Hebrew inscription opens: "Blessed be He who said," followed by biblical verses in the form of the menorah: Exodus 12:13, "I will pass over you, and no plague shall fall upon you to destroy you"; Deuteronomy 28:12, "The Lord will open for you his rich storehouse, the heavens [to give the rain of your land in its season and to bless all your undertakings]"; Deuteronomy 33:29, "Your enemies shall come cringing to you, and you shall tread on their backs." Below the branches, Deuteronomy 28:6, "Blessed shall you be when you come in, and blessed shall you be when you go out" (Photograph by Steven Fine).

A large arch at the gate of the main Holon synagogue, rebuilt by the Community Council in 1997, is inscribed in Samaritan Hebrew: "Blessed are you when you come, blessed are you when you depart" (Deuteronomy 29:6, Figure 7.11). As any Samaritan will tell you, this blessing, appropriate as it is, was first enunciated by the Children of Israel standing on the "Mountain of Blessing," Mount Gerizim. On the round arch of this portal is inscribed Exodus 25:8 according to the Samaritan version of the Torah cited above. A large brass menorah was added later. When first opened in 1963, the synagogue gate was marked in modern Hebrew simply as "Samaritan synagogue," with an Arch of Titus menorah above it— symbol of the State of Israel.

With increased comfort in their Israeli identity, this was replaced with a Samaritan inscription and a less statist menorah as part of an ongoing project to publicly mark off the Holon neighborhood. Neve Marqe, named for the late antique Samaritan midrashist and liturgical poet, is distinguished with street signs and exterior *mezuzah* plaques above or near each door—all in the uniquely Samaritan script and composed of apotropaic biblical verses (Figures 7.12-13). Similar exterior *mezuzah* plaques distinguish Kiryat Luza. Closing the circle, cloth *mezuzah* plaques are displayed within private homes and inside the Community Center on Mount Gerizim, some of which represent the Israeli state seal. The legend, "Israel," is written in Samaritan script.

For Further Reading

Yitzhak Magen. *The Samaritans and the Good Samaritan*. Jerusalem: Staff Officer of Archaeology, Civil Administration for Judea and Samaria, 2008.

Reinhard Pummer. "Samaritan Synagogues and Jewish Synagogues: Similarities and Differences." In *Jews, Christians, and Polytheists in the Ancient Synagogue: Cultural Interaction during the Greco-Roman Period*, edited by Steven Fine. London: Routledge, 1999, 118–160.

Benyamim Tsedaka. "Toward a History of the Synagogue Ritual: Between Jews and Samaritans." *A.B. – The Samaritan News* 357–358 (April 15, 1984): 9–16. [Hebrew].

Bracha Yaniv. "The Samaritan Torah Case." *Samaritan Researches*, edited by Vittorio Morabito, Alan D. Crown, and Lucy Davey. Sydney: Mandelbaum Publishing, 2000, 4.3–13.

---

1   Ed. Stenhouse, 182-184.
2   Bowman, 1977, 146.
3   Pummer, 2005, 106.
4   *Variae* 3.45; Pummer, 2002, 242–244.
5   Lieber, forthcoming.
6   Fine, 2012.
7   Ed. Stenhouse, chapter 34, p. 159.
8   Stiebel, 2007, 222-223.
9   Claridge, 2010, 71–73.
10 Mishnah Yoma 3:8-9; Tosefta Kippurim 2:4.
11 Rabello, 2002, 491.
12 Pummer, 2002, 274.
13 See Pummer, 1999; Magen, 2008.
14 Reich, 2002.
15 Reich, 2002.
16 Jacoby, 2000.
17 Fine, 1996, 118, 172; Fine, 2015, 45-46.
18 Gaster, 1925, 181, 183.
19 Yaniv, 2000, 6.
20 Ben-Zvi, 1966, 134.

8
Sukkot in the Garden of Eden: Liturgy, Christianity, and the Bronze Bird on Mount Gerizim

LAURA S. LIEBER

One night all the people were mustered, and ascended Mount Gerizim and Baba Rabba was in the van of the troops. Levi [nephew of Baba Rabba] then arose with the might and power of God and smote the guards of the king, the monks and the priests, crying out in a loud voice: "The Lord is a man of war. The Lord is His name!" And when Baba Rabba heard the voice of Levi, his nephew, they all raised their voices, saying as he had said. They unsheathed their swords and killed many of the Romans, not ceasing until they had wiped out everyone who was on Mount Gerizim.

Then they kindled the fire on the top of the [church] dome and all the Samaritans arose and killed all the overseers who had been put over them. Not one of them remained. And they continued throughout the whole night to burn the churches of the Romans, destroying them until they effaced their name from Mount Gerizim and round-about.

The memory of this [that is, the Samaritan triumph] has lasted up to our day: on the first day of the seventh month, the Samaritan children gather wood and burn it in the evening at the end of the first day of the seventh month.

— *The Chronicle of Abu l-Fath*, Chapter 44[1]

One of the more striking customs practiced among Samaritans today is the tradition of burning the dried palm fronds and dry leafy matter of the booths at the conclusion of the festival of Sukkot. Abu l-Fath, quoting a still earlier chronicle, provides the earliest source of this custom, which he associates with the stunning Samaritan victory over the Byzantine Christians under the leadership of the great Samaritan reformer, Baba Rabba.

By the fifth century, a series of churches had been built on Mount Gerizim, culminating in the great octagonal church of the Theotokos, the "Mother of God," built by Emperor Zeno in the fifth century and fortified by Justinian in the sixth (Figure 8.1). The Christianization of Mount Gerizim deeply distressed the Samaritans, who seemingly lost access to the Holy Mountain. The burning of churches described by Abu l-Fath is the culmination

of an intricate saga of resistance and success against the Christian empire. According to the story, the Christians had set up a mechanical automaton, a talking bronze bird on the mountain (a bird perhaps because Mount Gerizim hovers in the sky above Neapolis). Any time a Samaritan approached the mountain, we are told, the bird would scream out "Samaritan, Samaritan," alerting the Christians and allowing them to keep Samaritans from ascending this now Christian Holy Mountain. Interestingly, in rabbinic tradition the Samaritans were accused of setting up their own idolatrous bird on the mountain—a charge that Abu l-Fath's story quietly disputes. Baba Rabba, we are told, sent his nephew Levi to infiltrate and join the Church in Byzantium and rise in the hierarchy so that he could clandestinely support the Samaritan cause. This intrigue too reflects reality, as many Samaritans did succumb to Christianity and later Islam, maintaining their connections to the Samaritan community for generations. Returning to Shechem as an honored Christian prelate, Levi and his entourage ascended the mountain. Unfooled, the bird squawked at Levi's clandestine presence on the mountain. Levi managed to convince the Christians that the bird was thus defective, as no Samaritan was present, and had the bird destroyed. The saga concludes with the successful Samaritan conquest of Mount Gerizim cited above and the destruction of the hated churches.

This cleansing of the Blessed Mountain, Abu l-Fath tells us, was preserved in Samaritan memory and ritual to his own day: "On the first day of the seventh month, the Samaritan children gather wood and burn it in the evening at the end of the first day of the seventh month." This account aligns these momentous events and the wood-burning with the first day of the "seventh month," what Jews call Rosh Hashanah, the New Year. By the early twentieth century at the latest, the *Samaritan Chronicle II* (also known as *Sefer ha-Yamim*, the *Book of Days*), an expansion of the medieval chronicle tradition, records that the burning occurs at the end of the festival, on Shemini Atzeret, and it is the desiccated material from the *sukkot* that are burned, reflecting contemporary practice. This modern chronicle version has the story as follows:

© LAURA S. LIEBER, 2022 | DOI:10.1163/9789004466913_010

8.1 Church of the Theotokos, Mount Gerizim, fifth to sixth century (Amir Aloni, aerial photography courtesy of Moshe Alafi).

The Israelite community arose that night and overthrew all the Roman meeting-houses and all their posts, blotting out their name from the Mountain of the Divine Presence, Mount Gerizim Beit-El. From the day the Samaritan-Israelite community did this to the Romans, Samaritan children have set fire to the wood of the *sukkah*-booths on the night of the termination of the festive of the Eighth Day of Solemn Assembly, which concludes the festivals of the Lord. This episode has thus remained a memorial among them unto this day.

Over centuries, foundational stories from late antiquity, filtered through medieval historiography and developing ritual practices, transformed flames of victory into an enduring tradition of bonfires on the evening after Shemini Atzeret at the conclusion of the festival of Sukkot. A tradition of triumph over enemies, the purification of ritual space, the symbolism of fire and even the significant role assigned to children help us understand why Benyamim Tsedaka describes this celebration to outsiders as a kind of analogue to the Jewish festival of Hanukkah.

THE SAMARITAN *SUKKAH*

What does the *Chronicle II* mean by "Samaritan children have set fire to the wood of the *sukkah*-booths"? What is a "Samaritan *sukkah*"? The Samaritan "*sukkah*-booth" is a ritual response to the injunction found in Leviticus 23:40:

On the first day [of Sukkot], you shall take the fruit of *hadar* trees, branches of palm trees, boughs of leafy trees, and *aravah* of the brook, and you shall rejoice before the Eternal your God for seven days.

The "fruit of *hadar* trees" is interpreted by Samaritans as any beautiful fruit, and not specifically a citron (i.e., the *etrog*) of Jewish tradition, and the *aravah* is understood not specifically as a willow as among Jews but as any deciduous tree growing in Wadi Shechem, although there is a preference for the lilac chaste tree (*Vitex agnus-castus*), which is indigenous to the Land of Israel. Leviticus's injunction to "take" these four species provides little in the way of concrete ritual instruction—what is to be done with them, precisely? In Samaritan practice, by contrast they are "taken" and transformed into the materials from which the booths (specified in Leviticus 23:42–43) are made. This is very different from Jewish tradition, which sees the *lulav* bundle and *etrog* in these verses. While the *lulav* and *etrog* are emblematic of Judaism in Jewish art of Greco-Roman antiquity, these symbols never appear in Samaritan art.

As different as Samaritan practice is from Jewish practice, however, it recalls the celebration of Sukkot by the Jewish returnees to Jerusalem from the Babylonian Captivity, as it is recorded in the Jewish Bible (Nehemiah 8:14–16):

ⰥⰋⰀⰒⰔⰅⰓⰀ

They found written in the Teaching that the Eternal had commanded Moses that the Israelites must dwell in booths during the festival of the seventh month; and that they must announce and proclaim throughout all their towns and Jerusalem as follows, "Go out to the mountains and bring leafy branches of olive trees, pine trees, myrtles, palms and [other] leafy trees to make booths, as it is written." So the people went out and brought them, and made themselves booths on their roofs, in their courtyards, in the courtyards of the House of God, in the square of the Water Gate and in the square of the Ephraim Gate.

The community of the returnees, depicted in Ezra 4 as being in conflict with the Samaritan community, here builds their *sukkot* from the leafy boughs of trees, in a style strongly reminiscent of eventually attested Samaritan custom. It seems plausible that the Nehemiah passage records a once-familiar, unsurprising alternative means of constructing *sukkot* that, while eventually discarded by Jews during the Greco-Roman period, was once a normative practice—and one practiced by Karaite Jews down to the present day.

Few ritual items are as striking and unexpected by outsiders as Samaritan *sukkot*, the ritual booths built as an essential component of the autumn harvest festival. In contemporary Samaritan practice, *sukkot* are built inside the home, and thus not readily visible to casual passers-by. The *sukkah* has no walls. The distinguishing feature of the Samaritan *sukkah* is its roof; they are built on a metal frame (reused from year to year) that is suspended from the ceiling by chains or held up with poles (Figures 8.2-4). The frame is covered with mesh to which the "fruit of *hadar* trees," threaded with a wire, can be attached. While any fruits can be used, popular choices include citrus (pomelos, lemons, grapefruit, citrons, oranges, etc.), apples, peaches, pomegranates, and also eggplants and peppers. The ornate designs

are carefully sketched out and planned to create ornate patterns. The fruit may weigh upwards of seven hundred pounds. Above the fruit, over the metal frame and mesh substrate, palm fronds are layered in a pattern (alternately right side up and upside down); over the palm fronds, thick tree boughs are fashioned into a thatched roof and edged with branches from the lilac chaste trees (or other native species). In this way, the four species mentioned in Leviticus 23:40, "fruit of *hadar* trees," are brought together as a remarkable display of craftsmanship within the Samaritan home.

Nineteenth-century European travelogues and ethnographies—some based on direct observation and others on secondhand accounts—describe Samaritans as building their booths for Tabernacles outdoors in fields and in courtyards. It is possible that some *sukkot* were built indoors, as well, but the records are silent on this. We should also note the absence of polemics (whether in Byzantine or Islamic law or among Jews) against Samaritan custom, which likewise suggests that the Samaritan preference for erecting *sukkot* indoors became widespread only recently. It is possible that the tradition of building *sukkot* indoors is relatively recent, but such an observation only highlights the ongoing, dynamic nature of Samaritan practice, as we see in other religious communities as well. Among contemporary Samaritan families, the interior location of the *sukkah* has turned into an opportunity for outreach and hospitality, with members of the community opening their homes to curious neighbors and visitors, as well as to each other, in what Benyamim Tsedaka describes as a "*sukkah* hop."

Among contemporary Samaritans, the practice of building *sukkot* indoors is considered not only a legitimate alternative to outdoor construction but one that is preferred both out of practicality and out of respect for tradition. One explanation for the interiority of the *sukkot* understands the decision to build indoors as

8.2 Matzliaḥ (Najah), Wafa, and Brito Cohen in their completed *sukkah*, Kiryat Luza, Mount Gerizim, 2019 (Photograph by Moshe Alafi).

LAURA S. LIEBER

9
"This Covenant of Peace for the Samaritans": The Prophet Muhammad's Encounter with a Samaritan, a Jew, and a Christian

DANIEL BOUŠEK

Nathaniel was succeeded by the high priest Eleazer who was the great high priest for 25 years. At the end of the high priesthood of this Eleazer, Muhammad came. All the years from the disappearance of the *Radwan* to the coming of Muhammad, were 1,993 years. And the total from Adam, upon whom be peace, to the coming of the aforementioned, was 5,047 years.

At this time [of Muhammad's coming] there were three men, astrologers very skilled in their professions. The first was a Samaritan called Sarmasa from Askar. The second was a Jew whose name was Kab al-Aḥbar. And the third was a Christian, a monk called Abd al-Salam. They knew from their craft and from their astrology that the Byzantine Kingdom was gone and that the Kingdom of Islam had begun in the person of a man from the sons of Ishmael, from the Beni Hashim with a characteristic mark on his back, between his shoulder blades – a white birthmark the shape of the palm of one's hand. Some say that it was yellow.

When they heard that he had been seen, the three of them came together and said: "Let us set off and see if the man is he about whose appearance we foretold; and [let us confide] our secret to him concerning the Masters of the Books and sects so that we will not suffer at his hands what we suffered from those who went before him." So the three set out and came to the city in which he was. They asked one another, "Who will go in first?" Kab al-Aḥbar said, "I [will] go," and he went into him [first] and greeted him. He returned the greetings and asked him, "Who are you – a Jew?" He said, "I am one of the leaders of the Jews and I found in my Torah that a king would arise from the stock of Ishmael to rule the world; and that no one could prevent him." Abd al-Salam [then] went in after him, and said, "That is what I found in the Gospel" – although they did not know anything except from matters of their craft. Then Sarmasa went in and said to him, "You will be the one to profess [the Muslim] faith and law, and rule over the necks of the world. There is a sign for us on you – it is between your shoulder-blades." Muhammad was delighted at their words. He undressed, and behold! There was a big white birthmark between his shoulder-blades. Then Kab al-Aḥbar and Abd al-Salam became Muslims and he rejoiced exceedingly at the two

and sat them both by him and said to Sarmasa, "Why do you not do as they have done?" He permitted him [to approach closer] but Sarmasa was not able to approach closer to him. He said to him, "I have what I regard as necessary for me – namely the Law and [my] Faith. I am happy in my Faith and cannot come over to you. I cannot forsake my Faith. Muhammad was ill-pleased at him and asked him, "What do you want, O Samaritan?" Sarmasa said to him: "O my master, I have come to you to get a covenant and a treaty that we can rely upon, I and the people of my faith and my religion: a covenant of peace and security as a protection for persons and families and property and religious endowments, and for freedom to erect houses of worship." So Muhammad instructed a scribe to draw up a covenant of peace and security for them according to what he had requested.

The scribe entered his presence [and wrote]: "I Muhammad son of Abd Allah son of Abd al-Muttalib, have commanded that a treaty of peace and security be written down for the Samaritans concerning themselves and their families and their property and houses of worship and religious endowments throughout all my realm and in all their territories. And that this be effective for them and as a covenant of peace among the people of Palestine; and as a safe conduct." Then Sarmasa took it and left his presence. But Amir ibn al-Rabia and Abd Allah son of Jaḥsh advised him to get the covenant endorsed by Ali ibn Abi Talib. So he went back to Muhammad and stood before him and said: "O my master, I have come to you from an extensive, vast and distant land and from a religious group which is weak and which the polytheists have persecuted and which the idol-worshippers have overcome. We look for deliverance to God, by means of you. I have been advised to obtain the endorsement of Ali ibn Abi Talib for this covenant." So he instructed Ali to sign the document, and he wrote for them from him [as follows]: "I append to this covenant of peace for the Samaritans, a guarantee for themselves, their families, their belongings, their houses of worship and their religious endowments throughout all my lands in every place and throughout all my possessions that it be for them a safe conduct." This was written on a piece of leather, and he [Ali] gave it to him. Sarmasa kissed the ground at a respectful distance and said farewell. Muhammad said, "O Samaritan, Be gone! In this life it shall be yours to say, 'Touch [me] not!' And truly for you there is a tryst [a meeting] that you cannot fail to keep. Now observe your god, to whom you remained devoted: we shall surely burn it and scatter its ashes in the sea."[1]

This was the work of Kab al-Aḥbar since [Sarmasa] had not done [i.e., converted] as he did – every affliction that comes upon us is due to the Jews. Sarmasa then returned to Palestine and announced the good news to the Samaritans about what God had done to make his path successful and how He protected him. May God have mercy and compassion on this man! Kab al-Aḥbar and Abd al-Salam stayed with him [Muhammad] and Kab al-Aḥbar became his secretary, organized [affairs for him] and advised him on all issues.

— *The Chronicle of Abu l-Fatḥ*, ch. 54[2]

In the year 1352 Abu l-Fatḥ ibn Abi l-Ḥasan, the Samaritan, complained to the high priest Pinḥas about a "lack of familiarity with the knowledge of the affairs of past generations" among Samaritans. He further decried the "disarray" of their chronicles. Pinḥas subsequently charged Abu l-Fatḥ with "compiling a Chronicle of all the records of events that involved the Fathers, from the beginning of the world […] up to recent times." Abu l-Fatḥ embarked upon this task three years later, in 1355, when he again met the high priest and was reminded of his earlier charge. *The Chronicle of Abu l-Fatḥ*, in Arabic titled simply *Kitab al-Tarikh*, *The Book of History*, documents the period from Adam until the coming of Islam (Figure 9.1). It concludes with the story of the prophet Muhammad's encounter with three astrologers, representatives of three monotheistic religions: Sarmasa, a Samaritan, Kab al-Aḥbar, a Jew, and Abd al-Salam, a Christian monk. According to the *Chronicle of Abu l-Fatḥ*, astrologers saw in the stars the end of the rule of Byzantium and the rise of the rule of Ishmael. That is, Islam. They therefore travelled to Muhammad in Medina to find out whether he was, in fact, the man from the stock of Ishmael who would initiate the rule of Islam. When assured that Muhammad was the king promised in Scripture, the Jew and the Christian converted to Islam. The Samaritan, Sarmasa, however, stayed steadfast to his religion. Sarmasa negotiated with Muhammad and received full protection for his people under Islam. This treaty was dictated by Muhammad himself and endorsed by his cousin and son-in-law, Ali ibn Abi Talib. Despite the promised protection Muhammed sent off Sarmasa, Muhammed using a Quranic statement by Moses to al-Samiri, "the Samaritan": "O Samaritan, Be gone! In this life it shall be yours to say, 'Touch [me] not!' And truly for you there is a tryst [a meeting] that you cannot fail to keep" (Sura 20:97). The Chronicle continues: "this was the work of Kab al-Aḥbar since [Sarmasa] had not converted as he did – every affliction that comes upon the Samaritans is due to the Jews."

Abu l-Fatḥ's narrative presents a unique Samaritan version of a polemical story that was widespread among the Christians and Jews in the Middle Ages, especially in the Near East. It is intended to explain the coming of Islam and the roles that particular each communities played in this newly installed empire. There can be little

doubt that the Samaritan legend rewrites the Islamic, Christian, and Jewish narratives concerning the coming of Islam— with a Samaritan twist. This Samaritan retelling was based on motifs adopted from the Prophet's career. It is based in Muhammad's contacts with the Jewish leaders in Ḥijaz, in the holy region of Islam in Arabia that includes Mecca and Medina. Some of these Jews did indeed convert to Islam. Among them was a former "rabbi," Abd Allah ibn Salam, who became Muhammad's adviser. Abd Allah ibn Salam serves in Islamic tradition as a symbol of the Islamization of the Jews. He is the prototypical Jewish convert who recognized in Muhammad the prophet promised in Scripture and wholeheartedly made public confession of his prophethood. The same role is played by Kab al-Aḥbar, a Yemenite Jewish renegade and important authority on *Isra'iliyyat*, Judaism. The Prophet's biographies also mention Christians who recognized Muhammad's prophetic vocation on the basis of a series of miracles and informed reading of their own religious tradition. Christians possessed a book containing signs of the Prophet's future coming, as well as a detailed list of the bodily signs by which the long-awaited Prophet could be identified. The most famous of these Christians was the monk Baḥira, also called Sergius, who confirmed Muhammad's prophethood.

These conversions elicited a response from both Jews and Christians. Abd Allah ibn Salam was reappropriated and re-Judaized in Jewish legends concerning Muhammad. Likewise, a parallel re-Christianization of legends about the monk Baḥira was current in Christian circles. Both responses primarily polemicize against the notion that the Quran is a divinely revealed text, and against the Muslim claim that their Prophet was sent by God to all peoples— Christians and Jews alike. In the Christian Baḥira legends, the monk is portrayed as Muhammad's mentor, whose basically Christian message to the Arabs was corrupted by the Jews after Baḥira's death and made into today's Quran. The "Ur-Quran" that Baḥira is said to have given to Muhammad was a kind of simplified, man-made version of the "Gospel for the Arabs." This was intended to guide Arabs to the faith in ways that would not conflict with their traditional worldview and customs. Kab al-Aḥbar is portrayed as the falsifier of the Quran's in the Baḥira legend. In Islamic tradition Kab el-Ahbar is said to have converted only during the rule of the second caliph, Umar ibn al-Khaṭṭab. In both the Christian polemical tradition and Abu l-Fatḥ's *Kitab al-Tarikh*, Kab al-Aḥbar is considered to have been a companion of the Prophet. Jews as a whole are responsible for all the misguided teachings of the Quran, as well as its anti-Christian statements.

Once Muhammad has received his elementary training in Christianity, the legend records, promises to grant the monk anything he might wish of him. Baḥira asks for protection for his fellow-Christians and particularly for monks, who will soon be subjected to the foreordained rule of Islam. Muhammad pledges to order the Muslims "not to take *jizya* or *kharaj* from monks" and "not to act unjustly towards the Christians, and that their ceremonies will not be changed, and their churches will be built […] And whoever oppresses one of them – I will be his adversary on the day of the resurrection."

The anti-Jewish barbs in the Islamic and Christian versions of the story did not escape the notice of Jewish apologists, who wrote their own version of the encounter with Muhammad and the early history of Islam. This response first appears in a mid-eighth century apocalyptic Hebrew text, *The Secret of Rabbi Shimon bar Yoḥai*.[3] This document mentions "great men of Israel" who joined Muhammad. Jewish versions of the tale were widely current in Jewish circles from at least the tenth century. The earliest of these is a short Judeo-Arabic text known as the "Story of Muhammad's Jewish Companions." Most versions of the legend developed the basic elements that appear in the Muslim and Christian versions, and added new characters. The Jewish story relates that the Quran was actually co-written by a group of ten Jewish sages who converted to Islam with the intention of preventing Muhammad (or the monk Baḥira) from harming Israel. In addition to Kab al-Ahbar and Abdallah ibn Salam, later versions include among the ten Jewish sages the "rightly guided" caliphs Abu Bakr, Umar ibn al-Khatab, and Ali. The Jewish version is a response to the Muslim accusation that the Torah is corrupt. It argues that the Quran has been tampered with, not the Torah of Moses.

How does the Samaritan version in *Kitab al-Tarikh* differ from the Christian and Jewish versions of the story and how does it resemble them? As we have seen, Abu l-Fatḥ knew not only the Chris-

9.1 *Kitub al-Tarikh, The Chronicle of Abu 'l-Fatḥ,* open to chapter 9, describing the Abisha Scroll. The colophon of this scroll is reproduced in Hebrew in red. Arabic interspersed with Samaritan Hebrew, 14th century, Nablus, 1872. Scribe: Jacob son of Marḥiv (Yeshiva University, Mendel Gottesman Library, Joshua Finkel Collection).

tian and Jewish versions, but also was acquainted with the Quran and other Muslim traditions. He retains some elements of these sources, and reworks them. First, though, Abu l-Fatḥ describes a Christian monk. This monk is not named Baḥira, as in the Muslim, Christian, and Jewish traditions. Rather surprisingly, he is Abd al-Salam or Abd Allah, the Jewish convert to Islam Jewish convert of the other traditions.

The *Kitab al-Tarikh* relates that while standing before Muhammad, the Jewish and Christian astrologers claim that they found in their Scriptures— in the Torah and the Gospels— "that a king would arise from the stock of Ishmael to rule the world." Abu l-Fatḥ, however, counters their claim, arguing that unlike the Samaritan Sarmasa, "they did not know anything except from matters of their craft." They did not find heir proof in their Scriptures, he argues, but merely through astrological observations. This sequence appears at the beginning of the story, where Abu l-Fatḥ writes of the sources of the knowledge obtained by the three astrologers concerning the coming of the Kingdom of Islam, its founder, his origin and physical traits. Unlike the Jew and the Christian, Sarmasa does not refer to his Scripture as the source, but outright and without resort to any authority proclaims Muhammad to be the founder of a new religion that will rule the world. As if to counter the Muslim tradition that Muhammad's coming is foretold in the Scriptures, Abu l-Fath asserts that the Torah does not presage Muhammad's coming, nor his physical traits. This is known only from astrology.

While the Jew and the Christian become Muslims, the Samaritan, despite Muhammad's insistence, refuses to convert: "I am happy in my Faith and cannot come over to you. I cannot forsake my Faith." Though offended by Sarmasa's strident reply, Muhammad asks: "What was your purpose, O Samaritan?"—*ma khatbuka ya samiri*? Abu l-Fath sets the dialog between Sarmasa and Muhammad into the frame of a conversation in the Quran (20:95–97), in which Moses asks al-Samiri the same question:

He [Moses] said, "What was your purpose, O Samaritan?"

He [al-Samiri] said, "I saw that which they saw not. So I took a handful [of dust] from the footsteps of the messenger, and I cast it. Thus did my soul prompt me."

He [Moses] said, "Be gone! In this life it shall be yours to say, 'Touch [me] not!' And truly for you there is a tryst [a meeting] that you cannot fail to keep. Now observe your god, to whom you remained devoted: we shall surely burn it and scatter its ashes in the sea!"

After Sarmasa discloses the purpose of his coming, Muhammad grants his request immediately and without comment grants a covenant of security for the Samaritans.

Nonetheless, the Prophet scorns the departing Sarmasa. Abu l-Fath puts these words in the mouth of Muhammad, reproducing the conversation in the Quran where Moses condemns al-Samiri. The Samaritan chronicler writes: 'Touch [me] not!' (*la misasa*) for the rest of his life, as a punishment for inducing the Israelites in the desert to throw their ornaments into a fire and producing a "Golden Calf." But could Moses, the singular prophet of the Samaritans, really be the author of this condemnation, the only unequivocal reference to the Samaritans in the Quran? The following sentence serves as a clue: "This was the work of Kab al-Ahbar since [Sarmasa] had not done as he did [i.e., had not converted]– every affliction that comes upon us is due to the Jews."

How are we to understand these words? We have seen that Kab al-Ahbar plays the role of the falsifier of the Quran in both the Jewish and the Christian tradition. The latter even portrays him as the author of the anti-Christian statements in the Quran. A very similar meaning is conveyed by the Abu l-Fath's insistence that: "Every affliction that comes upon us [i.e., the Samaritans] is due to the Jews," albeit in this case not with regard to the Christians, but the Samaritans. It seems that Abu l-Fath could not accept that the only unequivocal reference to the Samaritans in the Quran contains a condemnation addressed to them by Moses. Therefore, he put it

into the mouth of Muhammad, the "author" of the Quran. At the same time he impugned the authenticity of the statement – "this was the work of Kab al-Ahbar," i.e., the author of the condemnation is not Muhammad, but Kab al-Ahbar, who inserted it into the Quran just as he had done before in other places concerning the Christians. The reason, we are told, is jealousy. Kab al-Ahbar was jealous of Sarmasa, who had not converted as he did in order to protect his community.

Abu l-Fath worked creatively with the Muslim, Jewish, and Christian versions of Muhammad's encounter with the People of the Book. This is especially evident in the statement that asserts that "Kab al-Ahbar and Abd al-Salam stayed with Muhammad and Kab al-Ahbar became his secretary, organized [affairs for him] and advised him on all issues." Indeed, in the Muslim tradition Abd al-Salam "stayed" with the Prophet and did become his counselor. Only the Jewish and the Christian traditions mention Kab al-Ahbar's conversion during Muhammad's lifetime. West Syrian recension of the legend of Bahira even identifies him as the one who taught "the Sons of Ishmael...many things from the Torah and the Prophets and also some of the stories of theirs." He is frequently referred to as "Kab the Scribe."

The aim of the Christian version is to explain the appearance of Islam and its difference from Christianity and its anti-Christian bias, the result of the Jewish tampering with the Quran. The purpose of the Jewish version, by contrast, is to show that the Quran is corrupted, and not the Hebrew Bible. The Samaritan version, by contrast, uses the story only as scaffolding for the story of how the Samaritans obtained a treaty of peace and security at the dawn of Islam. In the Islamic tradition this treaty, or pact, is usually titled *Ahd Umar* (the Pact of Umar, or *Shurut Umar*). It is construed as a treaty between the Muslims and Christians and contains a list of rights and restrictions applied by the Muslims to the non-Muslims (*dhimmis*) under their rule. While in the Islamic narrative this treaty was agreed between the caliph Umar ibn al-Khattab and the Christians of Syria or Jerusalem. In the the Samaritan treaty, however, it is given by the Prophet Muhammad himself and is endorsed by Ali. In this regard, the Samaritan version rather resembles the so-called "Muhammad's Writ of Protection." Different versions of this document circulated both among Jews and Christians, who presented it to Muslims as admonishment for ill-treatment. It was used to expose transgressors as ungrateful violators of a sacred covenant afforded to them by the Prophet himself. The aim of this pseudepigraphic tradition was to protect personal safety and the safety of possessions and freedom of worship.

Similarly in the Samaritan version, Muhammad's Writ of Protection was purported to have been dictated by Muhammad himself to Ali or even addressed by Muhammad to Ali. In the Jewish versions of the document, Muhammad extends his protection to the Jews and their progeny and grants them extensive privileges. These include physical security for their person and property, safe conduct, immunity from any injurious treatment, the free exercise of their religion, and exemption from the payment of taxes. In most versions the Jews claimed to be descendants of the Jews of Khaibar,

9.2 Boys in the Synagogue, Kiryat Luza, Mount Gerizim, 2019 (Photograph by Moshe Alafi).

an oasis 150 km. from Medina, to whom Muhammad purportedly gave such a treaty after his defeat of the local Jewish community in 628 CE. For example, Ibn Qayyim al-Jawziyya, the famous Hanbali jurist (Syria, d. 1350), claims that in the year 1301 some Jews of Damascus produced a book of treatises dictated by Muhammad and written by Ali which exempted them from the payment of *jizya*, the religiously sanctioned poll tax paid by the *ahl al-dhimma* ("the protected people") living under Islamic rule. Abu l-Fath's story of a treaty given to the Samaritans by Muhammad and written by Ali was not unique. On the contrary, the Samaritans followed in the footsteps of both the Jews and the Christians.

In this context we may ask what the attitude of *Kitab al-Tarikh* is to the prophet of Islam. About Muhammad himself the story says next to nothing. Only later, at the end of the book, does Abu l-Fath flatter the Prophet: "Muhammad [himself] never mistreated any of the followers of the Torah." He follows with the tradition of the ancestors that "Muhammad was a good and mighty person because he made a treaty of friendship with the Hebrew People." Muhammad is pointedly not a prophet, but a ruler and founder of a new religion.

Other Samaritan sources do not contradict this. The *Tulida*, an earlier Samaritan chronicle (circa 1200), has it only that Muhammad did good to the Samaritans.[4] The *Continuatio* of Abu l-Fath's chronicle, a later text that brings the history into modern times, follows the pattern and goes a little further. It claims that "The prophet of Islam did not cause anyone distress throughout his life. He would present his belief before the people, accepting who came to him, [yet] not compelling one who did not."[5] Undoubtedly, these statements had the aim of winning the favor of the Muslim majority without violating Samaritan scruples. Muhammed is a prophet sent only for the Arabs, and for other Muslims— but certainly not for Samaritans. This tongue-in-cheek stance toward Islam was adopted by Samari-

tans, Christians and the Jews in Islamic countries in the Middle Ages. It is already hinted at in the *Tulida*. There we read that "Muhammad prophesied among the Arabs in the town of Mecca."[6] Even when the *Continuatio* marks Muhammad as a prophet, it does not mean that he was also sent for the Samaritans. Nowhere is there any hint that Muhammad's mission is universal; that he has been sent by God as a messenger for all of humankind, as the Muslims claim. Though Abu l-Fath's Sarmasa admits that Muhammad will "profess faith and law," the Samaritans have no need of it, since they have their own law and faith: "I have what I regard as necessary for me – namely the Law and [my] Faith. I am happy in my Faith and cannot come over to you. I cannot forsake my Faith." Abu l-Fath has no interest in Muhammad nor in the teachings of Islam. He presents Muhammad as a ruler and a lawgiver of the preordained Kingdom, with its own faith and law, from whom it is necessary to obtain a treaty in order to assure the future well-being of the Samaritan community.

What was the purpose of Abu l-Fath's story of the covenant with Muhammad? Why was it written in the mid-14th century, under the Mamluks? This period in Egypt and Syria is characterized by the waning of tolerance generally and a worsening of the social, economic, demographic, and legal position of religious minorities— including the Samaritans. The laws enshrined in the so-called Pact of Umar were enforced by the Mamluk authorities with ever-increasing vigor. The aim was the conversion of non-Muslims to Islam, or minimally their exclusion from the imperial administration. The first major campaign to crack down upon "transgressors" against the Pact took place in 1301 in Egypt, during which a number of churches and synagogues were vandalized or closed. At this time, Muslim lawyers debated the legality of the construction, repair, or continuance of the sacral buildings of non-Muslims. This threat was painfully palpable to the Samaritans. During the high priesthood of Joseph son of Uzzi (1290–1308/9), the Muslims expropriated the Samaritan religious center in Nablus and turned the Samaritan synagogue on the "Parcel of Land" thought to have been precured by the patriarch Jacob (Genesis 33:19) into a mosque. In 1354, Sultan al-Malik al-Nasir (1299–1309) reasserted a set of discriminatory regulations concerning the *dhimmis,* to which a few new ones were added. Unlike the decrees of previous sultans, al-Malik al-Naṣir mentions the Samaritans explicitly, along with the Christians and Jews. One of his new ordinances stipulated that the Samaritans wear red turbans to differentiate them from both Muslims and other *dhimmis*— a color choice that continues to this day (Figure 9.2). Not coincidentally, two years earlier, in 1352, the Samaritan high priest Pinḥas had encouraged Abu l-Fatḥ to write his history.

In this context we may better understand why Abu l-Fatḥ's story emphasizes the protection of personal and communal property. When the *Kitab al-Tarikh* has Muhammad instruct the scribe to draw up a covenant for the Samaritans, it includes "their property and houses of worship and religious endowments throughout all my realm and in all their territories." The same formulation is also repeated by Ali, who is asked to endorse the covenant. Altogether,

the formulation is repeated three times in the text, by Sarmasa, Muhammad, and Ali. When Sarmasa asks Muhammad to give the Samaritans by treaty "freedom to erect houses of worship," he actually goes against the wording of the Pact of Umar. After the expropriations of Samaritan property and especially of their religious buildings, which took place at the end of the 13th and in the first part of the 14th century, the "freedom to erect houses of worship" was intended to persuade the Muslim authorities that the Samaritans had been given a special right to erect new houses of worship by the prophet Muhammad himself and his cousin Ali.

The Mamluk period was marked by a steady flow of Muslim polemical literature against *dhimmis*, including the Samaritans. A sub-genre of this literature consists of tracts directed against the employment of *dhimmis* in the civil administration. Many converted in order to keep their jobs. Moreover, in the first part of the 14th century Ibn Qayyim al-Jawziyya authored a comprehensive law book that deals exclusively with Islamic law for *dhimmis.* Islam generally considers the Samaritans as a "People of the Book" and therefore entitled to the status of *dhimma* (protection), which is related to their duty to pay the poll tax. The Samaritans form a sort of sub-

9.3 Synagogue, Kiryat Luza, Mount Gerizim (Photograph by Steven Fine).

group among the *dhimmis,* since their right to the status of *dhimma* is conditioned by the conformity of their basic beliefs with those of the Jews and Christians. Ibn Qayyim dedicated a whole chapter of his law book to the question: "The Different Opinions of the Jurists Concerning the Samaritans: Are They Entitled to *Jizya,* or Not?" After surveying the opinions of a number of Muslim scholars he concludes that even though they are "the most foolish and most opposed to other communities," it would be unjust to strip them of the duty to pay the poll tax.

We may thus conclude that *Kitab al-Tarikh* was written in the time when anti-*dhimmi* propaganda and legislation was at its height. We can therefore interpret Pinḥas's instructions to Abu l-Fatḥ to write a chronicle that concludes with the story of the treaty with Muhammad as part of his efforts to prop up the religious identity of the community. Abu l-Fatḥ's version of Muhammad's encounter with a Samaritan, a Jew, and a Christian was a Samaritan attempt to rewrite the history of rival communities that the intellectual historian Amos Funkenstein identified in Jewish-Christian contexts as "counter-history." This strategy retells and reverses the sense of Samaritan powerlessness in the face of Muslim enmity. It asserts a different history, "distorting the adversary's self image, of his identity, through deconstruction of his memory" — leading to a more positive attitude by the Islamic majority toward the powerless Samaritans.[7]

The Samaritan encounter with Muhammad presented by Abu l-Fatḥ, and the resulting charter of protection given them by the Prophet and then by Ali, exemplifies how counter-history is employed by marginal groups in challenging the historical narratives of the majority. The Samaritan transformation of Christian and Jewish accounts of encounters with Muhammad write the Samaritans into Islam's constitutive moment as a protected "People of the Book." Jewish and Christian stories reflect vague memories of their own participation at the start of the new religion, and of personal contacts of their Arabian brethren with its founder. The Samaritan account, however, is a fiction. Muslim sources do not recall encounters of Muhammad with the Samaritans. This did not keep the Samaritans, however, from appropriating Muslim, Christian, and Jewish historical accounts and reshaping them to accord with their own understanding of Islamic origins. Less scathing toward Islam

than either Jewish or Christian stories, this Samaritan appropriation asserted Samaritan presence at the dawn of Islam. This bolstered their place in Islamic society—both for their own self-understanding and for Muslim consumption. Abu l-Fatḥ wrote his chronicle, the *Kitab al-Tarikh,* to reinforce Samaritan legal protections against widespread challenges under the Mamluks. His counter-narrative shielded Samaritan communities from conversionist pressures, and in later generations even from death. Samaritans had reason to fear. One need only recall the extinction of the once prosperous Samaritan community in Damascus in the early seventeenth century; the near destruction of the Nablus community in 1842; and in our own day, the relocation of the community from its historic quarter in Nablus during the first Intifada (1987–1991) to Kiryat Luza, a protected enclave a top Mount Gerizim (Figure 9.3).

For Further Reading

Daniel Boušek, "The Story of the Prophet Muhammad's Encounter with a Samaritan, a Jew, and a Christian: The Version from Abu l-Fatḥ's Kitāb al-Tārīkh and Its Context" *The Samaritans in Historical, Cultural and Linguistic Perspectives,* edited by Jan Dušek. Berlin: De Gruyter, 2018, 105–130.

Milka Levy-Rubin, editor, *The* Continuatio *of the Samaritan Chronicle of Abu l-Fatḥ al-Sāmirī al-Danafī.* Princeton: The Darwin Press, 2002.

Simon Shtober, "Present at the Dawn of Islam. Polemic and Reality in the Medieval Story of Muhammad's Jewish Companions," *The Convergence of Judaism and Islam,* edited by Michael M. Laskier and Yaacov Lev. Gainesville: University Press of Florida, 2011, 64–88.

---

1   Dakake and Lumbard. 2015.

2   The article is dedicated to the late Paul Stenhouse, the editor and translator of Abu l-Fatḥ's *Kitab al-Tarikh.* Translation follows Stenhouse (pp. 242–246) with slight changes and additions based on Vilmar, 1865.

3   Even Shmuel (Kaufmann), 1954, 171.

4   Ed. Florentin, 1999, 93.

5   Ed. Levy-Rubin, 2002, 53/207.

6   Ed. Florantin, 93.

7   Funkenstein, 1996, 36.

10

"These Are the Jews of Shomron Who Are Called Samaritans": Jews and Samaritans in the High Middle Ages

JESSE ABELMAN

Six parasangs from here is Caesarea, the Gath of the Philistines, and here there are about two hundred Jews and two hundred *Kutim*. These are the Jews of Shomron [*ha-Yehudim ha-Shomronim*], who are called Samaritans [שניטרמש].The city is fair and beautiful, and lies by the sea. It was built by Caesar, and called after him Caesarea.

From there, it is a day's journey to Sebastiya, which is the city of Shomron [Samaria], and here the ruins of the palace of Ahab the son of Omri may be seen. It was formerly a well-fortified city by the mountain-side, with streams of water. It is still a land of brooks of water, gardens, orchards, vineyards, and olive groves, but no Jews dwell here.

Thence, it is two parasangs to Nablus, which is Shechem on Mount Ephraim, where there are no Jews; the place is situated in the valley between Mount Gerizim and Mount Ebal, and contains about one thousand *Kutim*, who observe the Torah of Moses, peace be upon him, exclusively, and are called "Samaritans." They have priests of the seed [of Aaron], and they call them "Aaronim," who do not intermarry with *Kutim*, but wed only among themselves. These priests offer sacrifices, and bring burnt offerings in their place of assembly on Mount Gerizim, as it is written in their Torah—"And you shall set the blessing on Mount Gerizim" (Deuteronomy 11:29). They say that this is the house of the Presence [*ha-Maqom*], blessed be He. On Passover and the other festivals, they offer up burnt offerings on the altar that they have built on Mount Gerizim, as it is written in their Torah—"You shall set up upon Mount Gerizim the rocks" [paraphrasing Deuteronomy 27:4] that Joshua and the Children of Israel set up at the Jordan. They say that they are descended from the tribe of Ephraim. And in the midst of them is the grave of Joseph, the son of Jacob our father, the peace be upon him, as it is written—"And the bones of Joseph they buried in Shechem" (Joshua 24:32). Their alphabet lacks three letters, namely: Hey, *ḥet* and *ayin*. *He* is taken from *Abraham* our father, because they have no dignity [*hod*], the letter *ḥet* from *Yitsḥak* [Isaac], because they have no kindliness [*ḥesed*], and the letter *Ayin* from *Yaakov* [Jacob], because they have no humility [*anavah*]. In place of these letters, they make use of the *aleph*, by which we can tell that they are not of the seed of Israel, although they

know the law of Moses with the exception of these three letters. They guard themselves from the defilement of the dead, of the bones of the slain, and of graves; and they remove the garments that they have worn before they go to the place of worship, and they bathe and put on fresh clothes. This is their constant practice. On Mount Gerizim are fountains and gardens and plantations, but Mount Ebal is rocky and barren; and between them in the valley lies the city of Shechem.

—*The Itinerary of Benjamin of Tudela*[1]

Benjamin ben Yonah of Tudela (1130–1173) was a Rabbanite Jew from the Kingdom of Navarre, part of what is today Spain. He traveled across Europe and the Middle East in the late twelfth century, leaving behind a record of his journey in a travelogue known as *Masa'oot Rabi Benyamin* (*The Itinerary of Benjamin of Tudela*). This travelogue was enormously popular, and was copied in manuscript and then in print many times over. It has been translated into many languages and read by diverse people around the world, Jew and Gentile alike. During the late twentieth century, author Sandra Benjamin used *Masa'oot Rabbi Benyamin* as an access point to the high medieval Mediterranean world, writing a series of fictionalized letters that Benjamin might have sent home. In her book, *The World of Benjamin of Tudela* (1995), she combines her own research with the text of the *Itinerary* in order to more richly depict the world through which Benjamin traveled, and to grant a modern audience access to it. One of these letters, purportedly sent from Nablus, describes how impressed our traveler was with the wide variety of heretics he encountered along his route, including Samaritans: "The people who are more-or-less Jews! Karaites, Vlachi, Khazars, Kaphrossin, Samaritans. The closer I get to Jerusalem, the more of the Jews are heretics."[2] Sandra Benjamin puts the word "heretic" in his mouth, but would Benjamin of Tudela have characterized the Samaritans as "heretics"? This raises a key question about how Benjamin, and Rabbanite Jews in the High Middle Ages in general, understood their relationship to Samaritans. Were they a kind of heretical Jews? Were they another people altogether? How should their claim to Israelite descent and a biblical tradition be understood? Three significant encounters are preserved in the historical record: Benjamin's description, Nachmanides's report from Acre, dated 1264, and letters from the Cairo Genizah. These documents provide narrow windows through which to view Rabbanite Jewish interaction with Samaritans during the High Middle Ages.

BENJAMIN OF TUDELA

The travelogue of Benjamin of Tudela describes a journey to the western edge of China in the mid-twelfth century. Little is known about Benjamin's life outside of his journey. His book describes communities that he encountered on his trip in anthropological detail, discussing how they lived and related to one another. Benjamin's work is one of the few sources we have that describe relations between Rabbanite Jews and Samaritans, as well as Samaritan culture independently, in the High Middle Ages.

The travelogue includes descriptions of Samaritan communities in Caesarea Maritima, which is on the Mediterranean coast to the west of Samaria—since Roman antiquity a place of Samaritan habitation in addition to Shechem. The numbers of Jews and Samaritans in Caesarea was equal—two hundred each. In Ashkelon, he reports that "two hundred Rabbanite Jews dwell here, at their head being Rabbi Zemach, Rabbi Aaron, and Rabbi Solomon; also about forty Karaites, and about three hundred *Kutim*."[3] The numbers of each community were of interest to Benjamin, who in general did not bother to mention the population sizes of gentile communities. His comment on Damascus is particularly enlightening. Benjamin wrote that "One hundred Karaites dwell here, also four hundred *Kutim*, and there is peace between them, but they do not intermarry."[4] In fact, the large number of Samaritan manuscripts copied in Damascus at about this time points to the prosperity of this community. The sense of a tripartite Israelite community that maintains "peace between them" even as they maintain their distance in marriage. This is a far cry from the absolute separation one might expect from more theoretical Jewish legal literature.

Clearly fascinated and perplexed, Benjamin describes the *Kutim* to his audience as "following the Torah of Moses, peace be upon him, alone. They have priests from the line of Aaron whom they call 'Aaronites' who do not marry *Kutim*, but priests only marry priests so they will not mingle with them. They are the priests of their Torah [*Kohanei toratam*] and they make sacrifices and raise burnt offerings as it says in their Torah 'And you gave the blessing on Mount Gerizim.' They say that this is the seat of the Blessed One. They bring an offering on Passover and on other holidays on the altar they built on Mount Gerizim as it says in their Torah." He goes on to describe the Samaritan belief that they derive from the tribe of Ephraim, which he does not dispute, and that Joseph is buried in their community in Nablus. Benjamin here attempts to capture how the *Kutim* present themselves. He ties their practices closely to the Pentateuch, which he is always careful to refer to as "their Torah [*Toratam*]," rather than "the Torah" despite his introductory statement that they "follow the Torah of Moses" (Figure 10.1, 10.2).

Our author frequently cites Torah verses that are shared by the Samaritan Pentateuch and the Masoretic text to explain elements of Samaritan practice. This is significant, given the distance that he creates between the two. On the one hand, it seems important to him to contextualize Samaritan life through reference to the sacred text that Samaritans share with Jews. On the other, he wants to make it clear that Samaritans are not Jews. He emphasizes this with the false assertion that the Samaritan alphabet, a close descendant of the Paleo-Hebrew alphabet, lacks three letters that the Jewish Hebrew alphabet has—*hay*, *ḥet*, and *ayin*. He then explains this lacking in homiletical terms. Benjamin asserts that the Samaritans lack an essential attribute of each of the biblical Patriarchs: "*Hay* is taken from *Abraham* our father, because they have no dignity [*hod*], the letter *ḥet* from *Yitsḥak* [Isaac], because they have no kindliness [*ḥesed*], and the letter *ayin* from *Yaakov* [Jacob], because they have no humility [*anavah*]." These three letters are weakened and silent, Benjamin reports. In fact, this is the case in the Samaritan reading tradition, though seldom not in the written text of the Torah itself. Thus, a Samaritan would "read" *Abrum, Yetsuq, and Yuqob.* For Benjamin, who certainly could not read a Samaritan text himself, difference from his own textual and reading tradition is a clear sign that the Samaritans do not descend from the biblical Patriarchs. Through this homiletic explication, Benjamin makes clear how close Samaritans are to Judaism, yet how far! His characterization of the Patriarchs resonates with rabbinic conceptions. Thus, for example: "A generous eye, a humble spirit and a modest soul—he is of the disciples of Abraham, our father" (Mishnah Avot 5:19), and Moses Maimonides' assertion that righteous charity [*tsedaqa*] is a characteristic of "the seed of Abraham our father."[5] To differentiate Samaritans from Jews, Benjamin questions their connection to the Patriarchs by disparaging their character traits. Owing to this minor discrepancy (he missed the larger ones), the Samaritan Pentateuch is not the true Torah, the Samaritan alphabet is not true Hebrew, and the Samaritans are not truly descended from Israel—even if they do perform their religion in ways that Benjamin well recognizes. They are uncannily close—so close that Benjamin found it necessary to state that Samaritans are "not of the seed of Israel, although they know the law of Moses with the exception of these three letters."

Benjamin's interest in noting what Rabbanite Jews share with Samaritans, even as he clearly explores the important distinctions between them, corresponds with how he describes the lives of the Israelite communities in Palestine. He describes the cities in which each community lived, sometimes together, sometimes separately. He discusses their peaceful coexistence alongside Karaite Jews as well, but mentions explicitly that Samaritans do not intermarry with Rabbanite or Karaite Jews (who did intermarry). It is an open question exactly how Benjamin actually understands the place of the Samaritans as Jews (*Yehudim*) in his work. In describing Nablus, he makes it clear that he does not consider Samaritans to be Jews, as he says: "There are no Jews … and there are a thousand *Kutim*" there. In discussing the population of Caesarea, however, there are "two hundred *Kutim* and these are the Samaritan Jews (*Yehudim Shomronim*)." It has been suggested that this latter explanatory phrase entered the text at a later date from a marginal annotation.

10.1 Dedicatory Inscription to the "Holy Synagogue of Kefar Qalil," Mount Gerizim, 1214. Donor: Abraham son of Emunah Ab-Yetrana of the sons of Badua (Beit HaNassi, Jerusalem. Photograph by Steven Fine).

Though this is certainly possible, and would explain the discrepancy, it is entirely speculative, as the phrase appears in all extant manuscripts. My suspicion is that Benjamin was not particular about his terminology, as he struggled to fit Samaritans into the taxonomies with which he was familiar. It is likely that his description of the Samaritan as a kind of Jew is drawn from Muslim perceptions, where due to their obvious affinities, Rabbanites, Karaites, and Samaritans have often been grouped together.

The Samaritans were thus perceived by Benjamin as living adjacent to the Jewish communities but as separate from them. It is difficult to tell from his text itself to what extent Benjamin saw Samaritans as a completely distinct people from Rabbanites, and to what extent they were seen as siblings, or even aberrant cousins.

His treatment of the Karaites, whom he mentioned in passing four times, is somewhat instructive. When Benjamin mentioned Karaites, he did not explain who they were, but assumed that his audience recognized them. The one time he discussed their practice, it was to note that they did not intermarry with Samaritans in Damascus (Figures 10.2-3). Also, intriguingly, in his discussion of the Jews of Cyprus, he refers to "Rabbanite and Karaite Jews." There are also heretical Jews who are called *Apikorsim* and "Israel excommunicates them everywhere."[6] Whether or not Benjamin considered Karaites to be heretics (and this may be evidence that he did not), they were known to him and were accepted by him as a subgroup of Jews who did not need to be marked as heretical or excommunicated. Samaritans—very much of interest—were more difficult for him to cate-

10.2 Samaritan Torah Scroll, Genesis 1:1—Exodus 9:35. ca. 1166. Scribe: Shalma son of Abraham son of Joseph of Sarepta (Museum of the Bible, The Signatry Collection, Photograph courtesy of Sotheby's, New York).

gorize. This tension and confusion persists throughout Benjamin's treatment of Samaritan communities. What is clear, however, is that the communities of Rabbanite Jews and Samaritans whom Benjamin describes coexisted in peace and cooperation.

MOSES NACHMANIDES

Rabbi Moses son of Nahman (1194–1270), known as Nachmanides, emigrated from Catalonia to Palestine at the end of his life, arriving in the port of Acre in 1264. This move to Palestine allowed him to incorporate new ideas about the geography and archeology of the Land of Israel into his works of Talmudic and biblical exegesis. One example is the weight of the ancient silver *sheqel* coin, half of which is taken as a head tax, discussed in Exodus 30:12–17. In his comment to Exodus 30:13, written while he was still in Spain, Nachmanides followed the position of the North African scholar Rabbi Isaac Alfasi (1013–1103) regarding the weight of the *sheqel* coin. In a letter sent back to Catalonia, which was appended to some early manuscripts of his Torah commentary, Nachmanides changed his mind:

> The Lord blessed me so [greatly] that I merited to reach Acre. I discovered there in the possession of the elders of the land a silver coin that was engraved. On one side, it had a sort of figure of a branch of an almond tree, and on the other side a kind of jar, and around both a very clear inscription. They showed it to the *Kutim*, who could read it at once because it is the *Ivri* script that remains for the *Kutim*, as it says in

[Talmud] *Sanhedrin* [21b]. On one side it read "Sheqel of Sheqels," and on the other side "Jerusalem the Holy."[7]

The coin was stamped on one side with what Nachmanides identified as the almond branch staff of Aaron, and on the other side with a jar of manna. It had Paleo-Hebrew (*ketav Ivri*) inscriptions on both sides. From this description, it is clear that Nachmanides was shown a silver *sheqel*—a tetradrachm—of the First Jewish Revolt against Rome (66–74 CE), and not a biblical coin as he thought. By weighing this coin, Nachmanides believed he could empirically determine the weight of the biblical *sheqel*, and he revised his position to accord with Rabbi Solomon son of Isaac (*Rashi*), who held that it weighed one-sixth less than Rabbi Isaac [Alfasi] did. More significant for our purposes, however, is how Nachmanides attempted to understand the Paleo-Hebrew inscriptions.

Nachmanides relates that the coins were shown by "the elders of the land" to the "*Kutim*." They did this because the inscriptions were engraved in "the *Ivri* script that remains for the *Kutim*, as it says in *Sanhedrin* [21b]." This Talmudic text cites Babylonian rabbis:

> Said Mar Zutra, and some say that it was Mar Uqva:
> Originally the Torah was given to Israel in *Ivri* [Paleo-Hebrew] script and the holy tongue, Hebrew.
> It was given to them again in the days of Ezra in *Ashurit* ["Assyrian" Hebrew square] script and the Aramaic language.

Israel selected *Ashurit* script and the holy tongue, and left *Ivrit* script
and the Aramaic language for commoners.
Who are these commoners [*hodyotot*]?
Rav Ḥisda said: The *Kutim* …

The Samaritan script is a continuation of the ancient Paleo-Hebrew
script (*ketav Ivrit*), distinct from the square Jewish script known as
the "Assyrian" script (*ketav Ashurit*) that was used by Rabbanite and
Karaite Jews. The Babylonian Talmud is aware that this script was
used by Samaritans, and by doing so connects them back to ancient
Israelites. It does so in dismissive language, identifying *Kutim* as
hedyotot, as "commoners," "untrained," or "unlettered." Though
precisely what this statement refers to in context is unclear, Nachmanides cited it to grant rabbinic legitimacy to the ability of the Samaritans of his day to read and understand Paleo-Hebrew. This is
quite different from the approach we saw in Benjamin's travelogue.
Benjamin included his canard about the alphabet, which delegiti-
mated the Samaritan claim to pronounce Hebrew, suggesting that
they lacked certain letters in their alphabet. Where Benjamin attempted to destabilize the relationship between Samaritans, Jews,
and the Torah, Nachmanides saw them as a link back to a time when
Jews used a different script to write and as a legitimate source about
historical practice.

It seems that Nachmanides himself did not speak with Samaritans; rather, he reported what he was told by the Jewish elders. It is
not clear whether the citation from the Babylonian Talmud is strictly academic, his own justification for consulting the Samaritans, or
was provided by the elders. It functions as a means to tie the consultation into the textual tradition, identifying the contemporary Samaritan community with the *Kutim* of rabbinic and biblical sources.
Nachmanides legitimized their identity according to his own Rabbanite Jewish mode, which granted him permission to make use of
their expertise. In addition, the consultation demonstrates an exist-
ing relationship between the Rabbanite "elders" and the Samaritan
community of Palestine. Nachmanides felt compelled to justify to
his audience his turn to the Samaritans through a Talmudic citation
that legitimized their claim of continuity with biblical Israel. This
discomfort is conditioned by the generally negative deployment of
Kutim in medieval rabbinic thought—especially in Europe, where
rabbis were disconnected from actual Samaritans.

LETTERS FROM THE CAIRO GENIZAH

While Benjamin and perhaps Nachmanides likely met Samaritans
for the first time during their travels in the East, in the world of Islam
the fates of Jews and Samaritans were closely linked. An Arabic-language letter found in the Cairo Genizah, dated 1038, well reflects
the interconnectedness of Samaritans and Jews in medieval Fustat,
old Cairo. This text mentions one Sheikh Abu al-'Imran Musa ibn
Yaqub ibn Ishaq, who was a Jewish court physician and chief of the
Jewish community in Fustat. The community included Rabbanite
and Karaite Jews and Samaritans. A Muslim author writing in 1188
mentions a "cemetery of the Jews and Samaritans" in Cairo. Reinhard Pummer suggests that "the fact that the cemetery was used by

Jews and Samaritans is an indication that the Samaritan community
was too small to have its own cemetery."[8] The very fact that these
two communities shared this consecrated plot points to proximity
that goes beyond mere necessity between Samaritans and Rabbanites. For the smaller Samaritan community, this association with
the Jews was vitally important, as it strengthened their ever insecure
dhimmi status as a protected "People of the Book."

A number of Samaritan texts made their way into the Genizah.
This in itself reflects the proximity of Jews and Samaritans. These
include a Samaritan commentary on Exodus 9:13, a fragment of a
Samaritan chronicle, and biblical manuscripts. Among these documents is a cache of alms letters, some written to the trustees of
the Rabbinate's charity funds and others to individuals. Two of
these were written during the twelfth century by one Joseph son of
Ishmael the Priest. Joseph was a Samaritan carpenter writing to a
Rabbanite charity fund in flowery Hebrew square Jewish script. In
this letter, he requests not alms, but work. The letter begins with
extended praise for God before reaching the point of this correspondence:

> Your brother and friend Joseph, the Samaritan priest, the poor and needy.
> In the name of the Lord we act and prosper.
> These are the names in the tongue of the pure.
>
> Peace be upon you, brethren, in the name of the Lord, the one, the sure,
> the enduring, the ancient, the first, the possessor, the holy, the power-
> ful, the giver, the supporter, the lofty, the comforter, who pardons, who
> gives life and death, who makes to live, who heals, long-suffering, giving
> increase, near and far off, triumphant, the deliverer, the peaceful, who
> brings together, who hears and knows and answers, the helper faithful
> and excellent, praised and exalted, who blesses and supplies, mighty
> and great, the strong, the master most high, all-seeing, the head, the
> good, the ancient: the restorer pure and perfect, the maker, the true,
> the commander, the judge, revealing, rewarding, strong and glorified,
> the saviour, [glori]fied, the opener, interpreter (?), maker, redeemer,
> preserver, enlightening, guiding, rich, creator, king, … , remembering,
> who begins and ends, who does good, enduring, (our) desire and (our)
> great support, the hidden, who receives, … , holy, lord of the place(?),
> wonderful, terrible, the true witness, who attains and searches out, who
> nurtures, who restores, who strikes (?), who makes to tremble, the mer-
> ciful, the pitiful. God, the God of the spirits of all flesh, God of things
> hidden and revealed, God of signs and wonders, God of all great deeds,
> God of the holy angels, upright, perfect, just, the ruler, merciful [and
> gracious], the God of these terrible and wonderful names give ear and
> hear all my blessing upon you. … Amen. For he is merciful and gracious,
> and hears the crying of the poor: Blessed be He! The Lord reward [you
> with goodness] and favor and truth for the words which you spoke on
> the Sabbath to the distinguished elder, the Lord preserve him.
>
> Now, my brethren, if the word which you spoke before him had been
> (spoken) to a stone or a flint which can neither answer nor speak a word
> back, it would have been ashamed and confounded before you, but up
> to the present he has not given me any help, nor will he. I know the Sa-

maritans to be without intelligence, caring only for the things that are seen (?), and that they have not done good in the sight of God, and will not. For they seek only a reputation in this passing world, whereas if they took pleasure in what is lasting they would have shown kindness to the poor, the afflicted and needy, the strangers and priests, such as I am.

Now, brethren, I did not ask him for either gold or silver. I am a carpenter. I can make boxes, bedsteads, doors, and beams. I asked him to speak to the head carpenter for me that he should take me with him to work every day for wages enough for me and my family to live upon. He has not done so for the Lord, nor according to your instructions, nor for my sake. And now it is right that we turn our faces to the Lord our God, the source of goodness which is not shut up, and the well of mercy which is not stopped. All goodness is found in the streams of his mercy, and all kindness is inherited as a gift of his deep. All eyes hang upon him, all souls are lifted to him, all hands are stretched out before him, and beside him is none that gives life. All his deeds are uprightness, all his work is wisdom, and all his ways are justice. There are no errors in his way, no injustice in his judgement, no corruption in his work. We ought to serve him, fear him and trust in him, for he is the Lord of truth, and all beside him vanity. Let us seek Our faithful God for this, and let us trust in him and love him, for he is merciful, gracious, and forgiving, who will not leave us out of his mercy. For these reasons may the Lord fulfill the blessing of Moses his servant for you: "May the Lord God of your fathers increase your numbers a thousand times" [Deuteronomy 1:11]. Amen and Amen.

If I have made mistakes in my letter, forgive my mistakes in the night that I wrote it.[9]

In his long preamble, Joseph son of Ishmael the Priest, the carpenter, asserts theological continuity between himself and the Rabbanites to whom he writes, and ends his letter with evocation of "the blessing of Moses, his Servant." Joseph describes himself as a *Shemaroni*, decidedly not as a *Kuti*, but also not as Samaritans identified themselves, as *Shemarim*, the keepers of the Torah. He positioned himself as a close-by foreigner, as a member of a community that was contiguous with the Rabbanites. Joseph emphasized both his diverse skills as a carpenter and describes the "unwillingness" of the Egyptian Samaritan community to help him. It was, to his mind, "too worldly minded" to give alms to a poor member of their community. Joseph acknowledges the Rabbanite critique of Samaritans as "without intelligence, caring only for the things that are seen (?), and that they have not done good in the sight of God." He disparages his own community, seemingly with anger, saying that "if they took pleasure in what is lasting they would have shown kindness to the poor, the afflicted and needy, the strangers and priests, such as I am."

The emphasis on his status as a foreigner may be surprising, but it should not be. Genizah documents show evidence that Jews from outside Egypt often applied for charity from the Rabbanite community, as well as others who could be construed as foreigners. In some cases, Rabbanite law suggests that foreigners should be given preference in charitable gifts over locals, though this is in tension with other statements that prefer locals. Whichever view prevails, it was not unusual for outsiders to turn to the community of Rabbanite Jews in Cairo for aid, and this carpenter would have been one of many such foreigners to do so.

The carpenter's statement that the Samaritan community was "too worldly" to offer aid to the poor of their own community should not be taken as strong evidence about the Samaritan community of Egypt. Though the Rabbanite community did often give aid to foreigners, it was generally when they did not have another place to turn to for succor. The carpenter would have had to justify his application to the Rabbanite trustees and to explain why he was unable to receive charity from his own community. In addition, the Rabbanite trustees would have had to assess the validity of his claim to poverty before agreeing to distribute charity to him, or in this case to decide whether to introduce him to the foreman. Thus, these letters cannot tell us very much about the Samaritan community itself.

This fascinating letter does not say very much about the relationship between the Rabbanite Jews and Samaritans of Cairo. We know that this Samaritan carpenter felt he could turn to the Rabbanite community for aid when he was in financial trouble, and it seems that he had been denied aid by the Samaritan community. We cannot know how common such appeals were. The fact that he positioned himself as a foreigner demonstrates that the communities were distinct, but beyond that we cannot say. Perhaps his reference to the head carpenter's unwillingness to take him suggests a bias or distaste for Samaritan or other foreign workers, but without more context it is impossible to know. Additionally, as we do not have the responses to his letters, we do not know how they were received by the Rabbanite community. The most we can say is that this individual Samaritan thought he had a chance to receive some aid from the Rabbanites. Nevertheless, the letters are tantalizing for what they suggest.

Though limited evidence of contact between Rabbanite Jews and Samaritans remains, what does exist points toward a degree of communal comity alongside an ideological tension. Numerous travelers encountered the Samaritan community in Shechem, and Rabbi Ovadia of Bartenura (died circa 1515) described the community in Old Cairo in some detail. Rabbi Jacob Tam son of David ibn Yaḥya (born in Portugal, died in Istanbul, 1542), for example, was asked whether a synagogue in Bornova, near Izmir, could hang a Torah curtain "with six lines of Samaritan writing," which had been brought from Egypt and donated to the community, before the Torah shrine.[10] The rabbi's answer was ultimately negative, though the act of donation and the question itself suggest a level of proximity. In 1566, Samuel Sulam printed a Samaritan legend, the "Epistle of Joshua son of Nun," as an appendix in his Istanbul edition of Abraham Zacuto's *Sefer Yuḥasin*.[11] Sulam, who had spent some time in Egypt, introduces this text by saying: "I found and saw [this] in a book of the chronicles of the *Kutim*, and they told me that they saw it in a *midrash* of the Jews." We cannot know exactly when in the centuries prior to Sulam's discovery this midrash was exchanged back and forth between the two communities—but a small fragment in Judeo-Arabic, in Jewish square script, was found in the Genizah. Sulam borrowed this text from a Samaritan chronicle and accepted it as Jewish. It was quickly integrated into Jewish works. This is the other side of the coin of Samaritan borrowing Jewish texts and traditions—from legends that appear in the chronicles to Saadia Gaon's Arabic translation of the Torah. There was continuous commerce between the two communities during the medieval period. Rabbinates and Samaritans were reading and using each other's works and at some level were learning from each other. This would continue through the early modern period.

Returning to Sandra Benjamin's *The World of Benjamin of Tudela*, "heretic" was likely not a term that Benjamin would have used to describe Samaritans. Having never met a Samaritan before his journey, Benjamin viewed them with curiosity. They existed at the fringe of the Jewish people. He directly polemicized against Samaritan claims to biblical ancestry, even as in other cases he identified them as a subgroup of Israelites. Nachmanides, who had also likely never met living Samaritans before, found them to be useful in interpreting the biblical heritage. The situation was more complex in the Islamic world, where "Rabbanites, Karaites and Samaritans" were vitally linked. We have seen that a lone Samaritan carpenter, unemployed in Egypt, turned to the Rabbanite community for aid in his time of need. Samaritans and Jews lived apart, if sometimes side by side. They were far more related, each begrudgingly knew, than either was to the Muslim rulers or to Christians. As Benjamin put it, describing Damascus: "There is peace between them, but they do not intermarry."

For Further Reading

Steven Fine. "'They Remembered That They Had Seen It in a Jewish Midrash': How a Samaritan Tale Became a Legend of the Jews." *Religions* 12 (2021), https://doi.org/10.3390/rel12080635.

S.D. Goitein. *A Mediterranean Society: The Jewish Communities of the Arab World as Portrayed in the Documents of the Cairo Geniza*. Vol. 2: *The Community*. Berkeley: University of California Press, 1972.

Martin Jacobs. *Orienting the East: Jewish Travelers to the Medieval Muslim World*. Philadelphia: University of Pennsylvania Press, 2014.

Reinhard Pummer. "The Samaritans in Egypt." In *Études sémitiques et samaritaines offertes à Jean Margin*, edited by Christian-Bernard Amphoux, Albert Frey, and Ursula Schattner-Rieser. Lausanne: Éditions du Zèbre, 1998, 213–232.

---

1   Adapted from Adler, 1907, 32–34 = Hebrew: 22.
2   Benjamin, 1995, 166.
3   Ed. Adler, 1907, 44.
4   Ibid., 48.
5   *Mishneh Torah*, Gifts to the Poor, 10:1.
6   Ed. Adler, 75.
7   Ed. Chavel, 2:507–508.
8   Pummer, 1998, 219.
9   Adapted from Cowley, 1904, 478–481.
10 Tam ibn Yaḥya, 1622, no. 204; Kelman, forthcoming.
11 Fine, 2021.

11

"Do You Have the Chronicles of the Kings of Samaria?": Jewish Knowledge, Christian Hebraists, and the European "Discovery" of the Samaritans

MATTHEW CHALMERS

Do you have the Chronicles of the Kings of Samaria as do the Jews to this day? Do you have the Book of Psalms of King David as do the Jews? Do you have appointed times and other convocations in addition to the appointed times of the Torah and the holy convocations? Do you slaughter the Paschal lamb, for the Jews do not slaughter it anymore? What are your thoughts and hopes about the King Messiah and about the Day of his Coming?

…These are the questions which I ask of you. Now if you deal kindly and truthfully with me, please write answers to each question in the holy tongue, and because of the kindness that you are showing me, do not send me away empty- handed, because I fear the Lord the maker of heaven and earth. And these are the books which you should sell to me for money:

…The place of your community which has been in Egypt for some years, now also who was the King, and what is his name, who deported you there from Samaria?

…What are your psalms, songs and prayers? In your community, or your refuges, or in your holy books, or where they are kept, do you have a manual for the intercalation of the year?

…The Jews say that once Kings reigned in Samaria, and later it was Hoshea that Shalmaneser the King of Assyria conquered, and the ten tribes of Israel he deported to Assyria and brought from the land of Cuth people to Samaria to dwell there, which is why they are known as Cutheans to this day. Are these things true?

— Excerpts of a Letter from Joseph Justus Scaliger to the Samaritan Community in Egypt.[1]

In the name of the Lord, the great, the mighty, and the terrible. And the peace of the Lord with Moses son of Amram, prophet for all the generations, than whom there is no greater in mercy, prayerfulness, fasting, and abstinence. May God sustain you, and favour you, and remain with you just as he remained with your fathers, and hate those who hate you, and may our Lord be exalted highly just as he is exalted highly among us and amongst you also the works of our righteous fathers, and your fathers, Abraham, Isaac, and Jacob—peace be upon them. This is a letter from the whole community of Israel in Egypt, the worshippers on Hargarizim-Beit-El, to one most favoured of our Lord, the pillar of the community, the first among the custodians of the guardians of the Torah, the lover of the law of Moses, called Joseph Scaliger, Christian and Frank, may the Lord guard him and equip him and remember him well. Amen.

The contents of your letter included these questions to us. We respond to you that we submit to the law and the judgements and the teacher, that is to say, the teacher of our community Moses son of Amram; we believe in the Lord, and in Moses the prophet son of Amram, and in the holy Torah and in Hargarizim-Beit-El.

Our Torah has five books from Genesis; these and no more. The light to celebrate Passover yearly on Mount Gerizim is lit by the hand of the high priest Eleazar son of Pinḥas from the line of Pinḥas son of Aaron the priest, on the fortieth day of the first month. And we celebrate the festival of Shavuot, observed for the count of fifty days, and the Sabbath of Amaleq (?), and the night of the congregation, and the day of reading. We also celebrate the festival of Sukkot in the seventh month, on the fifteenth day, for eight days. And Yom Kippur comes on the tenth day of the same month. This tenth day is for the sealing away of sin and the binding of sacrifice by the sons of Levi. We also celebrate Shabbat on the seventh day, just as the Lord said, and we do no work [o]n it, just as the Lord said: "Keep the day of the Sabbath, and do not kindle a fire on it"; just as the Lord said, thus: "Do not kindle a fire in any of your dwellings on the day of the Sabbath." And we observe the covenant of circumcision on the eighth day, just as the Lord said: "A woman who has given birth, at the time of the eighth day afterwards let her circumcise

12

Two Minorities on the Brink: Jews and Samaritans in Nineteenth-Century Nablus

REUVEN GAFNI

In 1842 the Samaritans were cruelly persecuted because they would not embrace the Moslem faith, and the Mohammedan Ulemas threatened to murder the whole of their community, on the plea that they had no religion, not even believing in one of the inspired books … A sect which acknowledges the inspiration of any one of those five books is legally tolerated by the Mohammedans. This being known to the Samaritans, they endeavored to prove their faith in the Pentateuch; But the Mohammedans, not being acquainted with the holy language and characters in which it was written, disbelieved them. Then they applied to the chief Rabbi of the Jews in Jerusalem— a recognized representative and head of the Jewish faith—who gave them a written declaration certifying, "That the Samaritan people is a branch of the children of Israel, who acknowledge the truth of the Tora" … This document, accompanied with presents, put an end to the persecution for a time. I mention this merely to show in what light the Samaritans are regarded by the superior and learned Jews.

— Mary Elizabeth Rogers, *Domestic Life in Palestine*, 1863[1]

In early 1842, Rabbi Ḥayyim Abraham (Mircado) Gagin, presiding at the time as the *Ḥakham Bashi* (Chief Rabbi) of Jerusalem, issued an extraordinary declaration from a historical-cultural perspective. Gagin, the first rabbi to be awarded the official Ottoman title of *Ḥakham Bashi* of Eretz Israel, only a few months prior, decreed that the Samaritans were to be considered "a branch of the children of Israel, who acknowledge the truth of the Torah."[2]

This affirmation made by the Jewish Chief Rabbi—the background to which will be described in greater detail below—can with some certainty be said to have had far-reaching consequences, both in terms of protecting the Samaritan community in Nablus from immediate harm, and, to some extent, in terms of shaping social relations and mutual perceptions between the Samaritan and Jewish minority communities in the city over the following decades. This complex and unique relationship, manifested in a number of encounters over the course of the second half of the nineteenth century, illustrates both the challenges faced by the Samaritan community and its attempts to enlist to its aid any relevant, locally active force, including Jewish actors in Palestine and beyond.

COMMUNITIES FIGHTING FOR SURVIVAL: BACKGROUND AND FIGURES

After several centuries during which testimonies to the growth and status of the Samaritan community in Nablus are relatively few and far between, from the beginning of the nineteenth century reports proliferated about the Samaritans in Nablus and the challenges they were facing. These make it possible to estimate with greater accuracy the size of this small ethnic minority as well as its economic, religious, and social status. The reports available from this period come mainly from Jews—both locals and visitors—as well as from Christian institutions and individuals, who became more and more involved in the state of affairs in Palestine, especially from the time of the Egyptian conquest (1831–1840) onwards.

The various accounts indicate that at the beginning of the nineteenth century the Samaritan community in Nablus numbered roughly only two hundred people (about forty households), and that its numbers remained around the one hundred and fifty to two hundred mark throughout much of the century, out of a total local population of seven to fifteen thousand. Some scholars, including Nathan Schur, conjecture that one of the factors that prevented the Samaritan population's growth during this period was the overall propensity of Samaritans to marry exclusively within their own community (which meant marriages between relatives of various proximities). Over the course of time, this led to the rise of various genetic disorders, one of the outcomes of which was that the males in the population came to significantly outnumber the females, thus limiting the community's birth rate. Furthermore, there is little doubt that, during this period, several members of the Samaritan community converted to Islam for numerous reasons, and that the population's economic and material conditions also affected their numbers in various ways.[3]

In terms of its political and socioeconomic standing, the community similarly faced severe challenges. During this period—especially in the first half of the nineteenth century—the central mountain of Samaria was mired in conflict between various local entities seeking to gain control over the means of power and wealth. The ability of the Ottoman regime to enforce its authority in the area—including in the city of Nablus itself—was extremely limited. The

© REUVEN GAFNI, 2022 | DOI:10.1163/9789004466913_014

A Samaritan Lady.

Egyptian conquest of Palestine in 1831, despite the Egyptian ruler's relative openness to Western influence, likewise failed to put an end to the local skirmishes in Samaria. Thus, even though they had officially been defined, just like the Jews and the Christians, as a protected minority with rights in the land of Palestine, in reality, the Samaritans continued to struggle to survive in Nablus by making temporary—and only partially effective—alliances with various forces, as those rose to power in the city. It was not until roughly 1859 that the Ottomans managed to gain effective control over the central mountain, thus greatly stabilizing the political and administrative conditions in Nablus.

Economically, some members of the Samaritan community worked as clerks for the municipal authorities, but others were also employed in small commerce and crafts in and around the city. Some, it should be noted, were reduced to collecting alms from tourists and visitors, whose numbers increased over the years. In some instances, the community even resorted to selling ancient Samaritan manuscripts in order to help keep Samaritan families and institutions afloat. Most of the Samaritan households were concentrated in a crowded neighborhood (*Harat el-Somra*) in the southwestern part of the city, and throughout the period the Samaritan synagogue (*el-Kanis*)—a small, only partially illuminated space—was, in many respects, the heart of the cultural, religious, and social life of the community (Figure 12.1).

Despite the many difficulties it faced during the nineteenth century—or maybe in part because of them—the Samaritan community in Nablus became a focus of research and reports by various clerics, scholars, and visitors. These described—each in their own way—the Samaritans' way of life as well as how they expressed their faith. Over time, some—including British Consul James Finn and other officials at the British Consulate in Jerusalem—became self-appointed guardians of sorts of the community, taking on responsibility for the welfare and well-being of the congregation and mediating between them and the central Ottoman authorities and various Western officials. However, despite the best efforts of these and other agents, the material situation of the community in Nablus remained tenuous, and during the latter half of the nineteenth century many regarded it as a community on the brink of extinction.[4]

Like the Samaritans, the Jewish community in Nablus also experienced considerable hardships during the nineteenth century. However, whereas the Samaritans managed to survive in and around the city until after World War I, and then to gradually start building up their numbers again, the local Jewish community had disappeared almost completely by the turn of the century, and—with the exception of a few individual Jews who stayed in the city for short periods of time during the Mandate period—never reappeared.

In terms of population, the Jews in Nablus also numbered about one hundred and fifty to two hundred at the beginning of the nineteenth century, and this number appears to have remained quite stable over the first decades of the century. However, after that point, the number of local Jews began to gradually decrease, with only a few dozen people left in the city by the last decades of the century. Ethnically, most of the community comprised Sephardic and Mizrahi Jews, who engaged likewise mostly in crafts and local trade. Nevertheless, there had been several attempts, beginning in the 1840s, to establish a parallel Ashkenazi presence in the city, both by private figures and by representatives of Jewish philanthropic institutions operating mainly in Jerusalem. Yet, despite these attempts, the number of Ashkenazi Jews who lived in Nablus in the second half of the nineteenth century remained very small. To some extent, this was due to the opposition of certain leaders of the Jewish community in Jerusalem to such initiatives in Nablus and in other cities, mainly because they considered it a waste of valuable financial resources that older and more stable communities, especially the one in Jerusalem, desperately needed.

Like the Samaritans, the Jews in Nablus also resided (at least for the most part) in a small, crowded Jewish neighborhood, and the religious life of the local Jewish community, whose character and history was somewhat similar to those of the ancient Jewish community in Acre (which was also gradually dwindling during this period), also revolved around the small synagogue operated by the congregation. Despite the material poverty and small size of the community, the Jewish synagogue in Nablus (like the Samaritan synagogue) housed various holy books and sacred objects donated to it by community members themselves and by occasional philanthropists and visitors, who were mostly passing through on their way from Jerusalem to Meiron and Safed. In terms of religious authority, over the years the members of the Jewish community appointed various personalities to preside over their religious affairs. These local officials usually fulfilled a variety of simple religious roles simultaneously, for example, serving as butcher, circumciser, cantor, and synagogue caretaker (*gabbai/shamash*) all at once.

On many occasions throughout the nineteenth century, the Jewish community in Nablus sought to enlist the support of various elements from the Jewish world, both in the Holy Land and abroad. And indeed, from time to time the local Jews benefited from external financial aid, sometimes for themselves and sometimes for the synagogue operating in the city. For example, Moses Montefiore visited Nablus on at least one occasion, and made sporadic contributions for the upkeep of the community and its institutions. From 1882 onward, Baron Benjamin Edmund de Rothschild also donated various sums of money to the synagogue in Nablus through his official, Eliyahu Shayed, who visited the city and met with the few remaining members of the community.[5] However, despite the assistance provided to the community by various institutional and private sources, it failed to establish itself and develop institutionally and communally, as well as in terms of population. Thus, the local Jewish population remained sparse throughout the last decades of the century, until at last Jews left the city for good in the early years of the twentieth century.[6]

Certainly, like the Samaritans, the Jews' relations with their local Muslim environment were anything but straightforward, and many visitors described the Jews of Nablus as living under various restrictions and humiliations imposed upon them by their neighbors. However, there is no doubt that the Jews' situation was vastly better than that of the Samaritans, if only because of the existence of large Jewish communities in other historical cities throughout the country, and because of the connections of Jewish leaders in Eretz Israel with prominent figures in both the Ottoman government and the various Western delegations.

BETWEEN SUSPICION AND SALVATION: JEWS AND SAMARITANS IN NABLUS IN THE MIDDLE OF THE NINETEENTH CENTURY

Despite the fact that both communities were minorities in Nablus, often threatened, both religiously and economically, by their Muslim environment, relations between Jews and Samaritans in the city remained frigid throughout most of the nineteenth century. Thus, after visiting the city in 1838, Eliezer HaLevi—Moses Montefiore's secretary at the time—stated that "the Jews have nothing to do with the Samaritans who live in this city, unless there are negotiations to be made."[7] In addition, the French researcher Victor Guérin, in describing the city of Nablus, firmly stated that "between Jews and Samaritans deep-rooted animosity still reigns," and British scholar John Mills, who studied the Samaritans in the 1850s, came to the same conclusion.[8] This state of intercommunal relations is likewise reflected in the description given by Ludwig August Frankl, who visited the city in 1856, which shows that the general attitude of the Jews toward the Samaritans was fairly clear-cut:

> I asked the man if he had any intercourse with the Samaritans. The women retreated with a cry of horror, and one of them said: "Have you been among the worshippers of the pigeon?" [An offensive term for Samaritans] I said that I had. The women again fell back with the same expression of repugnance, and one of them said: "Do you know that they offer sacrifices on Mount Gerizim? Take a purifying bath!"[9]

On the other hand, in describing his visit to the Samaritans Frankl ascertains that their attitude to contact with the Jews was, at least in some instances, somewhat different:

> "Are you a Jew?" he asked in evident surprise, "and do you come to us, the Samaritans, who are despised by the Jews?" … "You are not the same as the rest! We would willingly live in friendship with the Jews, but they avoid all intercourse with us."[10]

We see from Frankl's description that Jews did their best to distance themselves from any unofficial or accidental interaction with the Samaritan community. Samaritans, however, were happy to make contact, albeit indirect in this instance—that is, through Frankl himself—with the Jewish world at large. This, of course, was in the hope of bolstering their religious, economic, and social survival efforts in Nablus. Others, including John Mills, who, as mentioned above, stayed in Nablus for short periods of time in the middle of the century, noted that the Samaritans' attitude toward the Jews was also overall quite hostile.[11]

Nevertheless, contrary to these descriptions, at least on some occasions contact was made between representatives of the two communities, both in and outside Nablus. Indeed, this was the case in 1841, in the face of renewed attacks on the Samaritan community by the local Muslim leadership and their repeated attempts to force the Samaritans to leave their religion and convert to Islam.

The unfolding of events in Nablus that year, and the background to the decision by the Chief Rabbi, Ḥayyim Abraham (Mircado) Gagin, to intervene in favor of the Samaritan community, must be understood as following on the heels of a number of previous incidents that occurred in Nablus, during which the Samaritans came under attack for being—in the eyes of the changing authorities—idolaters excluded from the rubric of "People of the Book" (ahl al-kitub), which, under Muslim law, entitled non-Muslims such as Jews and Christians to maintain their basic rights.

For example, this is how Eliezer HaLevi described one such incident, drawing on the testimony of a leader of the Samaritan community in Nablus (Jacob Shalaby, whom he calls Abba Shaalbi) in reference to events that occurred in the city during Egyptian rule:

> When Ibrahim Pasha took control of Syria and Palestine, he considered the Samaritans idolaters who had no place in his land. And they endured a time of hardship like no other, knowing that death awaits them from his hand, were it not for a great man of their creed who hastened to see the pasha, and argued to him that they were true Israelites, until he succeeded in changing the pasha's mind to allow them to remain and live on their land.[12]

From 1841 to 1842, a similar affair took place against the backdrop of a Samaritan woman's conversion to Islam and the congregation's decision to attempt to keep both her children under the auspices of the Samaritan community in order to continue to educate and raise them as Samaritans. This incident was reported extensively by Mary Elizabeth Rogers, sister of the British Consulate's delegate Edward Thomas Rogers, who was cited at the start of this article. In this case, too, her description of the events was probably based on Shalaby's testimony (Figure 12.2)

It should be noted that the Samaritans' appeal to Rabbi Gagin took place only after their previous petitions to some of the representatives of the European powers had fallen on deaf ears.[13] Even Gagin's assistance, despite its immediate and symbolic significance, failed to resolve the plight of the Samaritans in the face of societal pressures in the long term, and the Muslim residents continued to press the community again and again for years to come. On the other hand, in the 1850s and 1860s, the British Consul in Jerusalem, James Finn, who was highly influential with the Ottoman authorities, took up the cause of the Samaritans, and his activity on their behalf—as of on behalf of the Jewish community in Jerusalem—undoubtedly helped the community to maintain its very existence in the face of these ongoing challenges.[14]

It is difficult to determine the factors behind Rabbi Gagin's decision to come out in defense of the Samaritan community. It is possible, of course, that he felt a genuine responsibility, as part of his official role, to the members of the small Samaritan community, who saw themselves as being connected in various ways to the Jewish people. By the same token, he may have sought to prevent a danger-

12.2 "Samaritan High Priest and Original Roll of the Pentateuch, Shechem, Palestine." The Priest Shelama son of the High Priest Amram, Gelatin silver contact print for a stereoscope slide, Keystone View Company, 1903 (Keystone-Mast Collection, UCR/California Museum of Photography, University of California, Riverside).

ous precedent of Muslim oppression of a minority community, which could then be reproduced elsewhere and possibly target Jews in the future. In any case, it should be emphasized that Rabbi Gagin's intervention in favor of the Samaritans did not fundamentally change the relationship between the two minority communities and, contrary to Rogers's conclusion at the end of her description, remained an exception to the rule. It was only in the last two decades of the century that the intercommunal relationship underwent any real change.

"ONE SCHOOL FOR OUR CHILDREN AND THOSE OF OUR JEWISH BRETHREN": A SHARED FIGHT FOR EDUCATION

One of the most difficult challenges faced by the two communities throughout the nineteenth century was the lack of specialized educational institutions for the children of both communities, and a lack of means for retaining suitable teachers in the city. This problem, which led some of the children of both communities to be schooled in Muslim institutions (or schools in other cities), had a major impact on the inability of the Jewish community in particular to survive over time in Nablus and to develop like the communities in other historical cities throughout the country.

This common challenge only grew in complexity during the second half of the century. The gradual arrival of Christian missionaries to Nablus made it tempting for both Jewish and Samaritan families to send their children to the Christian educational institutions they had established in the city. And indeed, faced with this chain of events, after a long period of very tense relations, the Jews and the Samaritans made several attempts at educational cooperation in the hopes of establishing a joint school for the children of the two communities in Nablus.

One such attempt is attested to by letters sent by representatives of the two communities to the management of the Alliance Israélite Universelle (AIU), in which both parties expressed their desire to establish a joint educational institution for Jewish and Samaritan children, in order to prevent, for lack of options, their children from being sent to the Christian institutions operating in the city. In a letter from the Jewish representatives to the Alliance, the writers expressed both the plight of education in the city and their surprising willingness to cooperate in this respect with the Samaritans:

> But the one thing that stands against us most of all is our children's education, because we have no money to pay for a school to teach our children Torah and *Derech Erets* [ethical behavior] and we are unable to take them to Jerusalem to your school [the AIU]. Firstly, because Jerusalem is far from Nablus, and secondly because [Mr.] Bachar [the principal of the school in Jerusalem] will demand large sums of money … For now, the boys go to the Mission school where they are being diverted from the faith of Israel … And now we have joined forces with the Samaritans, for they too wish to teach their sons the holy tongue of the Jews, and we come together in a plea to the respectable company … to open a school here so we don't have to send our children to the Mission school, and peace be upon Israel.[15]

Similar sentiments were expressed by representatives of the Samaritan community in their counterpart letter to the company management written in two copies, one in Samaritan Hebrew and one in Arabic (with minor differences):

> Because of our inability to teach our children, our greatest sadness and apprehensions stem from the Christian pastors, as they spare no effort to take our children into their schools … since there is no Israelite in Nablus capable of opening a school. And so we are now asking for your support to open one school for our children and those of our Jewish brethren, and to have teachers to teach them the Hebrew languages—both Samaritan and Jewish—along with the French and Turkish languages.[16]

The Samaritans' letter indicated that the issue troubling them most was the disappearance of the Samaritan language. It therefore emphasized that Samaritan Hebrew and Jewish Hebrew instruction would be an essential part of the school's curriculum, if indeed it were to be established.

Even though—in light of the AIU's experience operating schools in very small Jewish communities in Eretz Israel (such as the one in Shefaram, for example)—it was reasonable to expect a positive response to the Nablus Jews' request, the evidence suggests that this did not come to pass, and that the unique common initiative bore no fruit. Meanwhile, the Jewish presence in Nablus was shrinking, and in a few short years the idea of a Jewish school became simply impractical. The Samaritans, on the other hand, continued to seek educational assistance from Jewish agencies around the world, and so in 1897 the community approached the philanthropic *Agudat Achim,* the Anglo-Jewish Association, with a similar request. This likewise went unanswered. When word of this last request got out to other Jewish entities around the world, some attacked the very initiative—and even the thought!—of cooperating with the Samaritans, given the strained relationship between the two communities throughout the ages, and given that the Samaritans are not considered Jewish according to *halakhah*.[17] Others, like Ahad Ha'am (Asher Ginzberg), who recorded his response in the pages of *HaShiloah*, sided with the Samaritans in their appeal for support from Jewish institutions:

> The Samaritan community, so the press decries, has founded a school for its children, yet as they have no means for the school's upkeep, they have turned to the Anglo-Jewish Association to ask for their help. As could be expected, they invoked historical memories to support their request, and even gave these memories a more pleasant turn, in order to emphasize "brotherhood" over hatred and war. Yet they are met with nothing but jeering and poisonous laughter from the Jewish press … Among them, even those who preach the *Haskalah* [Jewish Enlightenment] have responded to the pleas of the dying [Samaritan nation] with insult and scorn, giving the age-old answer, which to this day we know not whether it had been just at the time: "Ye have nothing to do with us to build a house" (Ezra 4:3) … It is not proper for decent people to gaze upon such a historical tragedy with mockery and disregard, let alone for the People of Israel, for they themselves are still standing by sheer force of miracle alone.[18]

And yet, despite the moral support lent by Ahad Ha'am, this initiative too failed to become reality, and joint initiatives in Nablus itself soon became impossible, with the disappearance of a permanent Jewish presence from the city.

CONCLUSION

The relationship between the Samaritan and Jewish communities in Nablus in the nineteenth century was shaped by a number of factors: ancient intergenerational grudges alongside religious and halakhic sentiments on both sides; shifting local and geographic concerns; and the conditions endured by the two nations over the years. Thus, despite departing from a point of total distrust and deliberate remoteness on the part of the two communities, local connections were nevertheless made between representatives of the two communities on several occasions: Rabbi Gagin's dramatic and surprising 1841 declaration of the Samaritans' inclusion in the Children of Israel (though pointedly not on the legal, halakhic level as Jews), and the Samaritan–Jewish initiatives for joint education, which failed to come to fruition. The final disappearance of a permanent Jewish presence from the city, followed by the events of World War I and its consequences, once again reshuffled the deck and opened new and divergent chapters in the history of each community.

For Further Reading

James Finn, *Stirring Times*. London: C.K. Paul & Co., 1878.

Yaron Har'el, "On the Common Educational Initiative of the Jews and Samaritans in Nablus." *Cathedra* 119 (2006): 121–132. [Hebrew].

John Mills, *Three Months' Residence in Nablus: The Modern Samaritans*. London: J. Murray, 1864.

Nathan Schur. "Samaritan History: The Modern Period (from 1516 A.D.)." In *The Samaritans*, edited by Alan D. Crown. Tübingen: Mohr Siebeck, 1989, 113–134.

1   Rogers, 1862, 273.
2   On Rabbi Gagin, see Elmalih, 1970, 182–203.
3   Schur, 2002, 622–626.
4   Ibid., 636.
5   Shayed, 1983, 190–192.
6   Schur, 1986, 229–301.
7   Ginzburg, 1844, 184.
8   Guérin, 1874, 394; Mills, 1864, 323–329.
9   Frankl, 1859, 334.
10 Ibid., 329.
11 Mills, 1864, 323.
12 Dvir, 1884, 35–36; Rogers, 1862, 273. See also Rogers, 1855, 29–30.
13 Barges, 1855, 65–71. See also Ben-Zvi, 1970, 51–52.
14 Schur, 2002, 621.
15 Quoted in Har'el, 2006, 125, based on the archival documents of the AIU in France: AIU, Pays isolés, Jordanie, nos. 3220, 2677.
16 Har'el, 2006, 128–129.
17 *A.B. – The Samaritan News,* 1993, 120–139.
18 Ahad Ha'am, 1887: 388–389.

13

"The Priest Salama son of Ghazal and the Tailors" Palestinian Arab Justice and the Samaritans

HASEEB SHEHADEH

This is a true story of a recent time. It had not been written down before we transcribed it from those who had heard it from their parents and knew it. The priest Salama was renowned for his piety, simplicity and spiritual contacts, as well as for his poverty and lack of means. He was skilled in the science of astrology, which he had learned from his father Ghazal. As a result he was close to Arab governors and leaders who ruled this town [Nablus] and who helped him a little to meet the needs of daily life and support his large family.

This is Salama the priest who was mentioned above in the survey of his father's and his lives. He was the only son of the priest Ghazal and his wife Hadiyya (or Hadiyye in colloquial) the Samaritan from Gaza and the sister of Ghazal son of al- Surur, his friend. The child was born after the family returned from Gaza [to Nablus]. At that time the Samaritans of Nablus refrained from giving in marriage one of their daughters because of a dispute between him and some influential Samaritans. Consequently, Salama moved to Gaza and lived there for a period of time with respect and honor among the Samaritans. They gave him the best of their daughters in marriage and did not let him go back without the strong urging and insistence of the notables of Nablus, who expressed their regret and sorrow for what they had done against him.

The priest Salama was extremely simple, religious and pious. He practiced tailoring as a profession, not because he mastered it but because he regarded it as the only occupation through which it would be possible to earn some money to support [literally: spend on] his family, especially because he had no other income and no one among his impoverished community was able to help him. Yet, some of them did help him in renting a very modest and small shop in the bazaar on the street [*wakala*, guild?] of the tailors in Nablus.

He worked for a long period making *qanabiz* [traditional men's robes] for simple villagers for a small fee. In spite of the fact that he was not skilled in this profession, people chose him as their tailor, causing envy among neighboring Arab tailors, who hated him and asked him to raise his fees and even threatened him. Since he did not pay any attention to them, they decided to harm him by accusing him of stealing and complained to the governor of Nablus, the oppressor Musa Bey Tuqan. To make the charge, they secretly placed in his shop some pieces of cloth that they stole from their own clients. Then a delegation of them went and met Musa Bey Tuqan. They presented to him the matter of this Samaritan priest who steals the property of Muslims, considering such action as lawful. They all testified and swore in front of the governor that they were telling the truth.

The Bey [governor], who knew the priest, did not believe them at first sight and rebuked them harshly. He said to them: You envy this poor and humble person and treat him unjustly. He is simple, pious and above any suspicion. They answered: Our lord, if you do not believe us you can immediately send some of your men to search his shop. We are sure that there are some stolen goods [pieces] in it. If our statement turns out to be false then we would be ready to accept the punishment that our lord imposes on us. The Bey agreed and commanded some of his men to go and search the priest's shop. He instructed them that if they found any stolen goods as charged by the tailors they bring both the stolen goods and the owner of the shop. If they do not find anything, they should not bring the priest nor bother him. They went and searched Salama's shop, though he did not know why they came and what they were looking for. When they found the stolen pieces that the complainants themselves had put there, they asked him to accompany them to the Bey, which he did. When they arrived before the Bey with what they found, the priest stood before him. The Bey, feeling pity for the priest, asked him to tell the truth. The priest denied having any knowledge of the stolen goods. The Bey, who did not suspect that the charge was a trick by the tailors, became furious and thought that the priest was lying and refusing to acknowledge the truth. So he raised his hand to slap him [nobody he slapped remained alive] but Salama moved aside from the blow. The Bey's hand hit the wall. The blow was so hard that the Bey fainted because of the intense pain. Before he regained consciousness one of his brothers led the priest Salama by the hand and said to him: "Go away and save yourself, you poor man," before you get killed. He opened the door for Salama and ordered the guards to let him go.

The priest took to his heels, not believing that he was safe. He also did not know the source of this misfortune. When he arrived home he hid in the cellar below a floor tile that had been intended for such purposes for a long time. He remained in hiding until a messenger of the Bey arrived. When the Bey regained consciousness he felt a great pain in his hand. He tried to move his hand but could not. Orthopedic therapists and physicians tried to cure him but their attempts to mitigate the pain or enable him to move his hand were in vain. Then the Bey asked about the priest and what they did to him. He feared that they might have killed him. His brother came close and informed him that he took the priest to his home. Musa Bey thanked him for doing that and requested him to go and apologize to the priest and fetch him, believing that no one else could help him. The Bey's brother hurried to the priest's house and after some difficulty the priest showed up and agreed to accompany him. When he arrived, the Bey apologized to him and asked him to appeal to God and pray for healing. Salama did so, and the pain vanished. The hand was healed. Salama was honored and rewarded with a large sum of money and gifts for his family and an outfit for him. Though the Bey believed in Salama's innocence, he could not understand how the stolen pieces came to the shop. When he brought the tailors who had complained and started beating them with sticks, some of them revealed the truth and confessed that they themselves had placed the pieces that they had stolen from their clients in the shop. They received punishment which they had brought upon themselves, and they paid a fine which was given to the priest. After that the Bey remained grateful to the priest and extended to him a helping hand."

— Yaqub son of Uzzi Abu Shafiq (Jacob son of Uzzi),
The Book of the Samaritans.[1]

The story of the high priest Salama son of Ghazal son of Isḥaq son of Ibrahim son of Sadaqa (known often as Salama al-Kahin or al-Lawi Salama) and the Arab tailors of Nablus is set during the first half of the nineteenth century. It is presented here as it appeared in an unpublished hand-written book in Arabic on the Samaritans completed in 1960 by the Samaritan scholar and high priest Yaqub son of Ghazal, known as Abu Shafiq. This story affords a glimpse into the complex and highly liminal place inhabited also by a small group of Samaritans in late Ottoman Palestine, the second tier status of the Samaritans within Arabic Islamic culture—their professions, poverty, and the dependance of Samaritans—even high priests—upon local governors. It is also a window into the equally liminal world inhabited by the story teller, Abu Shafiq during the twentieth century. In what follows I will present some of the "backstory" to his tale, focusing on the main characters: Salama son of Ghazal and Yaqub Abu Shafiq.

SALAMA SON OF GHAZAL AND HIS WORLD

Salama son of Ghazal son of Isḥaq son of Sadaqa (1784-1855) served as a high priest from 1799 to 1826 (Figure 1.3). All high priests since have been his descendants, affording Salama particularly high status as progenitor of a long line of Samaritan leaders. After the death of Salama's father Ghazal in 1787, the Samaritans lived about twelve years without a high priest. Salama was Ghazal's only heir, and at

age three, he was too young to take up the office of high priesthood. His training began early, at the age of nine, (January 23, 1793), and we know that he began to copy his own Samaritan Torah manuscript, a folio of which survives in the National Library in St. Petersburg. Salama married Sis Shelaḥ Ab-Sakuwwa ha-Danfi (Warda Salih Murgan al-Danafi) in 1805 at the age of twenty, as recorded of in their marriage document (*kitab al-'aris*), also preserved in the National Library of Russia. The couple had three sons, Imran, Harun and Isḥaq, of whom Imran (1809-1874) served as high priest, between 1826 and 1859. This period witnessed also a truly tumultuous period, which included an attempt by the Muslim *Ulama* to convert the Samaritan community in Nablus in 1842 to Islam. Those Muslims did not know or accept that Samaritans have their holy book, the Pentateuch and they are thus protected as *dhimmis* like Jews and Christians. Our tale falls within the genre of high priests exempla, a very popular genre of Samaritan folktales since ancient times.

At the beginning of the nineteenth century approximately thirty Samaritan families lived in al-Khadra area of Nablus, associated by Samaritan tradition with Genesis 33:19. This text describes the patriarch Jacob at *Ḥlqt al-Smrh* where "he bought a parcel of land (*Helqat ha-Sadeh*) where he had pitched his tent." The Samaritan enclave was generally called *Ḥlqt al-Smrh,* the "Samaritan district." As our story suggests, the governor of Nablus was Musa Bek Tuqan (died 1823), who was followed by Maḥmud Bek Abd al-Hadi (died 1865). The tax collector in the Samaritan community was Abd Ḥannuna son of Sadaqa al-Danfi. Salama is known to had fairly good relations with the governors, especially owing to his knowledge of astrology (*tanjim*) and his skill in writing amulets (bitaqat), which they found useful.

Other Samaritan stories relating to Salama preserved at the Israel Folktale Archive at the University of Haifa, reflect Salama's ability to predict the future by interpreting the stars. As in our story, Salama was treated as a kind of Samaritan holy man, a status conferred upon Samaritan amulet writers to this day.

Salama was the last high priest to live in the old, dark, and damp priestly house, a building that was divided into three parts. In the past that house was known by the name *Hashem*, that is to say, *the Name of God*, owing to the holy manuscripts containing the name of God (*Shema*) were preserved there in a small closet. Later those parchments were stored in a small golden box in a metal closet together with other old books in the synagogue. They are now kept in a safe in the synagogue on Mount Gerizim. Salama corresponded for almost two decades with the well-known orientalist Sylvestre de Sacy (1758-1838), writing in both Arabic and Samaritan Neo-Hebrew (called previously *Shomronit*). Salama's correspondence, significant in various respects, was published accompanied with French translation by De Sacy, the pioneer of Samaritan Arabic studies in the modern era. In addition, Salama met with European travelers who visited the Samaritan community in Nablus and they left us positive impressions of his character. Salama composed prayers in Samaritan Neo-Hebrew and poetry in Middle Arabic. Several of those prayers are included in the collection published by Arthur E. Cowley in 1909. Salama's correspondence suggests that from 1788-1808 the Samaritans were forbidden to celebrate their Passover on Mount Gerizim.

13.1 Willem van de Poll, Priests with the Abisha Scroll with Jordanian Officials. Right to left: High Priest Amram son of Isaac (reigned 1961–1980), Priest Asher son of Matzliah, Priest Jacob son of Uzzi (reigned 1984–1987), Priest Sadeq son of Abisha, and Asher son of Shilach Tsedaka ha-Tsafri, 1953 (National Archives of the Netherlands / Fotocollectie Van de Poll).

ABU SHAFIQ— JACOB SON OF UZZI— AND THE COMPLEXITIES OF MODERN SAMARITAN IDENTITY

Our story teller, Yaqub son of Shafiq (Uzzi) son of Yaqub son of Harun son of Salama son of Ghazal (afterwards, Abu Shafiq and in colloquial Arabic Abu Shafi. He is often referred to as Jacob son of Uzzi) was born circa 1899/1900 and died on January 26, 1987 (Figures 0.7, 2.5; 13.1-2). Abu Shafiq served as high priest from October 20, 1984 until his death. The complexities of his life, and the liminal space that he inhabited between Samaritan, Palestinian and Jewish/Israeli culture, were no less than those of his ancestor, the high priest Salama. At the age of seventy-five the future high priest wrote an autobiographical essay, upon which this description of his life is based.

Abu Shafiq's parents died when he was very young. He and his younger sister, Munira, were raised for ten years by their mother, their grandfather Jacob son of Aaron the Levite (1840-1916) and their paternal uncle Abu al-Ḥasan son of Yaqub (1883-1959). It is worth mentioning that Abu Shafiq's father, a bookseller in Palestine, visited London with three other Samaritans in 1905. The purpose of this well publicized visit, which lasted three months, was to sell Samaritan manuscripts, and to collect donations to assist poor Samaritan families and for opening a Samaritan school. Among the manuscripts sold to one Mrs. Elizabeth Anne (McCaul) Finn (1825-1921), a writer and a wife of the British consul in Jerusalem, James Finn, was a small but very old parchment, a *Finasiyye* (generally a Torah attributed to an ancient high priest) dating back to pre-Islamic times!

Abu Shafiq received his basic education, religious and secular, in three different systems. His teachers of Samaritan tradition, Salama son of Imran and Ibrahim son of Khadr, were quite demanding. As was customary, he was taught to read the Torah as well as prayers written in Samaritan Aramaic. Abu Shafiq attended the Protestant missionary school in Nablus, where he was supposed to study Arabic and English — though he reports that his old, liberal and modest teacher Abu Nadir was not particularly successful. Abu Shafiq then attended the Samaritan school founded by the American E. K. Warren in 1912, where he studied English, arithmetic, history, geography and the Samaritan religion, especially the basics of cantillation. That school met in two large houses in the Samaritan quarter, one for boys and the other for girls (Figure 15.4). The number of pupils in each house was about seventy, distributed into three classes. The ages of the pupils stretched between five and twenty. Truth said, Abu Shafiq was in large part an autodidact. He taught himself both modern Hebrew (called in one place, the

"Jewish language") and English, and was fond of reading books. In his youth, history, love stories, and novels attracted him. Later he turned to scientific and philosophical works.

In 1937 Abu Shafiq married Afaf (Yafa) the daughter of Ghazal son of Khadr the priest (1924-1998) and they had ten children, five sons and five daughters. The gap in education and in age between the new couple was great. The elder son was Shafiq. Uzzi, later the high priest, was known as Abu Shafi in colloquial Arabic. Abu Shafi tried to move from Jordanian Nablus to Holon in 1961. He hinted at this clandestine desire in an autobiographical statement, approximately two decades later, where he declared his wish to move to Ḥolon in order to serve as the priest of this otherwise lay community. If need be, he wrote, he was even willing to live in a tent! This aspiration was not realized, as he wrote, because of the interference of his cousin, the priest Sadaqa. The real reason behind the denial of his immigration request, however, was different. Reading the autobiography of Abu Shafiq, it is clear that the Israeli authorities needed him to stay in Nablus and continue to function as a source of information. He visited Israel after the 1967 war, met the president and the prime minister of Israel and with the prominent Samaritanist Professor Ze'ev Ben-Ḥayyim (1907-2013). Abu Shafiq worked diligently and clandestinely on behalf of the Jewish Agency during the Mandatory Period. He did this for more than eighteen years, endangering his life. After the Six Day War, he and his family did succeed, though, in receiving Israeli identity cards and new immigrant status.

Socially, Abu Shafiq had good relations with Jewish, Muslim, Christian, and Druze dignitaries. He was among a small Samaritan delegation that included Sadaqa son of Isḥaq, Nagi Khadr and Abd Ibrahim, that met the Jordanian king Talal (1909-1972) in 1951. His connections with some of his relatives, however, were not free from rancor, envy and jealousy.

Abu Shafiq left some significant hand-written books in Arabic, copied many manuscripts, corresponded with Izhak Ben-Zvi (1883-1963), the second president of Israel, and was a correspondent and served as a source of information in Nablus for the Hebrew press as well as the *Palestine Post.* His reports about aggression, fights and robberies, which were written in Arabic, were translated into Hebrew by the Jewish orientalist, journalist and writer Menahem Kapeliuk (1900-1988). His work in journalism caused Abu Shafiq political difficulties, particularly during the Arab general strike in 1936 and the peasants' revolt in 1938. He was also a palm reader and a distiller and seller of *arak*, an alcoholic liquor, and was involved in commerce — which he called "a despicable profession" (*mihna mardula*). Abu Shafiq put it clearly—the job of high priest since his grandfather's time, he wrote, "is equal to nothing and its holder will starve if he does not have another occupation. Special mention should be made of *A Partial Arabic Translation of Izhak Ben-Zvi's Sefer ha-Shomronim,* and the *Samaritan Sacrifice of Passover* in Hebrew published in 1934. A short treatise dealing with Samaritan scholars and their Arabic writings is included in this volume. Abu Shafiq translated manuscripts from Arabic into Hebrew, including a pamphlet entitled *Who are the Samaritans?* which was published in Holon in 1965 by his son-in-law Abraham Tsedaka. Abu Shafiq translated the Samaritan

Pentateuch into Arabic, exploring differences between the translations of Abu Said (thirteenth century), Saadia Gaon (882-942) and the Greek Septuagint. Now lost, this work took three years (1935-1938) to complete. It was given to Izhak Ben-Zvi, who failed to find a purchaser for it. The priest decided to sell this translation himself, because he needed money for his marriage. My attempts since the 1970s to find any traces of this translation have been fruitless. Abu Shafiq produced copies of the Samaritan Torah and the *Deftar,* the prayer book, with vocalization in order to teach his children and to preserve the traditional oral pronunciation. He claimed that some "ignorant, fanatic and reactionary persons" had attempted to forbid this, on the argument that the punctuation marks are an illicit addition to the holy text of the Torah (Deuteronomy 4:2, 13:1).

On a number of occasions Abu Shafiq described his life as a *tragedy* (*ma'sa*). As a father he did not derive much pleasure from the intellectual achievements of his sons and sardonically suggested that rational people should, in fact, give a celebratory banquet when somebody passes away. He wished that his coffin be made of strong wood painted green and his grave be two and half meters deep and one meter wide. Planting flowers and especially roses beside the grave, he suggested, would be appreciated. He did not like Samaritan mourning customs, including the wearing of black clothes. He beseeched his wife, his daughters and his grandchildren not to mourn over thirty days.

The complexities of being a Samaritan in the Holy Land are the leitmotif of the story of "The Priest Salama son of Ghazal and the Tailors" and the life of his descendant, the scholar, spy, *arak* distiller and high priest Abu Shafiq. Both are stories of perseverance. The story of Salama resonates with the life experience of Abu Shafiq. It provided historical and spiritual depth for his own life in Mandatory Palestine, the Hashemite Kingdom of Jordan, the "West Bank," under the Palestinian Authority and under the State of Israel.

Finally, it is perhaps not superfluous to mention that the high priest, the late Cohen Sallum son of Imran (Shalom son of Amram, 1923-2004), was a member in the Palestinian parliament. The current high priest and all his community— Israelis and Palestinians— are speakers of Arabic and Hebrew. As a tiny minority in the world and in particular in the Middle East, the Samaritans would be the first to welcome real, just and comprehensive peace between Israel, the Palestinian Authority and the Arab World. Will our children witness justice, democracy, peace, equality and security for all the citizens in the Holy Land?

For Further Reading

Mary Eliza Rogers, *Domestic Life in Palestine.* London, 1862.

Haseeb Shehadeh, " "A Case of Palestinian Arab Justice between Minority and Majority: The Samaritan High Priest Salāma b. Ṣadaqa and the Arab Tailors of Nablus in the Nineteenth Century," *Samaritans – Past and Present: Current Studies,* edited by Menachem Mor and Friedrich V. Reiterer, Berlin: Walter de Gruyter, 2010, 205–220.

———

1   Abu Shafiq, 1960, 183-186.

لبني شمعون نسبتهم لقبائلهم لآل آبائهم لعدد الأسماء للجلاجلهم كل ذكر من ابن عشرين سنة فصاعدا كل خارج جيش احصاؤهم لسبط شمعون تسعة وخمسون الفا وثلاثمية

نولد ٭ ٭ ٭

لبني جاد نسبتهم لقبائلهم لآل آبائهم لعدد الأسماء من ابن عشرين سنة فصاعدا كل خارج جيش احصاؤهم لسبط جاد خمسة واربعين الفا وستمية وخمسون

نولد ٭ ٭ ٭ ٭ ٭ ٭ ٭

لبني يهوذا نسبتهم لقبائلهم لآل آبائهم لعدد الأسماء من ابن عشرين سنة فصاعدا كل خارج جيش احصاؤهم لسبط يهوذا اربعة وسبعون الفا وستمية

نولد ٭ ٭ ٭ ٭

لبني يساكر نسبتهم لقبائلهم لآل آبائهم لعدد الأسماء من ابن عشرين سنة فصاعدا كل خارج جيش احصاؤهم لسبط يساكر اربعة وخمسون الفا واربعمية

نولد ٭ ٭ ٭ ٭

لبني زبولن نسبتهم لقبائلهم لآل آبائهم لعدد الأسماء من ابن عشرين سنة فصاعدا كل خارج جيش احصاؤهم لسبط زبولن سبعة وخمسون الفا واربعمية

نولد ٭ ٭ ٭ ٭ عشرين سنة

14

"And We Shall Be One People": Abraham Firkovich, Karaism, and the Samaritans

GOLDA AKHIEZER

In these days a Jewish Karaite sage named Abraham came to the city of Shechem from the land of Russia, who stayed in the house of Jacob son of Sedaka ha-Danfi. He loved the Samaritans with a great love for their truthful [faith] in the Holy Torah, and every Shabbat he prayed in the synagogue with the Samaritans both in the evening and in the morning, and testified that there is no other truthful community that is so truthful. He suggested to Amram the Priest, our sage, that the Samaritans and the Karaites were one, the same people. Amram the Priest, our sage answered him: "There are huge differences between us and you concerning observance of the commandments of the Holy Torah. If you will become like us—accept the way of the five books of the Holy Torah—we will be one people." The sage Abraham answered him: "I will remember your words, I will return back to my country and gather all the elders of the Karaite tribe so I may speak these words in their ears, and we shall be one people."

— *New Chronicle*, 1900[1]

Samaritan chronicles were ever expanded over the one thousand years during which they were created, new generations adding memories to those already committed to writing by their ancestors. The so-called *New Chronicle* is the latest addition to the library, covering all of the Samaritan past up to the dawn of the twentieth century. The entry cited above tells of the Samaritan encounter with the Karaite scholar, public figure, and manuscript collector Abraham Firkovich. He made a strong impression, for the chronicle has the high priest Amram son of Salama (r. 1855–1874) refer to him as "the sage Abraham." Amram here invites the Karaites to take on Samaritan mores and join them. As a result, he promised, "we shall be one people."

Abraham son of Samuel Firkovich (1787–1874, Figure 14.1), was a leader of the Eastern European Karaite community, descendants of Jews who broke with what they called "Rabbinic Judaism" beginning at the end of the ninth century CE, the age of transition between Christian and Islamic cultural and political hegemony. The Karaites developed their own biblically focused brand of Judaism. Karaites, literally, the "scripturalists," (*benei* or *baalei mikra*), expe-

rienced a "Golden Age" in Jerusalem in the tenth and eleventh centuries. They established communities across Persia and the Eastern Mediterranean from the tenth century, and the Crimean Peninsula and northward into Poland during the thirteenth and fifteenth centuries. Karaite and Rabbanite Jews, and, in medieval Cairo, Samaritans, had lived side by side for centuries with greater or lesser degrees of interaction and amity. Today, the Karaite community in Israel numbers around 30,000 members, with their "world center" in Ramle. Smaller communities live in the Crimea, Lithuania, Poland, Russia, and the United States.

A native of Lutsk, Volhynia (today Ukraine), Firkovich settled permanently in Eupatoria, in the Crimea, in 1882. He first visited Palestine in 1830, acquiring numerous manuscripts. In 1834, he was appointed head of the Karaite publishing house, which under his management published numerous volumes of religious literature. Firkovich was deeply influenced by the *Haskalah*, the Jewish Enlightenment movement in the Eastern Europe.[2] He was well versed in the literature of the academic field of Jewish Studies and in the writings of modern Russian historians. Firkovich was an autodidact, who learned historical methods and modes of scholarly presentation from the scholars and activists of the Jewish *Haskalah* movement and from their writings. He cultivated friendly relationships with these scholars, who helped him to formulate his ideas and to publish them in Hebrew-language journals. Firkovich was accepted by the Russian authorities and some Karaite leaders as the Karaite voice within the project of the modernization and "enlightenment" of his community, representing himself among Jewish scholars as a guardian of the pan-Jewish project.

In his public life, Firkovich fought to obtain civil rights for the Karaite community within the Russian empire. He deployed a rhetoric of modern scholarship learned from *Haskalah* scholars toward this objective. Firkovich based his political program in a rhetoric of historicism, producing "historical facts" in support of Karaite emancipation—some of which he invented himself. Among the most significant, Firkovich strove to demonstrate that the Karaites had settled in the Crimea during the biblical period—well before the

© GOLDA AKHIEZER, 2022 | DOI:10.1163/9789004466913_016

14.2 Samaritan Pentateuch in Arabic Translation, with Section headings in Samaritan Hebrew, paper, fourteenth century, folio 133r, Numbers 1:21-32. Purchased from Jacob Shalaby, November 1883 (British Library, London, Or. 2688).

ⵣⵎⵇⵙⵡⵎⵣ

was active for another decade. Deinard, well known for his sharp tongue, winked toward more nefarious motives.

The *New Chronicle* provides details concerning Firkovich's contacts with the Samaritan community from their own perspective, including reactions to Firkovich's visit. From what we know of Firkovich, though, the talk about the unification of the two communities and the prayer together with Samaritans is quite plausible. The fact that the community leaders agreed to sell him such a large collection of manuscripts strengthens this proposition—even if these texts originated from the *genizah*, and so were of no real use. The manuscript collection obtained by Firkovich consisted of 1,341 items, a total of 18,250 pages, and a number of antiquities that were sold in 1870 for 9,500 rubles to the Russian Imperial Public Library in Saint Petersburg, today the National Library of Russia. This is the largest collection of Samaritan manuscripts in the world.[15]

Deinard wrote, correctly, that Samaritans and Karaites shared a number of similar laws and customs.[16] These include strict observance of the laws of ritual impurity, abstaining from all use of fire (today including electricity) on the Sabbath, and the sighting of the new moon. Unlike the Rabbanites, who abandoned this practice and switched to the calculation of their calendar before the emergence of Karaism, Karaites continued the ancient tradition of sanctifying the new moon to determine a new month on the basis of its direct observation. Deinard's claim about the direct historical relationship of Samaritans and the Karaites, however, is not based on documentary proof, but upon historic rabbinic categorization of the Karaites together with the *Kutim* (and the Sadducees) as biblical literalists who do not accept rabbinic tradition. This similarity is a result of some common views and practices typical of a number of Jewish groups, and not a result of historical kinship. Karaites rejected rabbinic "Oral Tradition" exemplified in the Talmud, while the Samaritans had split off already in biblical times. Both tended toward literary interpretations of Scripture. Similarities between Karaites and Samaritans were used by Firkovich to curry favor with Samaritan community members.

Firkovich attached great importance to the very existence of the Samaritans as a community that "rejected" rabbinic Judaism, and that maintained its own history, traditions, and literary sources. This was in spite of major differences in the interpretation of biblical law, calendrical systems, and customs, and in contradistinction to Samaritan self-identification and history. Firkovich sought to outline some common denominator and to express it in historical terms that would bring the Samaritans into his self-constructed Karaite historical narrative. Firkovich's innate intellectual curiosity and strong desire to purchase Samaritan manuscripts should be understood in the context of the nineteenth-century Jewish Enlightenment, the *Haskalah*. This movement, with its noticeable impact on Firkovich, stimulated an interest in the history of distinct Jewish communities. However, unlike contemporary research, like the Christian Hebraists discussed by Matthew Chalmers in this volume, and traditional Karaite authors, Firkovich conceived Jewish history (including Karaite history) only through the prism of the biblical text.

Firkovich's goal was to write a Karaite history that would be comprehensive and acceptable for Christians (disregarding factuality)—particularly for Roman Catholic and Orthodox scholars, with their strong focus on tradition. He presented both the Samaritans and the Karaites, as ancient Israelites, with nothing in common with the Pharisees/Rabbis. His approach aimed to promote the legal status of his community by creating a positive, even romantic image of the Karaites in the eyes of authorities, who were strongly antagonistic toward the Talmud. Firkovich presented the Karaites as a group that originated at the same period as the Samaritans. He thus linked the biblical tradition of the destruction of Samaria with a narrative of his own creation concerning the settlement of proto-Karaites in the Crimea. This counter-history supported the social goals and emancipation of the Karaites, whom Firkovich presented as the true Israel.

For Further Reading

Golda Akhiezer. "The Research Project of Abraham Firkovich as an Outcome of *Haskalah* and *Ḥokhmat Israel*." In *Studies in Caucasian, Georgian, and Bukharan Jewry: Historical, Sociological, and Cultural Aspects*, edited by Golda Akhiezer, Reuven Enoch, and Sergei Weinstein. Ariel: Ariel University: Institute for Research of Jewish Communities of the Caucasus and Central Asia, 2014, 38–71.

——. *Historical Consciousness, Haskalah, and Nationalism among the Karaites of Eastern Europe*. Leiden: Brill, 2018.

Dan Shapira. "From Our Exile to Shechem: Abraham Firkovich Visits the Samaritans." *Cathedra* 104 (2002): 85–94 [Hebrew].

Tapani Harviainen and Haseeb Shehadeh. "How Did Abraham Firkovich Acquired the Great Collection of Samaritan Manuscripts in Nablus in 1864?" *Studia Orientalia* 73 (1994): 167–192.

---

1   Eds. Adler and Séligsohn, 1900, 113–114.

2   On his biography, activities, and ideas, see Akhiezer, 2014, 131–180.

3   On the assembly of Firkovich's manuscript collections, see Elkin and Ben-Sasson 2002, 51–95.

4   Firkovich, "Remarks on the Sadducees and the Origins of Eastern European Karaites" (1850s), National Library of Russia (NLR), f. 946, op. 1, no. 387.

5   Firkovich, 1872, 77.

6   Abraham Firkovich, "Essay on Krymchak History," NLR, f. 946, op. 1, FA, no. 174.

7   See the detailed description of his visit by Harviainen and Shehadeh, 1994, 170–183.

8   Saint Petersburg, NLR, Firkovich's Private Archive (FPA), F. 946, no. 343, 605, 607, 608, 609.

9   Ibid., no. 609, 1r–2v.

10 Ibid., no. 605, 12r.

11 Ibid., no. 605, 11v–12r.

12 Harviainen and Shehadeh, 1994, 173, n. 28.

13 Cf. NLR, FPA, F 946, no. 589 and no. 697, 3v.

14 Deinard, 1875, 17–18.

15 See, about this collection, Lebedev, 1992, 12–20.

16 Deinard, 1875, 100–101.

15

Samaritans on the American Protestant Mind: William Barton, Edward K. Warren, and the American Samaritan Committee

YITZCHAK SCHWARTZ

The war made a sad break in our work for the Samaritans, and the death of Mr. Warren is for us a more serious matter. He was greatly interested in this work and his financial contributions far exceed all other sources of supply. I don't know if there is anything we can do for the Samaritans just now. During the first two years of the war we sent them help through Mr. [John] Whiting [a former American deputy consul in Jerusalem]. Unfortunately they quarreled with him. His report seems to indicate that their current need is self-reliance; a dependence upon their own exertions for support and an agreement among themselves as to their policy for the future.

Concerning the religion of the Samaritans, we have had this feeling. That we had no present call to force the hand of Providence. This little nation has been kept in existence for a very long time and it would be better for them to see in us a Christian spirit than that we should organize a campaign to proselyte them.

I am glad that they asked for your Arabic hymn book. It would be interesting to know that they are singing Christian hymns.

—Letter from Rev. William Eleazar Barton to Mr. Mortimore, June 14, 1920

In September of 1902, the Reverend William Eleazar Barton returned from a well-publicized steamship tour of Europe, North Africa, Egypt, and the Holy Land. Pastor of a large and prominent Congregationalist community in the Oak Park suburb of Chicago, Barton was an author of popular church literature and a future spiritual biographer of Abraham Lincoln. The cruise itinerary was, according to Barton, patterned on the journey undertaken by Mark Twain and described in Twain's 1867 *The Innocents Abroad*. Upon his return, Barton announced that he would soon publish a travel memoir of his own. The book, titled *The Old World in the New Century* (Boston, The Pilgrim Press, 1902), reads as a more religiously concerned version of Twain's. Barton takes a similar skeptical approach to the enterprise of tourism and to the peoples of the old world, and evinces a similarly wistful (if less humorous) perspec-

tive regarding the decline of ancient civilizations. Chicago newspapers mentioned Barton's forthcoming book in passing. They spoke at length, however, about a mysterious and exciting artifact that Barton had brought back from his travels: a Samaritan Pentateuch of purportedly ancient origins. Two years later, Barton published an English translation of the Samaritan Pentateuch based on his manuscript. Once again, Barton's book received passing mention in local newspapers, which, however, delighted in discussing Barton's Pentateuch manuscript.

The story Barton told, which was often somewhat embellished in newspapers, was as follows: on his visit to the Holy Land, he had sought out the Samaritans of Nablus and made the acquaintance of a leading priest, perhaps the high priest Jacob son of Aaron (Figure 15.1). Impressed by Barton's letter of introduction, the priest gave Barton the rare honor of a chance to see the Abisha Scroll, which was ascribed to Abisha the grandson of Aaron the high priest. The scroll is believed by Samaritans to be the most ancient copy of their Torah in the world, and it has generally been inaccessible to foreigners.

Outside the synagogue, Barton bought several small manuscripts produced by members of the community for sale to tourists. A young priest, noting Barton's interest, beckoned the minister away from the synagogue and into the adjoining courtyard of the high priest's home. There, they ascended a staircase to an upper room. The women of the priest's household realized what was about to transpire and, following the men, "made vehement protestations against what they judged he was about to do."[1] The priest succeeded in barring them from the room and bolted the door behind himself and Barton. From beneath the bed, the priest produced a large copy of the Samaritan Pentateuch in scroll form. The two men haggled for hours, the language barrier between them making negotiations very difficult. In the end, Barton secured a copy of the Samaritan Book of Genesis in a handsome tin case, a less precious replica of the sturdier brass case in which the older scroll was encased. The priest hid the case inside his flowing robes so as not to arouse the suspicion of his coreligionists and escorted Barton out of the compound as twilight descended on the city. Later newspaper accounts

© YITZCHAK SCHWARTZ, 2022 | DOI:10.1163/9789004466913_017

15.1 High Priest Jacob son of Aaron (reigned 1874–1916), with the Abisha Scroll, Magic Lantern Glass Slide, Brooklyn, Devereaux View Company, 1934 (Yeshiva University Museum).

would claim that Barton himself had secreted the manuscript out of the city beneath his coat.

To Barton's great joy, the next morning another young priest he had seen in the compound the day before approached the Americans' camp. He produced from beneath his robes the same scroll Barton had seen the day before. Barton would later claim this scroll to have been a copy of the Abisha Scroll itself. Barton and the priest reached an agreement on a price and Barton secreted his precious acquisition to Jerusalem, from whence he immediately sent it back to America.

Both upon his return, and, even more so, after he had published his translation, newspapers fixated on Barton's account of purchasing the Pentateuch. Many of them repeated the mistaken idea that Barton's copy was one of only twenty Samaritan Bibles in the world, although it was indeed a rare example of a Samaritan Torah scroll. Others proclaimed the Samaritan tenth commandment, which states that worship shall be eternally centered on Mount Gerizim, to be a new discovery made via Barton's manuscript. *The Chicago Tribune* proclaimed in a headline that "Chicagoan finds new Bible

verse." Several other newspapers similarly depicted the Samaritan Pentateuch as uncharted territory being explored by Barton, reframing Barton's story as a quest to discover the true location where God had commanded Moses to erect His altar. Another headline declared that Barton's discovery "ends a biblical dispute" and proved that the Temple was meant to be built on Mount Gerizim, as the Samaritan woman at the well had told Jesus.

Barton's visit to the Samaritans was, like his itinerary more generally, probably inspired by Twain's visit thirty-three years earlier. In fact, when Barton brought his manuscript home to Chicago, he tried to ascertain whether there were any other such manuscripts in the United States, and he corresponded with Twain:

After my return from Palestine, I chanced to notice in *Innocents Abroad* a sentence which stated that Mark Twain when there had procured from the high priest of this ancient Samaritan community, "at great expense, a sacred document of great antiquity and extraordinary interest," which, said Mark Twain, "I propose to publish as soon as I have finished translating it." Wondering if Mr. Clemens [Twain's birth name] had any

YITZCHAK SCHWARTZ

experience similar to my own, I wrote to him, asking him whether he also had a Samaritan Pentateuch, and have received his reply, stating that he had not seen a copy of *Innocents Abroad* for many years, and that all recollection of buying the manuscript referred to has entirely passed from his mind. I presume that what he bought was some of the smaller souvenirs, as he could hardly have forgotten a purchase like mine.[2]

Twain's account was influential in establishing the Samaritans as a staple stop along the American tourist route of the Holy Land. It also likely set a precedent for tourists visiting Nablus to purchase a Samaritan manuscript (Figure 15.2).

The stories told by Barton and Twain are examples of a genre of Samaritan tales popularized by mostly Protestant missionaries, researchers, and would-be explorers during the early twentieth century. Paralleling well-worn Orientalist tropes, these stories always involved Western, usually Protestant, men who make the perilous adventure to Nablus, where the leaders of the long-suffering Samaritan people entrust them with the purchase of sacred and rare manuscripts. The Samaritans in these stories bear motives that are often depicted as a mixture of financial desperation and greed and, in some cases, the desire that these Westerners will spread knowledge about Samaritan culture and belief. Some, but not all, of these authors evince the hope expressed by Barton's correspondent Mr. Mortimore in the letter transcribed at the beginning of this article, which was to convert what they saw as the unchanged-since-ancient-times Samaritan community to Christianity. And even Barton himself implied to Mortimore that "the hand of providence" would eventually have that result. The significance of the purchased manuscripts is often overstated in stories of this type. As Barton found out through correspondence in 1903, the New York Public Library owned two Samaritan Bible codices (Figure 3.3). The genre of which Twain's and Barton's accounts of Samaritan life are an example reflects antiquarian more than academic concerns.

Since the Renaissance, scholars have taken interest in the Samaritans in sporadic waves. Until the late-nineteenth century, these scholars were primarily interested in the Samaritan Pentateuch. As Mathew Chalmers discusses in this volume, this tradition began with Joseph Scaliger and continued on and off until the early nineteenth century. By that time, scholars came to a consensus that the Samaritan Pentateuch dated to a later period than the Masoretic text. To nineteenth-century scholars searching to recreate the original biblical text, this rendered the Samaritan Pentateuch of little value.

Shortly after the interest of textual scholars in the Samaritans had waned, however, the Samaritans became a focus of popular anthropological and religious interest. As steamships began to afford the middle class the means of traveling the world, the Samaritans became a staple stop on the tourist route for young bourgeois men and Christian pilgrims touring through Ottoman Palestine. In his travel book, Barton notes that the low cost and extravagant accommodations aboard his own cruise would have been impossible a generation earlier when Twain had taken the first cruise through the old world.

Tourist interest in the Samaritans was such that it spawned a new genre of Samaritan artifacts by the early twentieth century, namely

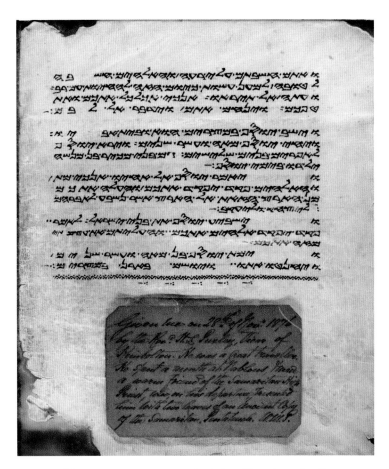

15.2 Leaf from a Samaritan Pentateuch Codex (Genesis 50:7b-26), probably Nablus, 12th century, procured by a Western visitor to Nablus. (Collection of Roger Harrison, Photograph Courtesy of Sotheby's, New York). The later label reads:

Given me on the 28th of Nov[ember] 1876 by the Rev[erand]. H[erbert] L[avallin] Puxley Vicar of Kimbolton [d. 1906]. He was a great traveler. He spent a month at Nablous, and made a warm friend of the Samaritan High Priest, who, on his departure, presented him with two leaves of an ancient copy of the Samaritan Pentateuch. W. M. P[uxley?].

Samaritan manuscripts and items produced explicitly for sale to visitors. In addition to the large tin Torah case, Barton brought home a miniature scroll contained in a small case that is an example of such an item. The miniature Samaritan scroll in the Temple Emanuel collection is an almost identical example of this genre of tourist scroll. Many manuscripts in codex form were also produced for the tourist trade, often containing one or another biblical book instead of the full Bible codices used within the Samaritan community. Drawings of the layout of the Tabernacle were also widely sold to visitors to the Samaritan community, and are found together in many collections, including Barton's, which is now archived at Boston University. In the United States, the Herbert Lehman collection of Temple Emanuel in New York (Figure 0.8), the Jewish Theological Seminary collection, and the Hebrew Union College collection also contain such drawings in addition to Samaritan manuscripts. This touristic interest meant that Samaritan manuscripts became a popular gift for libraries across America, and some of these were very significant. In a letter between the two men, the Samaritan high priest Jacob son of Aaron requested that Barton put him in touch with anyone who might want to purchase a Samaritan manuscript, as long as Barton would serve as intermediary:

> Therefore I dared to … ask you if any should ask about books of our law of our prayers I should be only willing to send them on to you. … I am willing to copy any of our books to any one that wishes to buy them, whether in Arabic or Hebrew. (Jacob son of Aaron to Barton, September 26, 1904)

Barton thus became a go-between for American individuals and institutions who wished to visit the Samaritans or purchase manuscripts from them. He also frequently lectured about the Samaritans and the Samaritan Pentateuch at venues such as the Chicago Society of Biblical Research.

To such tourists, Samaritans were of interest as a link to the religion of ancient Israel. They also became, during a period in which social Darwinist racial science was gaining popularity, important as racial specimens (Figure 15.3). An excellent example of the racial type of interest in the Samaritans is the article entitled "Samaritans: Anthropology," based on fieldwork carried out a young Harvard scholar named Henry M. Huxley, that appeared in the highly influential *The Jewish Encyclopedia* in 1905.[3] In it Huxley endeavors to locate the Samaritan race in relation to the Jews. He argues that they bear similarities to Jews and that they were indeed the only "pure" example of the ancient Jewish race but that they were, however, a "degenerate" version of that type:

> The pigmentation of the Samaritans, as indicated by the color of the hair and eyes, is shown in the following tables. …

> These tables make it clear that the Samaritans are by no means an exclusively brunette type. As seen by the presence of blue eyes and light hair or beards in a considerable percentage of the individuals examined, there is, on the contrary, a distinct blond type noticeable in the group.

> The general type of physiognomy of the Samaritans is distinctly Jewish, the nose markedly so. Von Luschan derives the Jews from "the Hittites, the Aryan Amorites, and the Semitic nomads." The Samaritans may be traced to the same origin. The Amorites were "men of great stature"; and to them Von Luschan traces the blonds of the modern Jews. With still greater certainty the tall stature and the presence of a blond type among the Samaritans may be referred to the same source.

> The cephalic [head size] index, much lower than that of the modern Jews, may be accounted for by a former direct influence of the Semitic nomads, now represented by the Bedouins, whose cephalic index, according to measurements of 114 males, is 76.3. The Samaritans have thus preserved the ancient type in its purity; and they are to-day the sole, though degenerate, representatives of the ancient Hebrews.

This text betrays a distinct prejudice against both Jews and Samaritans, ascribing greater "purity" to the Samaritans but also designating them as "degenerate," in addition to asserting Samaritan antiquity over Jewish claims. Surprising as that may seem, this is not the only place where anti-Jewish racial prejudice found its way into *The Jewish Encyclopedia*. Other examples include a supposed Jewish proclivity against art and the supposed prevalence of color-blindness among Jewish males.

The *Jewish Encyclopedia* article shows an interest in the Samaritans that was also expressed in Jewish tourist literature. Isaac Mayer Wise's *American Israelite* and other contemporary American Jewish newspapers published excerpts of travel accounts every few years that discussed the Samaritans. In Zionist travelogues of Eretz Israel, which were often intended to inspire European and American Jewish youth to immigrate to Palestine, the Samaritans were a common feature. David Ben-Gurion and Izhak Ben-Zvi's Yiddish language touring guide, *Erets Yisroel in Fergangenheyt un Gegenvart* (*The Land of Israel in the Past and the Present*; New York, 1918), approaches the Samaritans in a way that would later become a centerpiece of Ben-Zvi's research on this group and activism on their behalf. The authors describe the Samaritans in the course of their description of Shechem, noting that the Samaritans "live in their own little quarter of the city, which is called Haarat A-Samara, along the path that leads to their holy precinct on Mt Gerizim."[4] Ben-Zvi and Ben-Gurion (later Israel's founding Prime Minister) depict the Samaritans as both distinct from the Jewish people but also as part of their story. In this vein, they devote several pages to the history of the Samaritans, emphasizing that they, like the Jews, had tenaciously fought to remain in the Holy Land, describing the Samaritan wars against the Byzantines in heroic terms. They conclude their account of these bloody wars by noting that, despite the persecutions enacted by the Byzantines after the revolts,

> they were never completely exterminated, despite all of the attempts at doing so, and until today one finds the beloved and stubborn devotees of Mount Gerizim at the foot of their Holy Mountain in their old native city upholding the customs and the cult of more than two and a half thousand years ago.[5]

Like the *Jewish Encyclopedia*, the Protestant iteration of this wave of popular interest in the Samaritans often echoed anti-Semitic tropes. Protestant scholars who saw Samaritan practice as indicative of ancient Judaism prior to the Pharisaic "deformation" of the biblical religion were following a well-traveled trail of depriving the Jews of their day the honor bestowed by their ethnonym. Some members of the British Israelite movement, which claimed Israelite descent for the British, saw Samaritans as their kin but considered Jews to be imposters. Nineteenth-century European antiquarians had suggested that the Samaritans were descendants of the true Jews while European Jews were simply Khazars, an almost mythical Central Asian people who, according to legend, converted to Judaism during the eighth and ninth centuries CE. One newspaper proclaimed in its headline that Barton's discovery "affects Jewish belief."

"The Samaritans of
Nablus (Shechem).
Samaritan Youth,
Profile,": Amram son
of the High priest
Isaac, Matzliaḥ son of
Pinḥas, Ab-Ḥisda son
of the High Priest Jacob.
American Colony Pho-
tographic Department,
ca. 1914 (G. Eric and
Edith Matson Pho-
tograph Collection,
Library of Congress).

15.4 Girls Taught by the Priest Amram son of Isaac son of Amram in the School Founded by Charles Warren, Nablus. (American Colony Photographic Department, ca. 1914 (G. Eric and Edith Matson Photograph Collection, Library of Congress).

Barton never endorsed the sensational claims made by newspapers. He did errantly believe, however, that a Samaritan chronicle text that he had brought back containing the narrative of Jesus's life (a text discussed by R. Steven Notley and Jeffrey Garcia in this volume) was an independent witness to the New Testament. It was this Christian angle that motivated Barton and the Michigan industrialist Edward Kirk Warren to found a committee dedicated to aiding the Samaritans of Nablus in 1913. Over the next decade and a half, Barton would advise Warren on the acquisition of several important Samaritan artifacts. Robert T. Anderson suggests that Warren retained hope throughout his life that more Samaritan documents might be uncovered that would further corroborate New Testament narratives.

"The American Samaritan Committee," as Warren and Barton's project was called, hoped to support Samaritan purchase of land for a new, protected neighborhood in Nablus, to purchase the Samar-

itan holy precinct on Mount Gerizim, and to found a school where young Samaritans could receive a modern education (Figure 15.4). Fundraising ads for the committee were placed in various Christian publications, often including photographs of Samaritan life. This project was part and parcel of Protestant missionary activity directed toward Jews and Arabs in the Holy Land, though the American Samaritan Committee was ambivalent about outright proselytization, as noted above. This ambivalence may have been the result of Barton and Warren's fascination with the Samaritans as biblical relics to be preserved. Protestant missionaries sometimes expressed these attitudes toward Jews as well for similar reasons.

For his own part, Barton developed a relationship with Jacob son of Aaron, becoming the last Westerner to conduct an extensive correspondence with the Samaritan community by post, a tradition traced elsewhere in this volume. These letters contain a discussion of Samaritan history and practice as well as of practical matters relating to Barton's fundraising on behalf of the community and its internal affairs. After speaking at a World Sunday School Convention in Jerusalem at Barton's behest, Jacob wrote to Barton regarding the Chamberlain Warren Torah scroll case, which Warren's agent from the American Colony had apparently not yet fully paid for. He enclosed a copy of a manuscript he had written about Samaritan history that is now in the Barton Collection at Boston University:

> I had decided to send you a copy of our history, which is well translated in Hebrew. If you should have it printed in the Arabic and English languages, (I should like) that you send us a part of the edition … I searched for three years for material for this history. (Jacob son of Aaron to Barton, September 26, 1904)

Barton went on to commission several original works from Jacob. Several of these remain unpublished, but a few were, with an introduction by Barton, and can be found in libraries around the country.

In their attempts to raise money for the Samaritan community, Barton and Warren relied on the fact that the image of the Samaritans was by this time firmly engraved in the religious and visual culture of the West. The New Testament account of the Samaritan woman at the well was a key symbol of the new covenant (in which Christians would worship neither on Gerizim "nor in Jerusalem"). And the Parable of the Good Samaritan was a staple of popular visual culture, a symbol of Christian charity. In liberal nineteenth-century Protestant circles, the Good Samaritan had a further significance as a symbol of ecumenism and tolerance, key nineteenth-century liberal values. Hospitals, at the time generally charitable institutions, often included "Good Samaritan" in their name.

With the popularization of travel and photography, Samaritans also became a part of the visual culture of the tourism industry. Like other exotic communities, they were featured in stereoscope photographs intended to serve as both signifiers of worldliness in middle-class parlors and conversation starters for those who had taken a trip to meet them. The most important collection of photographs of Samaritans, which circulated around the Western world, was taken by the American Colony photographers beginning in 1914 (Figures 05, 1.8, 12.2, 15.3-5, 18.3, 4). The photographs in the collection were not simply photographs of Samaritan life, as they are often assumed to be, but examples of a type of ethnographic portrait common at the time. The subjects' positions and the staging of the photographs resemble, for example, those of well-known ethnographic photographers such as Edward S. Curtis, who worked on the cultures of Native Americans. Often set at biblical sites such as Jacob's Well and Joseph's Tomb, they were intended to portray both the greatness of the Samaritans' biblical past as well as their impoverishment in the present in the same tragic mode adopted by Twain and Warren. Photographs at this time were often taken at angles (i.e., profiles) that were commonly used by ethnographers to classify racial types. Jacob son of Aaron, who became an admired figure among Westerners with interest in the Samaritans, was a frequent subject of these portraits, a handsome man whose Middle Eastern features and luxuriant beard made his image a compelling feature in Western newspapers and magazines. The Samaritan Passover sacrifice also became a focus for ethnographic photographers and remains so to this day.

Barton and Warren believed that they could use this interest in the Samaritans as part of their efforts to raise money for the community. To this end, they commissioned an American Colony photographer to take a series of photographs of the Abisha Scroll (Figures 15.5) with the intention that the resulting images could be a resource for libraries and universities. An important textual scholar at the time identified the scroll in the photographs as a later copy of the Abisha Scroll rather than the original, and so this plan of Barton and Warren's ultimately failed.

It is unclear what plans Barton and Warren had for the artifacts they gathered. It seems from correspondence exchanged between Barton and Frederick W. Chamberlain, Warren's executor and brother-in-law, after Warren's death, that Warren had planned to exhibit these artifacts in a museum in Nablus geared toward raising money to help support the Samaritan community. When Chamberlain and Barton later determined that there were not enough funds in the American Samaritan Committee's coffers to fund such a museum, they feared that any artifacts remaining in the Holy Land might be claimed by the Samaritan community. To avoid losing the artifacts, they brought them back to the United States. The Samaritan community tried to have the artifacts returned, citing Warren's plans, but Barton and Chamberlain decided that the objects would be better preserved in an American institution. They were subsequently displayed for some time in the Warren family museum, but in 1950 the Warren family closed the museum, and the Samaritan items were given to Michigan State University in Lansing. According to the late Michigan State Professor of Bible Robert T. Anderson, "the materials, with the exception of a brass scroll case and several modern paper scrolls, were placed in cardboard boxes in a storage area under the bleachers of the football stadium until a renovation of the area led to their rediscovery." This discovery was made by Anderson in 1968.[6]

The Samaritan community seems to have appreciated the support of Barton and Warren's committee but wanted to be more involved in administering the funds collected and the manuscripts purchased. Samaritan high priest Jacob son of Aaron wrote the text for several of the committee's circulars and ads placed in Christian publications. In one such undated circular, he appeals to his American readers to help the Samaritans fulfill the biblical obligation of "Keep therefore the words of this covenant," a savvy choice of verses for an audience who saw the Samaritans as a link to a preserved biblical past.

With Warren's death in 1919, and the end of World War I, Barton's interest in the Samaritans waned. The next year, he and Chamberlain decided to cease the American Samaritan Committee's operations (though they never formally disbanded it) and distributed its small reserves to the community for its own use. This came precisely at the moment when the Samaritan community, decimated from the wartime draft and the scarcity of the war years, needed help most. The decline of American interest in the Samaritans at

15.5 "Details of the Oldest Scroll," American Colony Photographic Department, ca. 1914, (G. Eric and Edith Matson Photograph Collection, Library of Congress).

this time may have been in a large measure to the popularization of James Montgomery's thesis in his classic 1907 history of the Samaritans that the latter were merely a sect of the Jews that had broken away during the Second Temple period rather than the scions of the ten tribes.[7] By implication, this meant that there was very little the Samaritans could tell American Christians about the true nature of Judaism or of Christianity's roots.

As biblical scholar James Purvis notes in a 1969 article about the Barton Collection, the tone Barton and Warren took to the Samaritans after World War I became increasingly patronizing and condescending. During the war, the American Samaritan Committee learned that the school it had funded had been closed and that copies of the photographs of the Abisha Scroll taken by John Whiting of the American Colony had never been given to the community as promised. Members of the Samaritan community claimed that Whiting, who also served as the Committee's "feet on the ground" in Palestine, had led the Samaritans to believe that the Colony or Committee would support them during the hardships of the war years in exchange for the photographs. In a letter to Warren's son, Barton voiced frustration with Whiting but more so with the Samaritans:

My own present judgement would be that not too much attention should be paid to it [the Samaritans' claims against Whiting]. They are a childish people, with a covetousness and quarrelsomeness in their childhood and much has been done in recent months to stir up all manner of misunderstanding and bitterness. I do not wonder that Mr. Whiting is out of patience with them. (Letter from Barton to Paul C. Warren, March 13, 1919)

Samaritan claims that Warren's agent had not paid them in full for several manuscripts, including the Chamberlain-Warren Pentateuch, as well as their desire to keep Warren's artifacts in Nablus, went unheeded. Writing to Warren's son, Barton said that he doubted Warren had left any outstanding debts and that they could perhaps give the community a small amount as a final payment. "Nevertheless," he wrote,

I cannot help thinking that it would be better to bring that manuscript to this country and hold it until its future can be secured. If the Samaritans under claim of amount due on it [sic] should recover it they would quickly mortgage or sell it again. (Letter from Barton to Paul C. Warren, June 2, 1919)

YITZCHAK SCHWARTZ

In June 1920, the Committee met and resolved that it would not try to reopen the school and that:

> the hope of Mr. Warren that a Museum might be established at Nablus and a tract of land purchased for the Samaritan Committee appeared to the committee to be matters which the changes brought by the war had put well out of the foreground of probable events. (Minutes of the American Samaritan Committee, June 10, 1920)

In 1922, a group of leaders of the Samaritan community, including the new high priest, Isaac son of Amram, sent a letter via the English governor of the Nablus subdistrict to the treasurer of the American Samaritan Committee asking that they be returned. They made special mention of the ancient Pentateuch manuscript. Barton insisted that the Samaritan claims had no merit, writing that after the war the Committee had tried to continue to help the Samaritans. Whiting had, however, been "so disappointed in their reception of aid that it did not seem practicable to go forward with anything more than the completion of the undertakings commenced in Mr. Warren's life." When the Committee sent a token sum in an effort to settle the dispute, the governor wrote back that the community had refused to accept it.

In the early twentieth century, American popular writers and educators like Barton hoped the Samaritans would answer their questions about biblical Israelite religion. They and their rituals, and to a large degree their racial makeup, were described as "unchanged." For most American Christians, however, the Samaritans remained an abstract concept, protagonists of biblical stories or the namesakes of hospitals and charities, rather than a modern people. The American Samaritan Committee's efforts and similar efforts to raise funds for the Samaritans combined both of these perspectives. Barton seems to have ultimately been unable to come to terms with modern Samaritans being more than just objects of fascination and ethnography.

For Further Reading

Robert T. Anderson. "The Museum Trail: The Michigan State University Samaritan Collection." *The Biblical Archaeologist* 47, no. 1 (1984): 41–43.

William E. Barton. *The Old World in the New Century*. Chicago: The Pilgrim Press, 1902.

James A. Montgomery. *The Samaritans, the Earliest Jewish Sect, Their History, Theology and Literature*. Philadelphia: J.C. Winston, 1907.

James D. Purvis. "Studies on Samaritan Materials in the W.E. Barton Collection in the Boston University Library." *World Congress of Jewish Studies* 1 (1969): 134–143.

---

1   Barton, 1902, 208.

2   Ibid., 211.

3   10: 674–676.

4   Ben-Gurion and Ben-Zvi, 1918, 284.

5   Ibid., 283.

6   Anderson, 1984, 41.

7   Montgomery, 1907, 46–57.

16
"Joined at Last":
Moses Gaster and the Samaritans

KATHARINA E. KEIM

"And thou, son of man, take thee one stick, and write upon it, For Judah and for the children of Israel his companions: then take another stick, and write upon it, For Judah and for the children of Israel his companions: then take another stick, and write up on it, For Joseph, the stick of Ephraim, and for all the house of Israel his companions: join them for thee one to another into one stick, that they may become one in thy hand" (Ezek. xxxvii 16, 17). Some twenty-five years ago I gripped the stick of Joseph which is in the hand of Ephraim; and, little thinking what may be the outcome, I have endeavored during all these years to read the legend written upon it. Without fear and without favour, without historical prejudice or religious bias, I have tried to obtain a sympathetic understanding of the inner life and religious practices of the solitary remnant of the Ancient House of Israel. I did not formulate a theory, nor did I try to fit conclusions to preconceived notions. I did not allow myself to be swayed by the opinion of others, or my judgment warped by miss placed [sic] partiality. I went boldly on my quest. I travelled along untrodden paths. I have wandered through many an arid place, my only guide the meager writings still preserved by the Samaritans. I have scanned them with keen interest undeterred by their monotony and wearisomeness. As I arrived at the end of my journey, I became aware of the stick of Judah, which had meanwhile been pressed into my hands and that in my hands they became joined at last.

— Moses Gaster, 1925[1]

So wrote Moses Gaster in the preface to his 1925 volume, the product of his prestigious Schweich Lectures at the British Academy in London two years earlier. A towering figure in the modern study of ancient Judaism, Gaster was unique in his focus upon people and thus their texts—and not the other way around. A folklorist by training and by avocation, a rabbi, a communal leader, an early Zionist leader, a collector, and a public figure, Gaster took the "long way" to get to Samaritan Studies. Moses Gaster was born into a well-established acculturated Jewish family in Bucharest, Romania, in 1856. He received both a religious and a secular education and moved to Germany in 1873 to pursue a doctorate in Romanian phi-lology at the University of Breslau, which he completed at the University of Leipzig in 1877. There he became a renowned expert in the folklore of his native Romania. Gaster then obtained rabbinical ordination at the famous Jewish Theological Seminary in Breslau in 1881. Gaster was trained in the *Wissenschaft des Judentums* ("Science of Judaism") movement, a modernizing "scientific" approach to Jewish history, literature, theology, and philosophy using modern research methods that engaged with related academic disciplines. German Jewish scholarship at this time was highly philological, an approach that prepared Gaster for his larger project of bringing together the methods of *Wissenschaft* with his deep interest in people.

Gaster returned to Romania in 1881, teaching the Romanian language at the University of Bucharest. A fervent Romanian royalist, he agitated for Jewish emancipation and was an avid Zionist. As a result of his Jewish activities, he was expelled from Romania in 1885.[2] Gaster migrated to London, and in 1887 became the ḥakham, the rabbi, of the Sephardic community. He was a passionate educator, teaching Slavonic literature at Oxford in 1886 and serving as Principal of Lady Judith Montifiore College, a rabbinical college located in Ramsgate (1889–1896).[3]

Gaster's deep training in folklore was unique among Jewish scholars at this time. It accounts for his polymathic interest in all things Jewish. This interest corresponds with the identification of Jews as a national group in the Austro-Hungarian sphere, and not merely as a religious community on the German model. Gaster was an acolyte of the cultural approach to Zionism, whose leader, Ahad Ha'am (Asher Ginzberg), appealed for Jews to support the Samaritans as part of the national project. It is not inconsequential that Gaster named his son Theodor Herzl Gaster, or that the Balfour Declaration was composed in his salon. Gaster published pioneering studies that ranged from biblical subjects to Jewish legends, ancient magic, and even Samaritan script on ancient Jewish coins seen by medieval rabbis! This breadth accounts, in part, for his polemic, cited above, against "preconceived notions" among primarily Christian scholars regarding the antiquity of the Samaritans. It certainly explains his emphasis upon "a *sympathetic* understanding of the inner life and

© KATHARINA E. KEIM, 2022 | DOI:10.1163/9789004466913_018

religious practices of the solitary remnant of the Ancient House of Israel." Gaster was part of a small group of Zionist scholars who took a real and very human interest in the Samaritans—eventually weaving them into the Zionist narrative of return and ensuring their survival. Gaster's scholarship in Samaritan Studies has not been adequately considered, a situation that was not helped by his personal tendency to exaggerate his claims for the early dates of manuscripts and for the importance of his discoveries.

THE BEGINNINGS OF GASTER'S RELATIONSHIP WITH THE SAMARITANS

Moses Gaster's interest in the Samaritans predated his relationship with the community. He began publishing research in Samaritan Studies in 1900, with further articles appearing in years following that demonstrate his interest in the study of the Samaritan Pentateuch. Gaster began exchanging letters with the Nablus Samaritan community in around 1902 (if not before). The earliest letters are mostly lost, although some remain scattered among his scrapbooks and ephemera. Those that remain show the tentative beginnings of what was to become an intense correspondence with several generations of Samaritan priests over three decades. Years later, Gaster wrote with evident glee at meeting Samaritans face to face:

> At the beginning of the century four Samaritan priests came to pay me a visit. They showed me a wonderful old handwritten Bible on parchment and were not a little surprised when I flipped through the leaves to find the cryptogram indicating the date and name of the scribe. Seeing this they realized that I was somewhat familiar with Samaritan literature. We became friends, and this friendship has lasted over thirty years until today. I remain in contact with them, and have a large collection of letters we exchanged.[4]

Gaster's first in-person meeting with a Samaritan probably took place in the autumn of 1906, when the Samaritan priest Isaac son of Amram came to Gaster's home. The visit was reported in an article for the *Tribune* newspaper on November 25, 1906, headlined "Samaritans in London—Ancient Scroll for Sale." There was indeed a scroll for sale—a copy of the Abisha Scroll that was being offered by the Samaritan delegation for the enormous sum of £5,000. It was presented to the major collectors of the day for consideration—the British Museum, David Solomon Sassoon, and James Rothschild, but as far as I know it was not successfully sold. Nevertheless, Gaster and Isaac met several times over the months that Isaac was in London. The keepsakes in one of Gaster's scrapbooks show that Isaac tutored Gaster in Samaritan Hebrew, including pronunciation and script, teaching him the names of the letters of the Samaritan alphabet and to read aloud using the text of the early chapters of Genesis written in Samaritan Hebrew in Isaac's hand. Gaster annotated the manuscript with careful notes of the pronunciation of the text alongside other annotations in Hebrew and English to record details of these reading exercises.[5]

16.1 "Picture of Leading Samaritans from the second half of the nineteenth century," before 1874, labeled at the request of Gaster. Right to left, as identified by "Abisha the priest" son of Pinḥas at Gaster's request: "Isaac the Priest" [son of Amram], "Jacob the Priest" [son of Aaron, high priest 1874–1916], and "Pinḥas the Priest." The girl is identified as "Jacob's daughter," and by Benyamim Tsedaka as "Mariam, daughter of Jacob the Priest" (after Gaster, 1925, pl. 16).

GASTER'S SAMARITAN CORRESPONDENCE

Gaster only met Samaritans a few times in person, including during the Samaritan delegation's visit to London in 1906 and then when he visited Nablus in 1907. About five hundred letters between them survive. They are held at the John Rylands Library in Manchester, England. Gaster's letters are part of a European tradition of correspondence with the Samaritans that goes back to the first purchases of Samaritan manuscripts by European Orientalists in the sixteenth and seventeenth centuries, which was intensified around the turn of the twentieth century. American Protestant William Barton, discussed by Yitzchak Schwartz in this volume, corresponded with Jacob son of Aaron at about the same time.

Gaster's correspondence affords us a detailed picture of Samaritan life during the early twentieth century. Unique among modern missives, his letters with Isaac son of Jacob and the high priest Jacob son of Aaron (Figures 16.1, 3) were almost always conducted in a kind of biblicized Hebrew, a language that was comprehensible to both Gaster and his Samaritan interlocutors. This was no different than correspondence between Jews across linguistic barriers going back to the Middle Ages, which was carried out in a mix of Biblical and Talmudic Hebrew and Aramaic. Here, though, script was also an impediment to be overcome.

Samaritan writers sent Gaster handwritten letters in Samaritan Hebrew script on scraps of paper that were left over from the writing of manuscripts and other documents. Upon their arrival in London, these were transcribed into Jewish square script by Gaster and his assistants—often his own children, his wife, or recent Jewish immigrants. Gaster's replies were typed on a typewriter that he had converted to printing a Samaritan letter type of his own design (now at New York University, Figure 16.3). He later described this typewriter with considerable satisfaction:

> At this point you may be interested to learn that I created the first typewriter with Hebrew characters. I then had Samaritan letters cut to my specification and had the Samaritan letters put onto the typewriter in place of the upper case, so that I would have both alphabets together: with the upper case I write to the Samaritans in their script, while with the help of the lower case I transcribe Samaritan letters and writings.[6]

Carbon copies of Gaster's typed letters remain part of the Manchester archive, allowing us to see both sides of the conversation, a vital tool to the scholar of Gaster's Samaritan collections. The Samaritans preferred to receive letters in Samaritan script, as they were not fluent in the Jewish script. Gaster's typewriter allowed anyone to type easily in Samaritan script so long as they could read the square script printed on the keys. This overcame the challenge of recruiting assistants with an easy working knowledge of Samaritan Hebrew to whom Gaster could dictate his letters. Writing back and forth in Hebrew, by scholars who shared a sacred text and religious proclivities, allowed a level of intimacy between Gaster and his Samaritan correspondents. These were not shared with Barton and other Christian correspondents, who worked from translations and brought their Christian, often missionary and always condescending, baggage with them.

Gaster's Samaritan manuscripts and ephemera were procured mostly through this correspondence. His was a working collection, providing the raw materials for research. Gaster would generally inquire about texts held in the libraries of various priests and would in response receive lists of manuscripts along with the prices of copies. The precious originals were rarely for sale, since facsimiles provided Samaritans with vital income. The prices Gaster paid were considerably less expensive than the sums paid for by collectors like Sassoon for prize medieval manuscripts. Gaster would negotiate intensely over even two or three pounds. Both he and the Samaritans used whatever methods they could to reach the best possible prices.

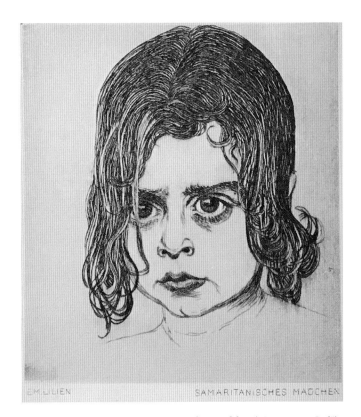

16.2 Ephraim Moses Lilien, *Samaritanisches Madchen* ("Samaritan Girl"). Mariam, daughter of the High Priest Jacob, photographed ca. 1870. Postcard. Berlin: Verlag von B. Marx, after 1907 (Collection of Leah and Steven Fine, New York).

So, for example, while the argument over the price to be paid for the production of manuscripts continued, Gaster was often asked to donate to Samaritan causes, such as the building of a school. The Samaritans often requested paper upon which to write Gaster's copies. These were returned by post in one go or in batches as they were completed. The correspondence thus reveals the source of the European paper upon which Samaritan manuscripts were copied, and gives us further insight into the process by which the Samaritans prepared, copied, and bound the manuscripts into quires or full codices in red leather. The manuscripts, sent to Gaster in installments, were bound in cloth and board covers in London. These letters provide a wealth of information about how Gaster commissioned and evaluated manuscripts of a variety of Samaritan texts, including treatises on law and tradition, answers to Gaster's lists of questions, liturgical texts, calendars, and marriage documents.

Gaster purchased and commissioned a number of Samaritan Pentateuch manuscripts. These include two Samaritan Pentateuch manuscripts written in parallel columns together with the Masoretic text.[7] A number of bilingual Samaritan–Arabic copies of the Samaritan Pentateuch, a trilingual Samaritan Pentateuch written in Samaritan Hebrew, Samaritan Aramaic, and Arabic in parallel columns. Gaster purchased a number of manuscripts of liturgical works, including a collection of liturgical texts in a manuscript that Gaster asked the Samaritan Priest Isaac son of Amram to perform aloud so that Gaster could record his voice using a phonograph.[8]

The recordings are now in the special collections of the Brotherton Library in Leeds, although whether they will be playable is uncertain: according to Gaster's son Theodor Herzl Gaster, the recordings sounded like "nothing on earth" when he heard them.

Annotations written on these manuscripts by Gaster indicate that he sought guidance from Isaac for the liturgical performance of ritual texts, especially service directions and liturgical responses. He made notes of the names of prayers and hymns in English and in Hebrew, and wrote marginal notes giving observations based on comparison of the two manuscripts. Gaster collected over forty manuscripts of liturgical texts, prayers, and hymns copied for him by a number of Samaritan priests, including Isaac, his son Pinḥas, and his grandson Abisha, over the course of thirty years. He also bought no less than five Samaritan Tabernacle drawings that were sent to him from Nablus. The drawings, discussed by Reinhard Pummer in this volume, are of varying size and produced with a range of materials including black and colored inks, wax crayons, colored pencils, and a paint used to simulate the effect of gold (Figures 0.8. 2.4, 13.2). Some are without annotation, some have annotations in Samaritan Hebrew, and one particularly vivid example is annotated both in Samaritan Hebrew and in English.

THE SAMARITAN BOOK OF JOSHUA

The Samaritan text that was of greatest interest to Gaster was the Samaritan Book of Joshua. This is not to be confused with the biblical Book of Joshua preserved by Jews. It is a uniquely Samaritan retelling of the entry of the Children of Israel into the Promised Land. Gaster saw Joshua son of Nun as a meeting point between Jewish and Samaritan tradition and believed that the Jewish biblical text was transmitted among the Samaritans in their own recension. In fact, we now know that the Samaritan Joshua is a Samaritan retelling of the Jewish Joshua, a counter-history that is part of the medieval genre of Samaritan chronicles.

Gaster acquired his first copy during his visit to the Samaritans in 1907 and was thrilled to have discovered what he saw to be a modern manuscript of an "ancient" version of Samaritan Joshua. The text was known to Western scholars, and a manuscript of Samaritan Joshua in Arabic was purchased in the sixteenth century by Joseph Scaliger from the Samaritan community in Cairo. Gaster believed, however, that his Samaritan Hebrew version was proof that there was a Hebrew text that predated the Arabic. The circumstances of this sale are discussed by Matthew Chalmers in this volume. Gaster announced his find with great fanfare in an article he wrote for *The Times of London* newspaper, dated Tuesday, June 9, 1908. It begins: "Out of the darkness of 2,000 years there emerges now for the first time into the light of day the Book of Joshua according to the Samaritan recension."

Gaster's tone is triumphant throughout, hailing his discovery as a watershed moment in the West's awareness of Samaritan tradition. He made a number of arguments for the authenticity and antiquity of the Samaritan Joshua manuscript he had purchased, both in newsprint and in his published works. Yet, his assertions were met with derision from a number of contemporaries, includ-

16.3 Moses Gaster's Samaritan Hebrew typewriter, with a letter typed upon it from Gaster to the High Priest Jacob son of Aaron, ca. 1910 (Typewriter: New York University Libraries, Letter: The John Rylands Research Institute and Library, The University of Manchester, Moses Gaster Collection, courtesy of Benyamim Tsedaka. Photograph by Steven Fine).

ing Elkan Nathan Adler, David Yellin, and Abraham S. Yahuda, and prompted a range of (mostly negative) responses in print. These were published initially as letters to the editor in British newspapers including *The Times*, *The Jewish World*, and *The Jewish Chronicle*, and subsequently in scholarly articles. Despite the largely negative reaction to Gaster's Samaritan Hebrew Joshua text, his pursuit of an ancient Samaritan Hebrew Book of Joshua manuscript was passionate and unwavering. Throughout his almost thirty-year correspondence with the Samaritan community, Gaster repeatedly tried to secure an "ancient" Samaritan Book of Joshua, despite the community's protestations that such a manuscript did not exist. The Rylands Gaster Samaritan Correspondence features a large number of letters in which Gaster cajoles Samaritan priests in the hope that they will reveal that they indeed were keeping secret from him a stash of ancient leaves proving Samaritan Joshua's antiquity. As a result of his consistent attempts to obtain an early version, Gaster collected over twenty-one Samaritan Joshua and other Samaritan chronicles manuscripts between 1907 and the early 1930s. These texts represent the largest subset of manuscripts in his collection.

Late in life, Gaster reflected that "my relations with the Samaritans are like something out of a novel, but I cannot go on about that here. ... But this is a matter for the future."[9] It is a pity that this memoir was never written, as it would surely give us a window into Gaster's fascinating relationship with the Samaritan leadership. Moses Gaster's interests in Hebrew philology, his focus upon folklore and all things Jewish, and finally his meetings with Samaritan priest Isaac ben Aaron in London gave flight to his engagement with Samaritans and Samaritan literature. His interest in the Samaritan community developed through his lengthy correspondence with the Samaritan priest in Nablus and his questions about Samaritan religious practice, history, and literature. He negotiated and commissioned and purchased copies of Samaritan manuscripts. Unlike other clients, Gaster knew exactly what he wanted to read and to know. This was no trophy collection of the sort obtained at great expense and some charlotry by major manuscript collectors and libraries across Europe and North America. Gaster collected every kind of Samaritan text that he could, regardless of economic value. Adhering to a strict budget, Gaster spent modest amounts on copies. In creating a working scholarly library, Gaster assembled a distinctive resource, uniquely including treatises containing Samaritans' responses to Gaster's queries about Samaritan history, culture, and liturgy. What his collection lacks in the antiquity of other Samaritan collections, it makes up for in diversity. Gaster once bragged, not without cause, that "I possess perhaps the richest Samaritan library in the world, in which there are innumerable valuable manuscripts written by their scholars according to my specifications and wishes."

Importantly, Gaster the historian accepted Samaritan claims about their unbroken presence at Mount Gerizim and Nablus nearby, and considered them to have "retained their faith unchanged." In the opening to his Schweich Lectures at the British Academy in 1923, Gaster remarked:

> The importance of the Samaritans lies in the dissenting position which they have adopted towards Judaism and later on towards Christianity, thus representing some of those forces which have contributed so greatly to the history of our modern civilisation. Their very antagonism to Judaism has been a powerful factor in moulding the character of the sacred Scriptures, the religious laws and the practices which through the Bible have dominated the world.[10]

Gaster saw Samaritan history as having been written by their late antique "adversaries"—Churchmen and rabbis, who represented the Samaritans in the ways that suited their own agendas. Gaster's pursuit of copies of Samaritan historical literature like the Samaritan Book of Joshua was partially driven by his interest in understanding Samaritan history from their own sources. He accepted Samaritan claims to rigor in the keeping of their law and tradition, and saw their texts as having high fidelity to presumed ancient originals—points that he reiterated with great frequency throughout his published work. His approach was one of (what he called) "biblical archaeology"—that is, he read Samaritan texts for what they had to reveal about biblical history. Gaster saw the study of the Samaritan Pentateuch and chronicle tradition as vital to filling in Jewish biblical history, and considered textual contradictions useful to our understanding of biblical history. Their stringent observance made the Samaritans reliable witnesses to tradition. Their continuous settlement at Gerizim, Gaster thought, would afford the highest possibility that the tradition was maintained intact.

Gaster's complete acceptance of Samaritan claims of continuous worship on Gerizim and their rigorous observance of the Torah went hand in hand with his Jewish and Zionist interests. He saw the Samaritans as faithful witnesses to a tradition that came from a common root with the Jews and that demonstrated the continuity of Israelite presence in the Land of Israel. As he vigorously defended the historical claims of Jews for the antiquity of their texts and traditions against what his contemporary Solomon Schechter called (not without justification) "the Higher Anti-Semitism," Gaster showed Samaritans the same courtesy—not a small thing in the Western and Jewish scholarship of his day. Defense of Samaritanism was in effect a defense of Judaism. Gaster treated the Samaritans as friends and long-lost relatives, and not just as curiosities and manuscript sources. This set him apart from most other Anglophone observers. Together with an international group of *fin-de-siècle* Zionist culturalists, notably Ahad Ha'am, David Yellin, and, most significantly, Izhak Ben-Zvi, Gaster, in his interest in the Samaritans and his "friendship" with their leaders, was apiece with his cultural and political Zionist work. His interest in their texts was theological as it was historical. This connection is alluded to in his preface to *The Samaritans*, but it is not explained to his British audience: "As I arrived at the end of my journey, I became aware of the stick of Judah, which had meanwhile been pressed into my hands and that in my hands they became joined at last."

For Further Reading

Moses Gaster. *The Samaritans: Their History, Doctrines and Literature*. London: The British Academy, 1925.

———. "The Story of My Library." Translated by B. Sabin Hill. *British Library Journal* 21, no. 1 (1995): 16–21.

Theodor H. Gaster, "Prolegomenon: Moses Gaster (1856-1939)." *Studies and Texts in Folklore, Magic, Medieval Romance, Hebrew Apocrypha and Samaritan Archeology*, New York: Ktav, 1971, I: xv-xxxxix.

Eli Yassif, "Moshe Gaster—A Groundbreaking Innovator in Folklore and in Judaic Studies." *Peamim* 100 (2004): 113–123. [Hebrew].

---

1   Gaster, 1925, preface, n.p.

2   Haralambakis, 1993, 109–110.

3   Ibid., 110, n. 16.

4   Gaster, *The Samaritans*, 20.

5   Gaster Papers Box 7, Rylands Gaster Samaritan Collection.

6   Gaster, *The Samaritans*, 20.

7   Rylands Gaster Samaritan MSS 805 and 2059.

8   Dated November 25, 1906; Rylands Gaster Samaritan MSS 830 and 831.

9   Ibid.

10 Gaster, 1923, 1.

17

"To This Day the Samaritans Have Never Left Shechem and Mount Gerizim": Izhak Ben-Zvi, David Ben-Gurion, and the Samaritans

ISRAEL SEDAKA ז"ל

Your Excellency, Our Master, the President:

We return a second time to the kingdom of David, after an interruption of some three thousand years. In light of this historic and important turn, the descendants of Menashe and Ephraim—the Children of Joseph the Righteous one, the remnant that survives of the kingdom of Israel, which was established in our holy house—Shechem-Beit-El—stretch out the hand of peace and brotherhood to the house of David as an expression of their loyalty to this house and to reestablish the covenant that was broken after the death of King David.

It is clear that these differences were not sufficient to necessitate a split, but once a small tear took place between the two brothers, Israel and Judah—who was larger and stronger than the other tribes of Israel—the historic dispute intensified and continued for many generations.

Even in those days, this divide left its mark. The two camps were easy prey for the enemies of Israel, who sent their swords against them repeatedly to annihilate them, without mercy. They cast them in every direction and debased them. From stable kingdoms they descended into the depths of poverty and weakness. The enemies carried out the judgement of the Lord upon them, as is written in His holy Torah, "And they will forsake me and break my covenant which I have made with them. ... Then my anger will be kindled against them in that day, and I will forsake them and hide my face from them, and they will be devoured; and many evils and troubles will come upon them" (Deuteronomy 31:15, Samaritan version).

It is important to highlight that the troubles did not afflict our brothers the Children of Judah to the same extent that they did the Children of Joseph, owing to the firm resolve and strong desire of Joseph to remain

faithful to the land of their fathers. As a result of decrees and persecutions and acts of annihilation under the cruel rule of numerous enemies over many generations, the large Samaritan nation dwelling in the homeland became small and depleted, both spiritually and physically. Of the luminance of the past there remained only a small spark that did not deplete in the course of many generations. Through these many years of hardship, they were sustained by their faithfulness to the Lord and to His Torah.

With full cognizance and abiding faith, that, heaven forfend, this spark will not burn out in the new State of Israel—which is based upon equality and judgement and especially the unification of the exiles of Israel from all of the lands of their dispersion—we have come today to renew the covenant with our brothers. This is accomplished through the agency of His Excellency the President. We know that there is no one of his stature in all of Israel who understands so profoundly the historical significance of this community and its traditions, who has dedicated to them his best hours of research.

We see in your presidency of the State of Israel a great and hopeful opening that will bring great blessings to our humble community. The moment has come for the Samaritans to take their place among the communities of Israel.

We are pleased at this time to express our appreciation of the President of the State of Israel, and convey to all the Children of Israel in the Land and in the dispersion, our heartfelt wishes for the festival of Passover. We bless you with the blessing of "joyous festivals" and great success in the future.

The Community Council of the Samaritans in Israel

Yefet Abraham Tsedaka of Shechem, of the Tribe of Menashe
Gamaliel Abraham Tsedaka of Shechem, of the Tribe of Menashe
Obadiah Yefet Tsedaka of Shechem, of the Tribe of Menashe
Abraham Nur Tsedaka of Tel Aviv, of the Tribe of Menashe
Abraham Simeon Atlif Dafni of Shechem, of the Tribe of Ephraim
Jacob Simeon Shoshoni, of Shechem, of the Tribe of Ephraim

17.1 The Priest Ithamar and his son Soleah, Passover Pilgrimage 2020 (Photograph by Eitan Bino).

17.2 Izhak Ben-Zvi with Amram son of the High Priest (to his left, reigned 1961–1980) and Nur son of Abraham, Mount Gerizim, Passover, 1932 (Yad Ben-Zvi).

Abraham Saad Marḥiv, of Shechem, of the Tribe of Ephraim
Benjamin Joshua Marḥiv, of Shechem, of the Tribe of Ephraim

This scroll was read publicly in Jerusalem before Izhak Ben-Zvi, the second President of the State of Israel. … Minister David Ben-Gurion, Prime Minister, in the presence of Mr. Israel Ben-Ze'ev of Jerusalem, and the Samaritan Community Council in Israel.

Nissan 16, 5713 [= April 1953]
First Intermediate Day of Passover
The Fifth Year of the State of Israel

This document was written by Abraham Nur Tsedaka.[1]

In his memoirs, *Essays and Reminiscences*, Izhak Ben-Zvi tells of his first encounters with the Samaritan community.[2] These began in about 1908, when he first met the elder Abraham son of Marḥiv Zedaka Hazafri (my grandfather). Ben-Zvi rented a room in Abraham's house in Jaffa, aiming to learn Arabic so that he could reinforce his ties to Middle Eastern Jewry. At the same time, he also became acquainted with the life of a Samaritan family, through which he met the Samaritan community in Shechem. Every morning, Ben-Zvi awakened to the voice of Abraham son of Marḥiv, who used to rise at dawn for the morning prayer. When the prayers were over, Abraham used to come into the great hall where the entire family gathered, and where, at the end of prayers and the morning meal,

they would start studying. It is from him that Ben-Zvi learned both Samaritan Hebrew and Arabic, in which he became fluent enough to speak within three months. Arabic enabled him to converse with Middle Eastern Jews, Yemenite Jews, and Arabs.

On his first visit to the Samaritan quarter in Shechem, Ben-Zvi was greatly moved by the dignity and nobility of the then officiating high priest, Jacob son of Aaron. He writes:

> I inquired into the state of the community and admired our remote tribe, dwelling among the hills of Shechem. How wondrous is the fate of the Samaritans … How impressive the strength of this small, meager tribe, persisting against the entire world for thousands of years.[3]

Ben-Zvi stood in the ancient synagogue in Shechem, facing the Holy Ark oriented toward Mount Gerizim, and saw for the first time the Scroll of the Torah, written in the ancient Hebrew writing in which the Torah was given to the tribes of Israel on Mount Sinai. He listened to the high priest's explanations. During Passover, when he climbed Mount Gerizim to observe the Passover sacrifice, Ben-Zvi said that in his imagination he could see the Passover sacrifice as it was celebrated on the Temple Mount.

These two earliest encounters with the high priest Jacob son of Aaron and the elder Abraham son of Marḥiv Tsedaka formed the foundation and source for the mutual, firm ties between Izhak Ben-Zvi and the Samaritan community. This solid and profound foundation grew deep roots and yielded fruit. It is the foundation from which grew the extraordinary, rare relationship between the tribes of Ephraim and Manasseh and a descendant of the tribe of Judah— whose deeds, integrity, and belief in justice singles him out as perhaps the first Jew to win the trust and love of the Samaritans.

Judah and Israel had parted ways when King David chose Jerusalem for a religious center, and even more so in Second Temple times, owing to religious and national struggles. Thus, when the Judean diaspora returned to its ancient homeland, it was but natural for them to seek out the last remaining Samaritans in the Land of Israel. What they found was a weakened tribe, struggling to survive and yet firm of faith and strong of spirit. History, which works in mysterious ways, brought about the moving and life-giving encounter between Izhak Ben-Zvi, a descendant of the tribe of Judah returning to rebuild and resettle his ancient homeland; the high priest Jacob son of Aaron, a descendant of the tribe of Levi, and Abraham son of Marḥiv Tsedaka Hazafari, an elder and descendant of the tribe of Joseph. These represent the "remnant that escaped out of the hand of the kings of Assyria" as 2 Chronicles 30:6 calls us, who have survived for some two thousand seven hundred years. This moment represents the historic encounter between Joseph and Judah, and is proof of the eternal existence of the people of Israel.

This time, however, despite his faith in Jerusalem and his struggle for it (but unlike Hezekiah king of Judah), Izhak Ben-Zvi did not attempt to convince the remaining descendants of Joseph to come to Jerusalem. He knew that ever since the days of Moses, the Israelites dwelling in Samaria had focused their faith on Shechem and on Mount Gerizim. Ben-Zvi understood and valued the historical truth expressed in our daily prayer: "...Mount Gerizim a temple of the Lord, every day of our lives."

The Samaritan community had indeed dwindled, so much so that scholars could already imagine the entire nation coming to an end. Not so Ben-Zvi, who saw then the eternity of the nation of Israel in all its glory. What other people or nation in the world was reduced to a few dozen living in the confines of a narrow, dark ghetto, and still lived on in the firm and unshaken belief that they are the chosen people, chosen above all nations? Ben-Zvi felt love and admiration for the Samaritans—the love of a descendant of the tribe of Judah, perhaps even of Benjamin, for the sons of his brother Joseph— the descendants of Ephraim and Manasseh. It was love, respect, and wonder—which I myself always saw and felt during our many encounters (Figure 17.2, 3).

Ben-Zvi made it his life's work to carry out a thorough and comprehensive study of the Samaritans, their faith, their literature, and their settlements. His studies strove to prove both their physical and spiritual existence in Israel's towns and villages across history, and to prove the presence of a Samaritan community in Israel even when the country was bereft almost entirely of its Jewish sons. We see this in his Hebrew books, *The Samaritans* (1935) and *Eretz Israel and Its Settlement under Ottoman Rule* (1955).

On appearing before the *Anglo-American Committee of Enquiry Regarding the Problems of European Jewry and Palestine* in 1945/1946, the Arab representatives raised the Samaritan issue. They asserted that the Jews have no need of a state of their own. Palestinian representative Awni Abd al-Hadi said: "Let the Jews live with us in peace, as do the Samaritans in Nablus (Shechem)." In reply to the Arab representative's suggestion, Ben-Zvi retorted:

> Historical truth does not bear out the Arab claims as to the status of the Jews in Arab countries. At the time of the Arab conquest, the Samaritans numbered approximately 135,000 individuals. Some 1300 years later their number has been reduced to 200 people in Shechem and some 60 people in Tel Aviv.

To this, I would like to add that in 1918, when Palestine was taken by the British, there were only 145 Samaritans in the country. Under British occupation and the State of Israel increased this number to six hundred and seventy-five individuals—an increase of 465% over a period of eighty-five years between 1918 and 2003. Today the Samaritans are a community with over 850 members.

During the course of his research, Ben-Zvi often visited the Samaritan community in Jaffa, and in Shechem— mainly on holidays. In 1933 he participated in the research carried out by a Italian genetic study expedition headed by Professor G. E. Gena. In 1935, he published *The Samaritans*, which was reissued in a revised edition after his death. In the introduction, Ben-Zvi writes:

> We should remember that this tiny community is the only one to have preserved a special version of our holy writings and chronicles, a version that contradicts at places our traditional [Masoretic] text. The important point here is not whether their version is right or wrong— but rather that this version is an independent source preserved by the most ancient Israelite sect. This source contains points that are invaluable to the understanding of our own text, and the differences and arguable points between the various religious streams that formed during our nation's long history.[4]

To the Samaritans, Ben-Zvi was more than just a scholar and historian. In his position as head of the National Council of the Jewish Agency, and then as Israel's second president, Ben-Zvi was a steady and loyal friend to this community, who regarded him as the right and fitting addressee for its needs—individual and general alike. To all of which he lent a willing ear. He found the rift that formed in the community as a result of the 1948 War extremely painful.

When Ben-Zvi wished to communicate with my uncle, Yefet Tsedaka, who was head of the Jaffa community but had moved to Shechem when war broke out, Ben-Zvi sent his letter to the principal of my secondary school, Gymnasia Herzliya in Tel Aviv, who gave it to me to deliver to my father, Gamaliel. From then on, my relations with Izhak Ben-Zvi grew closer with regard to the community. This was especially so during his term as president (1952-1963). In the 1960s, when I served as the secretary of the Samaritan community, the priests on Mount Gerizim, headed by the high priest, appointed me to ask President Ben-Zvi about the possibility of financial assistance that would enable the Samaritans to purchase land on Mount Gerizim. The idea, although agreeable to Ben-Zvi, was rejected because of possible political implications.

On the other hand, at the request of the community committee in Holon, the mayor of Jerusalem, Teddy Kollek, arranged for a donation on behalf of Meir Weisgal, head of the Weizmann Foundation, to build of the new synagogue on Mount Gerizim. The donation was given to the high priest Amram son of Isaac. Thus, Izhak Ben-Zvi managed to maintain steady contact with the priesthood in Shechem and to make sure the community there received material and financial aid, occasionally through the American Jewish Joint Distribution Committee.

In Israel, he assisted in moving the community to a single place and in the building of the Samaritan neighborhood in Holon. He laid the foundation stone for the Samaritan synagogue in Holon, and, despite being in a state of ill health only two months prior to his death, ceremonially opened the synagogue (Figures 17.3). This was his last public appearance, during which he called for the reunion of Samaria and Judea, since all the tribes of Israel are but one nation.

In one of our meetings during his term as president, while discussing historical and archeological matters, Ben-Zvi asked me to invite Professor Ze'ev Ben-Ḥayyim to visit him. I gladly fulfilled his request, and Ben-Ḥayyim was delighted to oblige. Discussing various Samaritan themes, Ben-Zvi made a request of Ben-Ḥayyim: "Please translate the *Memar Marqa* [the Samaritan midrash that is today generally called *Tebat Marqe* -SF] from Aramaic to Hebrew." Ben-Ḥayyim responded: "Your Excellency, it is not an easy matter and is still beyond me. However, I do hope to translate the *Memar Marqa* as soon as possible, at your request." Indeed, some twenty-eight years later, in 1988, Professor Ben Ḥayyim published the Hebrew translation of *Memar Marqa*.

In 1954, the World Zionist Organization held its first ever conference in Israel. In his opening speech, Prime Minister David Ben-Gurion noted that the conference was taking place for the first time in Jerusalem, which was chosen by King David as the religious center of the nation. As a young student, I wrote to him and noted that Israel had a religious center four hundred years prior to King David, that center being in Samaria rather than Judea. Two days later, I received a reply signed by the premier, where he wrote that although he himself was aware of the controversy between Israel and Judah— concerning Mount Gerizim and Jerusalem— it was history that determined that Jerusalem should serve as a national center.

Ben-Gurion was very much aware of the Samaritans, of whom

he had heard a lot from his friend Izhak Ben-Zvi. He, too, thought very highly of the history, faith, and principles of the Samaritan community. In 1959, the Israeli Bible Society met in Ben-Gurion's home. Among the fourteen meetings dealing with the Book of Joshua, was a lecture delivered by President Ben-Zvi on the Samaritan Book of Joshua. Although he spoke of the Samaritans with great sympathy and appreciation, on several points Ben-Zvi emphasized the Jewish point of view. At the end of the lecture, Ben-Gurion requested permission to speak. This is what David Ben-Gurion said to Izhak Ben-Zvi, as recorded in the resulting book, *Studies in the Book of Joshua*:[5]

I'd like to ask a few questions:

On what did you base your claim that the Samaritans changed the text of the Pentateuch? Perhaps their version that is the correct one? The fact is that they have lived in this country continuously. If there is any doubt concerning their origins can anyone know the biological origins of the Jews living here?

As to the question of "in the place which he shall choose" versus "the place which he chose" [in Deuteronomy], one should note that the Bible mentions only one chosen mount—Mount Gerizim. The Jerusalem mountain is never mentioned.

When Abraham came to the Land of Israel, the first place that is mentioned is Shechem. Does this have no historical or traditional significance?

When Abraham was told to sacrifice his son, he was sent not to the mount of Moriah, but rather to the land of Moriah ... upon one of the mountains (Genesis 22). Conceivably, Abraham would have chosen a familiar place—and Shechem was a familiar place, as he had twice built an altar there. The mount of Moriah is never mentioned, and Jerusalem is absent in the Pentateuch. It is mentioned only in the days of King David....

What is the basis, therefore, for the claim that they changed the text, and not us? Why not accept their version, confirmed by the Torah, that the Mountain of the Blessing is Mount Gerizim? Shechem is also mentioned in Joshua. There he established a covenant between Israel and the Lord.... How are we so sure that they erred in this matter? David indeed chose Jerusalem for his capital, but until then Jerusalem plays no part in our history.

A few days after the 1967 War, in my then capacity as the secretary of the Samaritan community in Israel, I introduced the leading Samaritan priests in Shechem, headed by the high priest Amram son of Isaac, to the then heads of state: President Zalman Shazar, Prime Minister Levy Eshkol, and Minister in Charge of Religious Affairs Zerach Warhaftig. The highlight of this encounter, however, was the unplanned meeting with David Ben-Gurion in his Tel Aviv home. The meeting was suffused with intense happiness and love, as though it was faithfully and hopefully anticipated for decades. Those present discussed the problems of the Samaritan community, as well as its history during the previous century—in particular since the inception of the State of Israel.

For Further Reading

Izhak Ben-Zvi. *Essays and Reminiscences*. Edited by Rahel Yanait Ben-Zvi and Yehuda. Erez. Jerusalem: Yad Ben-Zvi Press, 1966. [Hebrew].

——. *The Exiled and the Redeemed*. Philadelphia: Jewish Publications Society, 1957.

———

1   Israel State Archives (ISA), Private Collections, Izhak Ben-Zvi, 2049/3-פ, translated by Steven Fine. This article is slightly adapted from Sedaka, 2005.
2   Ben-Zvi, 1966, 119–120.
3   Ben-Zvi, 1966, 134.
4   Ben-Zvi, 1935, 8.
5   Ben-Gurion, 1960, 139-140.

18

Passover, 1968: Johanna Spector, Israeli Civil Religion, and The Ethnographic Study of the Samaritans

DAVID SELIS AND STEVEN FINE

The kitchen is on the ground floor of the high priest's house and has a comparatively large window behind a metal grill, several cupboards, a sink, two gas-burners, tables, chairs and an icebox or Frigidaire. Men and women of the high priest's family as well as guests watch the ritual of Matsa baking. … Amram [is] pronouncing the blessing over the Matsa. He wears his everyday outfit, namely a red turban and gray robe with wide, long sleeves. All men and boys have their heads covered, while from the women head coverings are not demanded. Some children wear striped pajamas under their striped coats, but these are by no means ceremonial. The attire of all Samaritans is a workday attire and somewhat casual. Eleazar, the "baker," has rolled up the sleeves of his navy shirt, wears a turquoise-grey-white knitted cap on his head, and an orange patterned scarf around his neck. The women wear dark brown and black woolen sweaters above their nondescript cotton dresses and some of the older ones knitted scarves of a dark color on their heads. The kitchen is dimly lit. A young woman arrives in a bright green, short-sleeved sweater, and short navy skirt. She wears a golden chain with a pendant around her neck and her hair is set in honor of the occasion, and people flock to buy Samaritan postcards and views of Nablus to send to their friends or for a keepsake. Small stalls are set up for the purchase of holy books and trinkets and soft drinks. It is still early, but throngs of people have arrived from all over Israel by car, taxi, or chartered busses. One meets friends of the Samaritans and scholars in addition to newspapermen and tourists.

What was new going up to the Qorban Pesach?

The Qorban Pesach [Passover sacrifice] itself which I had never seen before, only read about. The entire population: the pitched tents, the baking of matsoth, the life in the camp, the Mishmar Hagvul [border police] of the Druse [Israelis], the reception of the dignitaries by the high priest (Figure 18.1). Prayers in the synagogue and on Mount Gerizim I had witnessed at Succot. But then there were hardly any outsiders—only [Avigdor] Herzog with his crew from H. U. [the Nation-al Sound Archives of the Hebrew University] Jerusalem (Uri Epstein, a technician, a photographer), and a stray Arab, while this time there were at least 2,000 spectators. The Jerusalem Post reports 4,000.

I also have to correct them on the "many" Jewish wives the Samaritans took in the last years! The government had provided better roads for Succot, but for Passover there were elaborate preparations of bus-service, hundreds of policemen in black uniforms and hundreds of soldiers (in Khaki uniforms), wooden stands were erected for spectators, a post office was opened just for the day, refreshments could be bought, postcards and pamphlets pertaining to Samaritan history and lore, and police directed the traffic. According to the papers, 30,000 were expected, the President (Shazar), the Prime Minister [Levi Eshkol], the Defense Minister [Moshe Dayan] were to come along with scores of dignitaries. Perhaps they would have come if the Chief Rabbi would not have made a public statement in the newspapers that no Jews should attend the Passover sacrifice which had been abandoned by the Jews since the destruction of the Temple.

The ones who arrived were the Military Governor of Nablus, Zvi Ofer, the Mayor of Nablus, Hamdi Canaan, who had taken part in the festivities in previous years, Mr. Raphael Berdi, West Bank Military Governor, [Supreme Court] Justice [Moshe] Silberg, Dr. Israel Goldstein [World Chairman of Keren Hayesod-United Israel Appeal] with his foolish wife (who made loud derogatory remarks about the Matsa, etc.) reporters, a man from S.A. writing a book on Samaritans and tourists.

On the mountain itself the holiest places were fenced in, and stone and rubble cleared away. While the first ascent was difficult, this one was as smooth as could be. I was almost sorry that everything had been streamlined. I had the same feeling about the Old City of Jerusalem.[1]

This is how ethnomusicologist Johanna Spector described the Samaritan Passover in June 1968, the first after the 1967 Six Day War. It was a sea-change from previous Passovers, especially those of 1966 and 1967, which were traumatic for the Samaritans. As a

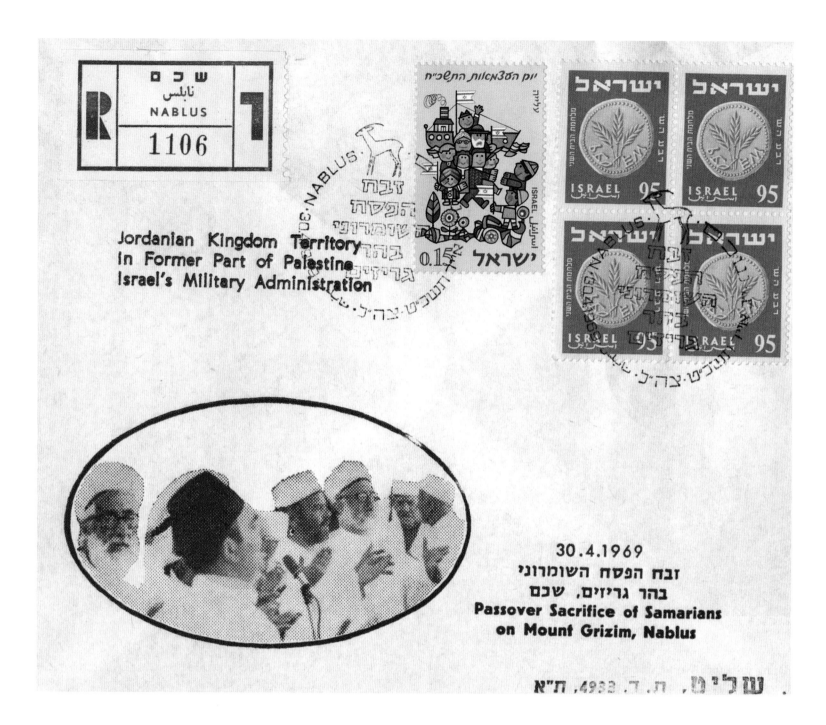

18.6 "Passover Sacrifice of Samaritans on Mount Grizim, Nablus," Commemorative Envelope, April 30, 1969 (Collection of Leah and Steven Fine, New York).

According to Spector's fieldnotes, cited above, the ceremony was protected by hundreds of Israeli policemen and soldiers. Bleachers were prepared for the visitors and rocks cleared. This was no small gathering, as Sukkot was in the fall of 1967, or as Passover was under the Jordanians. Spector comments in her fieldnotes that "the event was well attended, as busses made their way from Israel proper to Nablus, and then to the top of Mount Gerizim." She notes that up to 40,000 tourists planned to make their way on new roads, parking lots and infrastructure prepared for the purpose. This is on top of the roughly two hundred and ten Samaritans present and being watched! This event had a carnival-like feel. Souvenirs were readily available, and a commemorative brochure was published by the community, written by Abraham Tsedaka of Holon. Among the most interesting souvenirs were commemorative envelopes, their stamps cancelled by the Israeli postal service with a commemorative logo. Spector collected examples of these, which are preserved in her collection. They were clearly quite popular, and these commemorative envelopes are available for sale in considerable numbers today on the Internet. The complexities of the moment are clear even on these commemorative envelopes. An envelope from 1969 shows a photograph of Samaritans praying. To the right, the envelope is dated "30.4.1969. Passover

אשמורעל

Sacrifice of Samaritans on Mount Gerizim, Nablus." Above, and more interesting for its awkward language, one can read where it was from: "Jordanian Kingdom Territory in Former Part of Palestine. Israel's Military Administration" (Figure 18.6).

The Samaritan Passover of 1968 was intended to be a state occasion of the first order to be attended by no less than President Zalman Shazar, Prime Minister Levi Eshkol, and the hero of 1967, General Moshe Dayan. This makes sense owing to the priority that Ben-Zvi put on the Samaritans, who he supported economically through the Red Cross and the Joint Distribution Committee throughout his tenure. They have been especially close to Israeli presidents ever since. The State of Israel was publicly embracing the Samaritans, integrating the Passover sacrifice into the ceremonial cycle of Israeli civil religion. It was perceived by many as an "ingathering of the exiles" made possible by the 1967 War—the "bringing home" of indigenous Israelites, who had long been covered under Israel's law of return. Beyond that, this Israeli ceremony was a statement of Israeli indigenousness in the West Bank.

This integration of the Samaritans into Israeli society is precisely the development that may have stymied the presence of the national leadership. Spector's claims that the Chief Rabbi ruled that "no Jew should attend" the sacrifice reflects the fault line that both connects and separates Israeli civil religion and traditional Judaism. Beyond that, his reminder that Judaism "abandoned" the Paschal sacrifice with the destruction of the Jerusalem Temple in 70 CE is clearly directed toward his own constituency. A small religious Zionist group was agitating for the renewal of sacrifice on the Jerusalem Temple Mount. This group has coalesced today around the Temple movement, with its now annual faux Paschal sacrifice—theatrically modeled on the well-known Samaritan ceremony.[9] In 1968, the Religious Affairs Ministry forbade this Jewish sacrifice, reflecting the position of the Chief Rabbinate that Jews may not enter the Temple Mount.[10] Spector's swipe at the wife of Conservative rabbi and Zionist leader Israel Goldstein and her clear discomfort with non-Jewish matzah was an "inside baseball" comment from one JTS personality toward another. It most certainly expresses the discomfort of others in the audience observing and internalizing the sacrifice.

A year later, in 1969, Spector returned to Nablus with a full film crew to create *The Samaritans: People of the Sacred Mountain*, which appeared in 1972. This documentary was narrated by actor E.G. Marshall and directed by Israeli filmmaker Dan Wolman. It was produced by two groups, the Friends of the Samaritan Museum, Jerusalem, Israel and The Society for the Preservation of Samaritan Culture, New York, New York. There were indeed plans for a museum, organized by Ratson Tsedaka, and the New York society seems to have been a funding agent organized by Spector. This documentary fits the standards of its day for such films. It provides an outsider's perspective on Samaritan life, with an extremely graphic film of the Passover sacrifice. It ignores the thousands of tourists and politicians and philatelic agents observing the rite, and treats the sacrifice in isolation. Spector's presentation begins with matzah-baking and continues through the entire multi-hour process of the sacrifice with a particular focus upon the slaughtering and

preparation of the animals. Biblical resonances between the sacrifice and Exodus 12 are emphasized, with a major focus on the liturgical elements of the sacrifice. One reviewer noted:

> Documented in vivid detail, the significance of ritual in Samaritan life becomes readily apparent to the viewer. Even in so truncated a version as this (the actual ceremony takes many hours), the tension and exhilaration of the participants, i.e., virtually the entire population of Samaritans, is effectively transmitted cinematically.[11]

It was the very distance created between the well-known narrative voice of E.G. Marshall and this very graphic, sophisticated, detailed, and bloody depiction that made this presentation palatable to Western viewers. While numerous recordings of the ceremony were made during the twentieth century, this depiction is forthright and lacking in voyeurism and "Orientalizing" tropes.

The American context of Spector's work is important for contextualizing *The Samaritans: People of the Sacred Mountain*. The title itself invokes the kind of "pop spirituality" made popular by Religious Studies scholars at this time, most prominently Mircea Eliade and Joseph Campbell. It clearly resonated within the American Jewish community. In 1970, the Union of American Hebrew Congregations, the educational arm of the Reform movement, issued a filmstrip written by the polymath Orthodox Zionist author Tovia Preschel entitled, *The Samaritans: Their Traditions and Customs*.

Spector's research took place at a turning point for the Samaritans, as they negotiated their way between Israeli and Palestinian identities as Israel consolidated its control of the West Bank. Even more complex, Israeli Samaritans were committed Israelis and participants in Israeli culture. The Nablus community, and especially the priests, were rightfully suspicious and self-protective in the face of the myriad changes occurring around them. In a letter dated September 6, 1968, Spector reflected on these complexities through the lens of the hoped-for Samaritan museum:

> Negotiations with the Samaritans as to their museum do not proceed satisfactorily. While the young generation is community-minded, especially the one in Holon, Israel, the older people (Nablus) are only concerned with their own well-being and income. The family of the high priest wants the income from their books and artifacts, the building should be next to their house, and they want complete control. Without their precious manuscripts and books no museum is feasible, they remind me very much of Jews lacking security. And of course, the priestly family in Nablus have to be careful in whatever they do since they may have to live under the Jordanians again. Their sole income throughout the years was from tourists to whom they showed their precious books and manuscripts and writing "cameas" [*qeme'ot,* amulets] for the superstitious Arabs. At the moment, the high priest is paid a monthly salary by the Israeli Government, but everybody else has to earn his living at some profession or trade. This is difficult to understand for people who had no opportunities until recently, and precarious to accept in the present political situation. Half of the entire group are at the moment in Israel and more young people will come in the future since opportunities and education are better here.

Israel treats Samaritans legally as Jews and extends to them all the opportunities Israel has to offer. They can get scholarships to study and can enter any profession. (Rafi said unfortunately no application has been received until now.) The priests, however, have to stay at the foot of their Holy Mountain, and whoever remains in Nablus sits on a powder keg. At the moment, Israel controls the school system and everything else in Nablus and pays all the salaries. All adults and children study Modern Hebrew in an Ulpan. But for how long this peaceful situation is going to prevail, nobody knows. This is why I cannot blame the elders (high priest and brother) for their negative attitude towards a museum from which they would not derive any personal income. Nevertheless, I am going ahead with the discussions, hoping for a solution.

It must be said that it is much easier for working people with a steady job to envisage a communal enterprise like a museum or community center. People, however, with a precarious and uncertain future tend to hold on to tangible assets and would not think of sharing them with others. The high priest and brother also have another point; why should they give up a source of income for some esoteric reason? It is practically giving a gift that they can ill afford to the museum. We would not ask a man in the U.S. to give his most precious possessions, especially if they are part of his personal income, to a public institution whence he would not derive any benefit; perhaps we would have to find a way to compensate the priests; perhaps part of the museum dues should go to them. They certainly would not dream of selling the documents and books. It is easy for Samaritans who do not own any artifacts or documents to plan a museum; they have nothing to lose.[12]

In light of the promises made by William Barton and Edward Warren, the failure of their plan to create a Samaritan museum—and the resulting loss of precious manuscripts that Yitzchak Schwartz documents in this volume, it is no wonder that the Nablus Samaritans were so reticent! Israeli Samaritans, portraying themselves as a model minority, had periodically mounted exhibitions in the Israeli public sphere, most notably in a distinctive pavilion at the Levant Fair of 1934 in Tel Aviv, which is reported to have attracted twenty thousand visitors. Another exhibition took place in Nablus in 1985, which included "a small altar (bima) with two satin curtains, traditional dress, scrolls and Torah codices open and closed within cases." Only in 1997 was the Samaritan Museum opened, with similar exhibits. It was built in Kiryat Luza, atop Mount Gerizim and near the Passover sacrifice site. This is a private museum, owned and operated by Husney (Yefet) Cohen, nephew of the current high priest, who greets visitors in traditional garb. The complexities caused by the division of the Holon and Nablus communities were profound, and in many ways still are. Johanna Spector provides us access to this messy process for this small community early on, one that is unstated in more "official" press and communal documents. Beginning with Passover 1968 and continuing through her documentary work, Spector's research, archived at the Library of the Jewish Theological Seminary (Figure 18.7), provides a "snapshot" of the lives of the "People of the Sacred Mountain" at a moment of profound transformation (Figures 18.8-12).

18.7 Johanna Spector and High Priest Amram son of Isaac (reigned 1961–1980) (Photograph courtesy of the Jewish Theological Seminary Library, Johanna L. Spector Papers and Audio-Visual Materials).

For Further Reading and Viewing

Editor. "Thousands of Shechem Residents Visited the Exhibition of our Heritage and were Enthusiastic about its Many Exhibits." *A.B. – The Samaritan News* 379 (March 15, 1985): 1 [Hebrew].

Johanna L. Spector and Dan Wolman, producers. *The Samaritans: The People of the Sacred Mountain*. New York: Johanna Spector, 1970.

The Johanna Spector Archives. https://jts-spectorarchives.tumblr.com/ (accessed August 1, 2021).

John D. Whiting. "The Last Israelitisch Blood Sacrifice," National *Geographic* 37, no. 1 (1920): 1–46.

———

1   Johanna L. Spector Papers and Audio-Visual Materials, Box 51, Folder 25.
2   April 15, 1969, 3–4.
3   May 5, 1966, 12.
4   Sassoni, 1969, 3.
5   Cowley, 1909, 191.
6   Hutchinson, 1900, 2:584.
7   *The Prince of Wales's Journal*: February 6 – June 14, 1862, 45.
8   Ibid., 34.
9   *Times of Israel* Staff, 2017; Chen 2007, 146–160.
10 Cohen, 1969.
11 Loeb, 1975, 694.
12 Johanna L. Spector Papers and Audio-Visual Materials, Box 52, Folder 1.

18.8 Young Samaritans at the Passover Sacrifice. Left to right, Women: Salwa, Ramz, Rawan, Faten, Natalie; Men: Rezeq, Ibraheem, Yousef, Yousef. Kiryat Luza, Mount Gerizim, 2019 (Photograph by Moshe Alafi).

18.9 Preparing the Passover Sacrifice, Kiryat Luza, Mount Gerizim, 2016 (Photograph by Ori Orhof).

18.10 Burning of the Entrails of the Passover Sacrifice, Kiryat Luza, Mt. Gerizim, 2016 (Photographs by Ori Orhof).

ⵝⵎⵇⵯⵎⵝ

18.11 Yefet and Abed, sons of Netanel Cohen; Yefet, Yair, Isaac, sons of Pinhas Cohen, 2019 (Photograph by Moshe Alafi).

18.12 The Family of Matzliaḥ (Najah) and Wafa Cohen Eat the Passover Meal, Kiryat Luza, Mt. Gerizim, 2020 (Photograph by Ori Orhof).

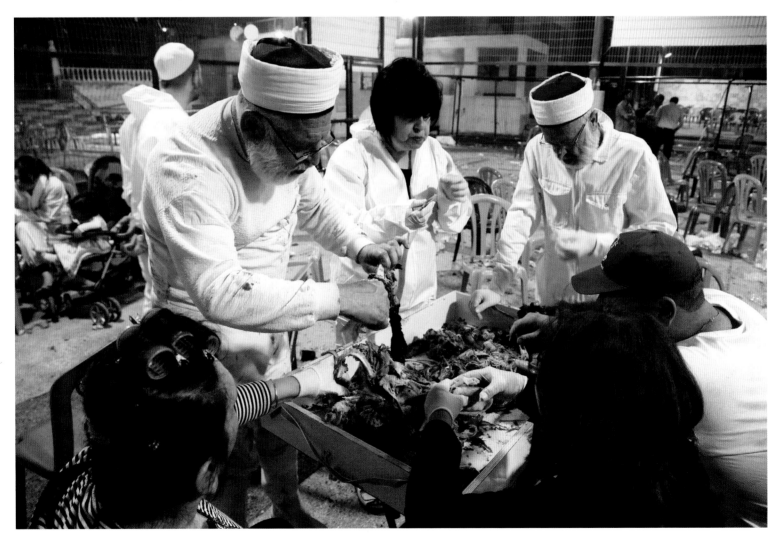

19

Samaritan Stories in the Israel Folktale Archives: Poetics and Cultural Exchange in Modern Israel

DINA STEIN

Dov, Shalom,

There has been a complaint regarding the book of legends that was published. The complaint of Israel Sedaka the Samaritan is that you treated historical events (according to the Samaritans) as if they were folk legends (for instance, the story of Baba Rabba).

I explained to him that such stories were included in the anthology as representing characteristics of folk tales and not of legends.

At any rate, it is always advisable to hear your opinion on the matter—although one cannot ignore a *family conspiracy* here!

Would you please explain that to him in a few words via mail.

With utmost admiration,
Benyamim Tsedaka[1]

The Israel Folktale Archives (IFA), named after its founder, professor Dov Noy, holds about thirty Samaritan folktales, twelve of which were published by the archive in 1965. The small anthology was authored by Ratson Tsedaka, and it was annotated and edited by Noy, who also added an extensive bibliography relating to Samaritan traditions (Figure 19.1). It was titled *Samaritan Legends*. In addition to the tales themselves, the archive holds correspondences between the people involved in the documentation of the stories, as well as information pertaining to their public activities. Among these is the letter cited above from January 26, 1967, written by Benyamim Tsedaka, Ratson's son, and addressed to Dov Noy. The letter was answered immediately, on February 3. Noy begins by reproaching Benyamim for having failed to apply what should have been his newly acquired knowledge of folklore as a student of Noy's at the university (the letter is even addressed to Benyamim Tsedaka, a student at the Hebrew University in Jerusalem). He then proceeds to provide a short overview of folk genres:

Folk-legend … is a kind of folktale, which is a story passed down from generation to generation, orally. What is unique to the legend is that it has a historical-geographical background (as opposed to the fairy-tale, anecdote and more that take place in a no-time and no-place). This explains that if Professor Louis Ginzberg, who was meticulous and believed firmly in the historical legacy of the people of Israel, named his monumental book … *The Legends of the Jews*, he means by this term stories that have a geographical-historical background … that is stories that are connected to biblical heroes identified by name. The question of the historicity or non-historicity of each legend is linked to belief and scholarship, but any story told about King Solomon, about a Samaritan high priest, or about any other historical hero, and told orally, by the people, and transmitted from one generation to another, scientifically defined is a legend whether it contains unreasonable super-natural elements or whether it has a realistic character.

Among our first eighteen files of the publication series, file no. 8, named Tsedaka, as is customary to name the files after the recorder of the tales, it is the only one in which the entire collection (all twelve stories with no exception) has a distinct historical-geographical background. Each one of the (other) seventeen collections contains a bigger variety of folktales: magic fairy tales alongside legends, anonymous love-tales alongside legendary anecdotes, and so forth. Hence it is the only file in the series that carries the title folk-legends and not a non-specific name: folktales.

Noy concludes by scolding his student, again, for failing to recognize disciplinarian terms; he signs off warmly but is careful to reinstate his academic rank, as he writes: "With greetings to you and your home and to the entire Shomerim congregation, Dr. Dov Noy."

The crux of the matter seems simple enough: the collection of Samaritan tales (unlike the other anthologies published by the archive) was named *Samaritan Legends* (rather than folktales), thereby eliciting uneasiness among those who hold the stories to be true historical accounts. The issue is tentatively resolved by framing the term "legends" within a formal disciplinarian taxonomy of genres. Yet, this short epistolary moment also embodies a more

lected consciously for that reason or (most probably) not, the tale of Susanna lays out a familiar platform that connotes issues of authentic narrative, of the "true" account of one's history. In other words, it may echo the crux of the dispute between Jews, modern scholarship, and the Samaritans regarding the history and origin of the latter. The Samaritan legend endows the high priest with the knowledge of true narrative/course of events and, by implication, suggests that he is the one who knows the true account of the history of his people.

The fear of losing credibility is exactly what prompted Israel Sedaka to criticize the anthology (according to Benyamim), which in turn drove Benyamim to write to Noy, voicing a concern that the title *Samaritan Legends* may imply that historical events (in Samaritan eyes) are treated in the anthology as fanciful tales, as false narratives. Note that there are two moments of mistrust in this cultural transaction: a mistrust toward the cultural broker (Benyamim is Ratson's son), and the related mistrust that is implied by the title of the anthology of traditional narratives. Again, Noy's reply is telling and is fraught with contradicting sentiments. He introduces Louis Ginzberg's *Legends of the Jews* as a model in which generic distinctions were employed. Ginzberg, he writes, "was meticulous and *believed firmly in the historical legacy of the people of Israel*, named his monumental book … *The Legends of the Jews*, he means by this term stories that have a geographical-historical background … the question of the historicity or non-historicity of each legend is linked to issues of research and belief." Noy's phrasing is subtle: he asserts that the "legend" is a purely formal concept, a story with historical-geographical markers, and adds a terse comment that questions of historicity are contingent on research and belief. He thus avoids directly addressing the contentious subject at hand, namely, the question of the Samaritan legends as historical truth. Yet he does address the question of "belief" and "history" indirectly by stating that Ginzberg "believed firmly in the historical legacy of his people." The key term here is "legacy," which is neither history nor fiction but nevertheless allows for a position of reverence toward past traditions as well as a sense of entitlement in the present. The facts that Ginzberg's book addresses biblical narratives/history, that the first story in the Samaritan anthology, according to Noy, dates back not to the biblical era but to the Roman period, and that the last one takes place in the nineteenth century are not acknowledged. Yet, paradoxically, in the Zionist context, where an assumed biblical origin plays a major role in the Jewish claim on Palestine, Noy's comparison provides the Samaritans with an equivalent sense of propriety based on their historical postbiblical heritage.

The following eleven tales in the anthology display recurring motifs and themes: a revered hero of ancient times (Baba Rabba); the perilous existence vis-à-vis foreign regimes and the ability to find favor in the eyes of capricious rulers; the sanctity and magical power of precious manuscripts; and last—the challenge of finding a bride to ensure the succession of a priestly leadership. External threats, while usually not posing an existential threat of annihilation, are matched in the tales by internal matrimonial crises. It is with the crisis surrounding the marriage of Pinḥas the priest, which is settled by Ratson's wife Batya's great-grandfather, that the anthology ends. The Samaritans

in Shechem, the concluding tale recounts, were reluctant to marry off their daughters to the young priest, future heir to the high priest Amram, because he lacked sufficient financial means. In the implied social hierarchy, money trumped nobility. The wealthy Marḥiv takes it upon himself to pay for the wedding and provide a sum of money for the couple's future. If chronology is the explicit compositional principle of the anthology, the thematic framework seems to delineate additional contours of the intercultural dialogue that is at stake—from metanarrative issues in the opening story of Susanna to practical social concerns of a small group striving to regenerate itself while upholding its lineage, identity, and boundaries in the last tale. This choice also gives voice to contemporary politics within the Samaritan community. Neither the founder of the Holon community, Yefet, the father of Batya, nor her husband Ratson were members of the priestly caste. Their authority was local and dependent upon Ben-Zvi's patronage. At the time when *Samaritan Legends* was produced, the impoverished Shechem community was financially supported quietly and clandestinely by Ben-Zvi—a direct result of the relationship between Ben-Zvi, Yefet, and then Ratson. That our anthology concludes with the assertion of lay power by the Tsedaka's of Holon over priestly authority is thus no accident.

The epistolary exchange between Dov Noy and Benyamim Tsedaka, and the extensive communication between Noy and Ratson Tsedaka, part of which is embodied in the layered anthology, revolve around folk narratives. That is, cultural poetics as cultural capital. These relations, one could argue, epitomize key aspects of the IFA project as an arena of cultural dialogue and appropriation. Granted, the IFA was predominantly engaged with collecting folktales of distinctly Jewish ethnic communities. However, not only was it part of Noy's vision to include in the IFA folk-traditions of all the ethnic, religious, and national groups that live in the State of Israel, but it may be the case that it is precisely because the Samaritans were perceived as a liminal group that the recording of their tales suggests an intensified model of cultural exchange that applies to the IFA in other instances as well. Be that as it may, as an almost invisible fraction of the archival collection that consists of twenty-five thousand mostly Jewish folktales, the Samaritan corpus, which includes the tales as well as written communication with archival agents, provides us with an intricate drama of Samaritan–Jewish (Zionist) relations, of texts, and of the people who acted as their agents.

For Further Reading

Moses Gaster. "The Story of the Daughter of Amram: The Samaritan Parallel to the Apocryphal Story of Susanna." In *Studies in Text in Folklore, Magic, Medieval Romance, Hebrew Apocrypha and Samaritan Archeology*, London: Maggs Brothers, 1928; reprinted New York: Ktav, 1971, I: 199–210.

Dina Stein. "Diaspora and Nostalgia: Traveling Jewish Tales in the Mediterranean." *Mediterranean Historical Review* 34, no. 1 (2019): 49–69.

Ratson Tsedaka. *Samaritan Legends: Twelve Legends from Oral Traditions*. Edited by Dov Noy. Haifa: The Israel Folktale Archives, 1965. [Hebrew].

---

1   Translated by Dina Stein.

2   Noy, 1965, 8.

20

A "Samaritan Renaissance": The Tsedaka Legacy and the Samaritan Community in Israel

DOV NOY ז"ל AND STEVEN FINE

I was born in Shechem, the holy city, located opposite Mount Gerizim, the Mountain of Blessings, to my father Benyamim and my mother Puah on the 24th day of the eleventh month, 6362 years since the creation of the world, which is 3,562 years since the settlement of the Children of Israel in the Land of Canaan, Shevat 15, 5692, according to the Jewish reckoning and February 12, 1922 according to the Christians.

When I was four years old my father placed me under the yoke of Torah and began to teach me the alphabet orally. When I was five my uncle Asher (my father's brother) began to teach me to read the Torah according to our custom: "For in the name of God I will call out" (Deuteronomy 33:3). He then taught me the first chapters of Genesis. After my reading of the first chapters became fluent, he continued until I completed all of the Book of Genesis. My father, of blessed memory [z"l], organized a large party in my honor. Naturally, this encouraged me to study with increased vigor. In less than six months, by the time I was six years old, I had completed learning the entire Torah. At that point, I entered under the yoke of the commandments. In honor of this event, a great party was arranged in my honor that continued all night long.

The next morning, I woke up quickly and rushed to the morning prayers. According to our customs, a boy who completes the entire Torah must participate in the prayers like an adult, and he may not skip even one prayer. Present at my "bar mitzvah" ceremony [called a ḥitma] was Mr. David Miller z"l. He was sent by the Jewish Agency in 1920 to teach the Samaritan students Hebrew in the school opened for the Samaritans in Shechem. In 1928 Mr. Miller was replaced by Mr. Abraham Rosen z"l. I consider it an honor to be counted among the students of these men. My Samaritan teachers were Abraham son of Pinḥas z"l and the priest Ab Ḥisda son of Jacob z"l. I also studied in the government school—Arabic, arithmetic, English, and other subjects.

During the Arab riots of 1929, the teacher Abraham Rosen was forced to abandon Shechem and thus ended my study of Hebrew … I would come to our *Knisha* (synagogue) each Sabbath preceding the festivals, and those who knew the prayers [*shira*] sang the "musaf of the festival"

which is added after the Sabbath prayers and the liturgical poems *kimei ha-shamayim al-aretz* ("as the days of the heavens and earth"), *dekor* ("remember") *maran qebel tsotkhon* ("our master, accept our prayers"), *yesh-tabaḥ* ("praise"), *milei-pot* (lit. "short words") and others. I was jealous of the singers and decided to strive to be like them …

My father merited to see my engagement to Batya, the daughter of the current head of the Samaritan community in Israel [Yefet Tsedaka]. Our first meeting was short. We met when her family, who lived in Jaffa, visited Mount Gerizim for the week of Passover, 1940. On Sukkot of that year, my father z"l received a letter from Batya, written in ancient Hebrew script and in rhyme. My father was taken with this letter and asked me to reply similarly. Thus, began our acquaintance, first through correspondence and then through visits. My first visit to Tel Aviv, in 1941, lasted seven days. I was embarrassed then that I did not know Assyrian [Jewish] script, called today "Hebrew." I resolved that for the sake of our developing relationship, I would learn it. [The] truth is, our ancient language and modern Hebrew are one language. With the aid of A. Elimelech's Hebrew-Arabic dictionary, I began to write letters to Batya—at first in Samaritan script and then in Assyrian Hebrew script. Batya was happy to receive my first letter in Assyrian script at the end of 1941. A month earlier, I had visited her, and we decided to become engaged (Figure 20.1)….

I would sin against myself were I not to mention the studies of Professor Ze'ev Ben-Ḥayyim, *Ivrit va-Aramit Nusaḥ Shomron* [*The Literary and Oral Tradition of Hebrew and Aramaic amongst the Samaritans*, Jerusalem, 1957–1961], which were awarded the Israel Prize two years ago [1964]. I was greatly honored (together with a few other members of the community) to aid in this project of reading and transcribing. Professor Ben-Ḥayyim breathes the study of the Samaritan language and has encouraged my interest. He is interested in the history of Hebrew and Aramaic pronunciation among the Samaritans. I thank him [so] much. I hope that my two sons, or at least one of them, will merit to study the various aspects of our community as a student at the Hebrew University of Jerusalem under the direction of Professor Ze'ev Ben-Ḥayyim.

— Ratson Tsedaka, Autobiographical Statement, 1965, excerpts.

20.5 Benyamim Tsedaka Lecturing at Yeshiva University, New York, November, 2018 (Photograph by Moshe Alafi).

20.6 Ovadia (Abed) Cohen and Yefet Tsedaka in *Samaritans - Icon/Sonic Opera* by Yuval Avital. Performed at *MiTo SettembreMusica*, Milan, 2010 (Photograph by Stefano Vaja forLEAV, 2010).

manuscripts and present public lectures, highlighted in *A.B.*, Benny has attracted individuals and groups of gentiles, mostly former Evangelicals. Some of these people have taken on Samaritan customs and consider themselves to be Samaritans. Tsedaka reports that eleven communities of new Samaritans have developed in Brazil (numbering "many thousands'"), smaller communities in California, Tennessee, various European countries, and even two in Indonesia.[6] The Brazil group is constituted as *Associação Aargarenzeem Israelita Samaritana dos Guardioês da torá* (The Mountgerizim Israelite Samaritan Association of Torah Guardians). All look to Benny as their spiritual guide. He communicates Samaritan customs to these followers weekly via Facebook messages in Hebrew, English, and Portuguese and through yearly visits. This project reflects Benny's understanding, from without and from within, of the fragility of Samaritan life caused by the dangerously small Samaritan population—an issue that he discusses in almost every public appearance. His missionary activities have not been sanctioned by the Mount-Gerizim-based leadership, and are seldom discussed in *A.B.*

Benyamim's many academic and communal projects, organized since 1981 as the *A.B. Center for Samaritan Studies*, have included the assemblage of a database of all Samaritan manuscripts scattered in libraries around the world, and the identification of those manuscripts. This is a passionate act of reclaiming a lost heritage, far from a disinterested exercise. Benny's finds are serialized in *A.B.* and occasionally in freestanding catalogues. Benny's extensive travels and his many contacts—from scholars to world figures—and his many lectures are well documented and presented as a source of pride for the community as a whole (Figure 20.5). During the 1990s, Benny organized a Samaritan chorus (which included a female Jewish vocalist) that appeared regularly in Europe and the United States. The choir starred in *Samaritans- Icon/Sonic Opera N.2,* a work written by Israeli Yuval Avital and performed at MiTo SettembreMusica in 2010 in Milan (Figure 20.6). This fascinating work "forms a new and fresh avant-garde concept by integrating the representation of an indigenous culture, multimedia elements and music, both ancient and contemporary. It presents an almost surreal tension between the opposite poles of antiquity and the present, the vocal and the instrumental, the traditional and the experimental."[7]

Continuing the bridge-building legacy of Yefet and Ratson, Benny has produced a vast literature that is directed both to non-Samaritan and Samaritan audiences. Prominent among the former are his article on the Samaritans in the monumental *Encyclopedia Judaica* (1971), his Torah translation into English (2013), and *Understanding the Israelites* (2017). Where Ratson produced a volume comparing the Samaritan and Jewish versions of the Torah in Hebrew (1965–1968) and prayer books directed toward Israeli Samaritan and Jewish readers, Benny's translation into English appeared with an American Christian publisher for an international readership. Benny's output directed toward Hebrew-speaking Samaritans and Jews includes collections of midrashim in modern Hebrew, his multivolume commentary on the Torah, and even cookbooks with an emphasis upon the experience of women. These continue Ratson's educational project, particularly within the Holon community, where a minority Samaritan Israeli identity has been forged—but also on Mount Gerizim, with its far more complex Samaritan-Palestinian-Israeli ethos.

Benny's outreach goes well beyond that of Ratson and beyond Israel, bringing him into contact with major world leaders on behalf of the Samaritans and their precarious position between Israelis and Palestinians. *The Samaritan Medal for Achievement in Peace, Humanitarian or Samaritan Studies* that he initiated in 2007 well expresses the assertion of communal pride and well executed *Realpolitik* that is essential to Benny's program.

The *Facebook* post translated at the start of this article well expresses Benny's message to Israeli Jews and Samaritans. It is a statement of his faith in the precarious balance between cultures that he lives. Writing in his native Israeli Hebrew and drawing on his background in Jewish Bible studies, Tsedaka uses a small fragment of a manuscript then thought to come from Qumran (most scholars now consider it a fake) that places the altar of God on Mount Gerizim, as the Samaritan Pentateuch does— and not on Mount Ebal as the Jewish versions do (Deuteronomy 27:4). Were this manuscript genuine, it would be an important support of the Samaritan version and tradition. Similarly, the fragment reads *Hargarizim*, Mount Gerizim, written as a single word as the Samaritan tradition does. These philological details are used by Tsedaka as both an icon and a "time capsule" from antiquity. Through this text, Benny gently asserts both the biblical tradition shared by Jews and Samaritans and the correctness of Samaritan tradition over the supposedly later Jewish tradition of the Masoretic text (which separates the words *Har* and *Gerizim*). This "Dead Sea fragment" is used as evidence by Tsedaka of Samaritan priority, even as it symbolizes the ancient Israelite tradition that both Jews and Samaritans share—but that Jews abandoned. This is quite a change from the Samaritan chronicles, with their epithet for Jerusalem—*Arur Shalem* ("Cursed Shalem") and their lament that "every affliction that comes upon us is due to the Jews."[8] Taking the stance of an "objective" academic scholar, Tsedaka ends the post where he began, downplaying and celebrating difference. He asserts familial and covenantal bonds between Jews and Samaritans over division and polemic, which he calls a "sin." This post epitomizes the liminal and deeply complex nature of the Tsedeka legacy—bullishly Samaritan, scholarly in tone, and proudly Israeli as it strives for its place in Israeli culture.

The "Samaritan Renaissance" that Professor Noy traced to Yefet, Ratson, and Ben-Zvi has continued for more than seventy years. Designed for communal preservation and internal Israelicization and to generate external support, the goal of this program has been broadened by Benyamim beyond immediate self-preservation and the Israeli context. It may well have transformed the deeply conservative Samaritan religion—or some part of it—into a missionary religion. As always in modern Samaritan history, the future is an open question, and Samaritan tenaciousness is a source of inspiration and spiritual power. The Tsedaka family has done much to ensure the community's success, as a new generation of Samaritans takes the helm.

— Steven Fine

For Further Reading

Michael Corinaldi. "The Personal Status of the Samaritans in Israel." In *Samaritan Researches*, edited by Vittorio Morabito, Alan D. Crown, and Lucy Davey. Sydney: Mandelbaum Publishing, 2000, 2.85–96.

Dov Noy. "Ratson Tsedaka z"l and the Samaritan Renaissance." *A.B. – The Samaritan News* 503–505 (February 15, 1990): 19–25 [Hebrew].

Miriam Tsedaka. "The Longest Way to Marry a Samaritan." *A.B. – The Samaritan News* 156 (March 15, 1976): 16.

---

1   Justnes, 2017.

2   This and the citation from Ratson Tsedaka's memoir at the top of this article are translated by Steven Fine.

3   Corinaldi, 2000.

4   Ben-Zvi, 1935, 164.

5   *A.B. – The Samaritan News* 169 (September 15, 1976): 16.

6   Tsedaka, 2019.

7   http://www.yuvalavital.com/samaritans-icon-sonic-opera-n-2

8   *The Chronicle of Abu l-Fatḥ*, ch. 54, ed. Stenhouse, pp. 244-246.

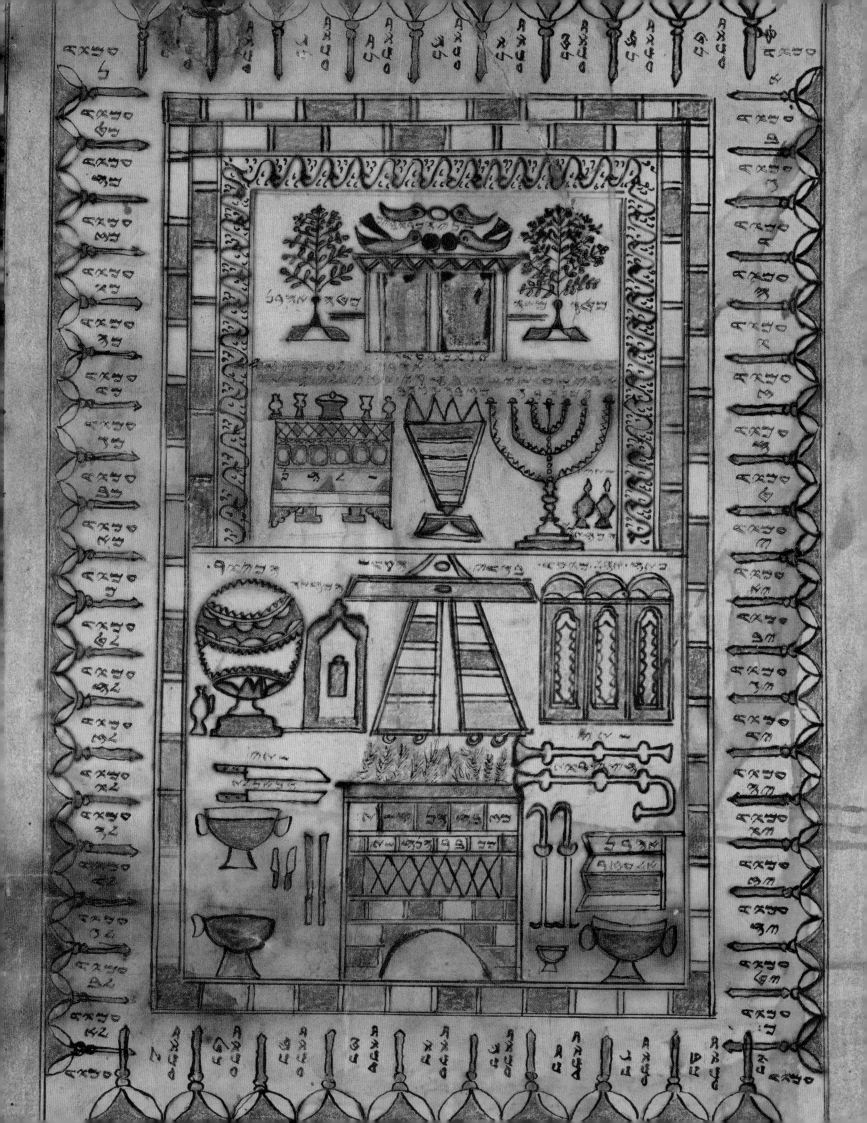

21
Tales of the Samaritan Elders

MOSHE ALAFI AND STEVEN FINE

The oral tradition will not wait. Over the last quarter century, many of the elders, the bearers of the tradition, have passed away and they did leave behind them suitable inheritors [of Samaritan oral tradition]. The new life of the Land of Israel is flowing swiftly, and there is reason to worry that many of the age-old traditions will disappear and be forgotten—if collectors (*baalei asufot*) do not rise and collect all they can. The time is now.[1]

So wrote Izhak Ben-Zvi in 1935. Happily, collectors and transmitters did take up the challenge—Samaritans, Western scholars, and often both together. In this volume, we have highlighted much of this important and, for the Samaritans, holy work. As part of the YU Israelite Samaritans Project, we undertook to preserve still more—this time in video form. Moshe Alafi interviewed elders of the Samaritan community, working with them to assemble and thus preserve their most beloved stories. Our volume opens with one of these, Badri Cohen's tale of a Passover miracle.

The stories were filmed in the reception room of the community center in Kiryat Luza. This precious collection of memories is translated here in full. Each of the Kiryat Luza storytellers concludes her or his formal presentation with a moralizing aphorism. Yefet Tsedeka, the sole resident of Holon, did not. Four of the stories are miracle tales set on Samaritan holidays in the distant past. Three are historical recollections of Samaritan life under Israel and Jordan. The women spoke in Arabic, the men in Hebrew—even those from Kiryat Luza, for whom Arabic is their first spoken language. The men chose to dress in traditional garb. All were recorded in 2019.

The printed word cannot express the beauty of the verbal performances of each of these elders. We are hopeful that at the conclusion of the YU Israelite Samaritans Project, Alafi's videos will be posted to yu.edu/cis and so be available to the public. They will be preserved at Yeshiva University Archives and at the Dov Noy Israel Folktale Archives (IFA) at the University of Haifa. We look forward to the next collections of Samaritan stories and the ones after those—for centuries to come.

MEHALEL SON OF BENYAMIM TSEDAKA, KIRYAT LUZA: "KHALIL, THE MASTER OF THE SECRET" (FIGURE 21.1)

Two hundred and thirty years ago, there was a man named Khalil. Khalil was a great man, though he hadn't studied the Torah. When he heard the children his age learning "Alef, Bet, Gamal, Dalaat …", he absorbed the letters. It is our custom, before we read from the Torah, to recite: "I will proclaim in the name of the Lord, and ascribe greatness to our Lord. The Rock, His work is perfect, for all His ways are justice, God of faithfulness and without iniquity, just and right is He" (Deuteronomy 32:3–4). Blessed be our God forever, and blessed is His Name forever." He picked that up, as well. He also learned "Hear O Israel" (Deuteronomy 6). On Yom Kippur, he didn't know how to read the Torah or the hymns or the other readings that they read [in the synagogue]. He had a strand of [prayer] beads in his hand and he said: "Alef, Bet, Gamal, Dalaat." No one heard him.

21.1
Mehalel Tsedaka, Kiryat Luza, Mount Gerizim, 2019 (Photograph by Moshe Alafi).

21.2 Mariam Al-Tef, Kiryat Luza, 2019 (Photograph by Moshe Alafi).

At that time, there were two extremely wealthy Samaritans, one named Faraj Zedaka and the other, Yitzhak Lutfi. It was the custom to go [after the Day of Atonement] to the *Kohen Gadol*, the High Priest, and ask: "How are you, my master, the Kohen? How was Yom Kippur?"

[On this occasion,] they went to Amram the Priest, the *Kohen*. Amram the *Kohen* said: "I had a terrible night." "Why, O Kohen? What happened?", they asked. He said: "I was pondering whether God has accepted our atonement, if He forgave us for our sins and misdeeds. And what can I tell you? An angel came to me in a dream and said: 'I have forgiven you for the sake of Khalil.'"

A year passed, and Faraj Zedaka went to Khalil and said: "After Yom Kippur, you will come and have dinner with me." And Yitzhak Lufti [who also visited Kalil] said: "Khalil, come to my house."

The next day, after Yom Kippur, they went to the *Kohen*. "O *Kohen*, how was Yom Kippur?" He said: "Thank God, I slept well last night. I and Khalil, my wife and children ate together." Faraj Zedaka said to Amram the Priest: "Khalil was at my table, and ate with me!" Yitzhak Lufti said to him: "No, Khalil ate at my house!" He [Faraj] said: "I am not telling a lie." The other [Yitzhak] said: "Are you saying, O *Kohen*, that we are lying?" "We would never lie to you; you are our priest." The *Kohen* said: "You know what? Let's go see Khalil."

Khalil lived in a simple house in the neighborhood. They went in

[and called]: "Khalil! Khalil! Khalil!" No one answered. They forced the door open, went in, and found Khalil dead. The *Kohen* said to them: "There is a mystery here and what I saw in my dream was true." From that day forward, they referred to him as *Khalil Isoriye*, "Khalil, the Master of the Secret."

MARIAM AL-TEF, KIRYAT LUZA: "I ASK YOU ALL TO PLACE YOUR FAITH IN GOD" (FIGURE 21.2)

My name is Mariam Al-Tef. I want to tell you stories our parents used to tell us. My father-in-law was fifteen when his father died. This was during the Ottoman period [before 1918]. His father left him to take care of his mother and five siblings. He had nothing. He had no work, so he tried to ask people for money and started to beg.

When one of the holidays was coming, his mother said to him: "Your siblings are hungry, they have nothing to eat. Take this metal tray, go to the merchant, pawn it and get some flour in exchange so that I can bake bread." He took the tray to the shopkeeper, but the shopkeeper refused to take the tray. He refused to give him flour. The boy cried all the way home.

On his way, in the darkness, he stepped on something. He thought it was a [dead] mouse. He looked up to Heaven and cried: "Dear God, I have no money for food and no money to go to the baths to purify myself. Please have mercy on my siblings and don't

21.3 Faiza Cohen Wasef, Kiryat Luza, 2019 (Photograph by Moshe Alafi).

make me step on something that will cost me even more money [having touched a dead rodent, he would need to go to the public baths to purify himself.—SF].”

When he went back to see what it was, he saw a small sack on the ground. He picked it up, looked at it, and saw something shiny. He took it, went on his way, opened the sack, and found it was full of gold coins.

The boy went back to the shopkeeper and said: “Give me flour, rice, and sugar.” The shopkeeper asked: “Where did you get this money?” He replied: “God sent it.”

He went home, and his siblings were asleep. He said to his mother: “Cook for them.” She said: “But they’re sleeping.” He said: “Wake them up.” She asked: “Where did you get the money?” He replied: “From God.” She cooked for the children, woke them, fed them.

The boy paid all the expenses of the holiday from the contents of the sack, without counting how much money was in it. After the holiday, he discovered that all the money had been spent.

God, praise His name, never abandons a person in need. God gives to those who ask. Let us thank God for all His deeds. I ask you all to place your faith in God.

FAIZA COHEN WASEF, KIRYAT LUZA: “BUT FROM THE DEPTHS OF TROUBLES, HELP ALWAYS COMES” (FIGURE 21.3)

My name is Faiza Cohen Wasef, mother of Abed.[2] You want to hear stories of the past. Here’s what happened in the Yasmin [Samaritan] neighborhood of Nablus.

We were five sisters and three brothers. Our father was a simple man. He had no money. He was poor. Eighteen of us shared a house—us and my uncle’s family. We had no bread to eat. Nothing. Little children with nothing to eat! Eighteen of us shared a single chicken. We had no meat to eat. The fruit ... we’d all share one orange. We were in dire straits.

My husband, Abu Abed, lived in the Yasmin neighborhood [as well]. When his father died, they [his family] were in dire straits. My mother-in-law wanted to feed the children, so she kneaded some dough.

One son was sent to [the Muslim] baker Abu Abed to bake the dough. He asked: “Do you have money?” He said “no.” “Go get it.” He went back to his mother and said: “He wants money.” She said: “I have no money. I searched your [dead] father’s pockets and didn’t find a *grush* [“a cent”]. Leave the dough here; I will fry it and feed you.” She fried the dough and fed them *zalabia* [“donuts”].

The next day, they wanted to bake. A figure appeared to the baker that night and awakened him. “Have you no mercy? You sent

21.4   Yefet Tsedaka, Holon (Photograph by Moshe Alafi).

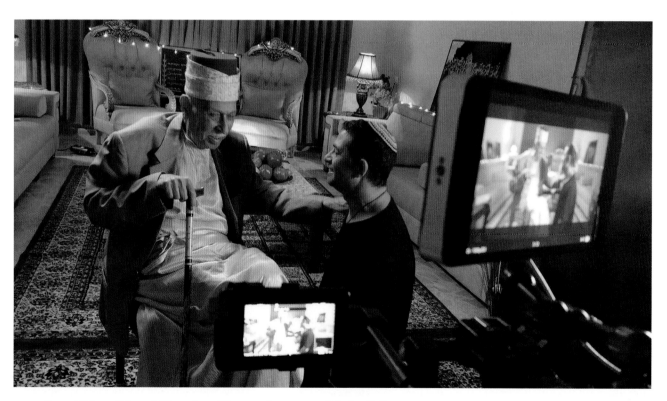

21.5   Shmuel (Ishmael) Sasoni, Kiryat Luza (Photograph courtesy of Moshe Alafi).

ⲩⲙⲇⲩⲩⲙ⳽   MOSHE ALAFI AND STEVEN FINE

the boy home without bread? Prepare to be punished by Allah." He tried to go back to sleep. His wife asked: "What's the matter?" He answered: "The Samaritan priest rebuked me in a dream." "What should I do?" She said: "It's because you wouldn't bake their bread." He said: "Okay, I'll deal with this later. I want to sleep."

Again the bearded figure in white appeared and shook him. He didn't actually shake him; it was all a dream. He said to his wife: "What should I do? He appeared again." She said: "When you see the boy with the dough, grab the dough from him, bake it and take the bread to his house."

The next day, he [the baker] went to his oven, grabbed the boy's dough, baked it, went to the boy's mother, and gave her the bread himself. She said: "Why did you bother?" He answered: "Give me a break. I can't sleep. His father appeared in my dreams: 'If you don't come and bake this morning, I'll come get the dough myself.'"

If God gives something to His righteous, one must not treat them that way. The weak should be treated kindly. One must not offend people. The Samaritans have always had troubles. But from the depths of troubles, help always comes.

YEFET TSEDAKA, HOLON: "HOW COULD ANYONE SAY THAT ABOUT THE SAMARITANS?" (FIGURE 21.4)

The year was 1956. I was in fifth grade. We had a teacher named Rachel. In one class, we were studying [the Jewish biblical book] Second Kings (Chapter 17), [which was] about people who came from Avva and Sepharvaim and Cuthah. She told the whole class that the Samaritans are Cutheans and that they worship idols, that they are dove worshippers, and that they don't belong to the people of Israel.

Naturally, I was very, very hurt. I went home very sad, and my mother, who was an educator, soon realized that I was out of sorts. She asked me: "What happened?" I told her the story. She said: "Oh, really? Okay, come with me right now."

She took me to Grandpa Yefet. "Tell Grandpa what happened." I told him what had happened, and I started to cry. He said: "Don't cry; tomorrow you are not going to school." Just like that. I said: "Then what will I do?" "You will go up to Jerusalem with me."

The next morning at eight o'clock, he took me to Jerusalem. It wasn't as it is now, an hour's drive to Jerusalem, or forty-five minutes. You had to go to Tel Aviv by bus, then take another bus, and, from the bus station in Jerusalem, take another bus to the President's Residence.

We went together and arrived at the President's Residence. Of course, there were guards at the entrance and my grandfather, who hadn't made an appointment, started to walk in. The guard said: "What are you doing here?" He answered: "I'm here to see the president." "Do you have an appointment?" "No." He [the guard] radioed in that Yefet Tsedaka was at the gate. He [President Ben-Zvi] told the guard: "Tell him to stay there; I'll come to him. Don't send him to me; I want to greet him."

The president came to the gate, and greeted us. We went into the reception room. I, a little boy, was trembling all over. Then grandpa made me tell the president what had happened. I told the president. The president was shocked: "How could anyone say that about the Samaritans? That they are gentiles? They are not gentiles!" And he wrote a letter and sent it by courier to the Minister of Education: "I want this dealt with—not tomorrow, today!" "This teacher may not teach classes with Samaritans in them. If she says this stupid thing again, even to other students, by the president's order, she may no longer work in the Ministry of Education." Our class got a new Scripture teacher and that was the end of that problem. They no longer spoke about this subject in the Book of Kings [in classes with Samaritan children]. When they reached that chapter, they just skipped it.

ISHMAEL (SHMUEL) SON OF AZAT SIRAWI SASONI, KIRYAT LUZA: "HAPPY ARE THOSE WHO KEEP THE SABBATH AND ANYONE WHO OBSERVES IT IS CALLED A SAMARITAN [A KEEPER OF THE TORAH]" (FIGURE 21.5)

I am from the Samaritan community. I keep the Sabbath very strictly, according to the commandments of the Torah. We studied in Arab schools [during Jordanian rule], and we got used to not going to school on the Sabbath. I completed twelve years of school; at the end there's a series of tests: it's called the matriculation test. You take it after high school and then move on to university.

To matriculate, in the old days, in Jordan, you needed five subjects. You were allowed to fail in one subject and take the test again, and if you passed, you passed. I was at home studying when a Samaritan friend came over: "Shmuel! Shmuel! I have the test schedule."

At first, I panicked. Why? Mathematics was to be tested half on Thursday and half on Shabbat. As a religious Samaritan, I don't go to school on Shabbat. So why take the test? Twelve years wasted, finished!

My poor father came home from work, saw that I was sad, and asked: "Why are you so sad?" I told him what was the matter. He took it hard, very hard. He was waiting for his son to graduate and help him in life, and so ….

He had a friend, Zedaka Cohen, a distinguished priest, known to the Jordanian royal family. My father told him about it. He said: "Tomorrow we will go to Amman [capital of Jordan] and we'll see what we can do. He and my father went to Amman, and asked to meet the Minister of Education. They met him.

He told the minister what happened: "Never mind, he can do a retest." "That's no good, the retest is also on the Sabbath." As they were talking, the minister looked at my father and saw a tear in his eye. The *Kohen* said: "Wait." "Why is the old man crying?" "That's why I'm here. Because of that tear." He [the official] fell silent. He said: "Look, priest, you have my word, give me one day and I'll get you an answer."

The next day, the *Kohen* came to our house, laughing. The minister consulted his colleagues, who told him: "If this person fails in one subject, the retest won't be on Saturday. It will be on a different day."

And so it was, I failed in math. The retest was on a Monday, and I took the test. For one Samaritan, they changed the whole program for a whole country, for me! After I passed, I said to myself: "Our Sages are right: 'Happy are those who keep the Sabbath and anyone who observes it is called a Samaritan [a keeper of the Torah].'"

21.6   Dan Hadani, Samaritan Pilgrimage to Mount Gerizim on Shavuot, June 18, 1967 (From the Collection of the National Library of Israel, Dan Hadani Archive).

ISHMAEL (SHMUEL) SON OF AZAT SIRAWI SASONI, KIRYAT LUZA: "WE FELT HAPPINESS THAT CANNOT BE FORGOTTEN."

In 1967, we lived in the Samaritan neighborhood in Shechem. We had a shop in the casbah. When war between Israel and Egypt broke out, the Arabs began to dance. They sang and danced: "We will throw the Jews into the sea." My father was afraid that the Arabs would threaten us, so he closed the shop, and we went home.

That Wednesday, we were at home; we heard the boom-boom-boom of the tanks. The Samaritans began to say among themselves that those were [the sounds of] Israeli troops. But we couldn't say it out loud; we couldn't say it. We whispered it among ourselves.

That morning, we awoke to the sound of tanks. Tanks were driving around the neighborhood. The flag of Israel was above the tanks. So we said: "Oh-ho, wonderful. Now we are under Israeli rule!"

My father, may his memory be blessed, immediately wanted to go to Jaffa, to Tel Aviv, to see what was there. He started to dance. He was seventy-eight or eighty years old, and he started to dance!

He thought that he could go straight to Israel to see Ratson Tsedaka (Figure 19.1, 20.2) and his other relatives.

His first encounter was with two or three Samaritan soldiers serving in the Israeli army. They entered the home of the High Priest. The High Priest was Amram son of Yitzhak, and his brother was Zedaka son of Yitzhak.

They went in, and … oh, what joy and kissing and … "How are you? Did anything happen to you during the war?" "No, we're fine. The war is over and we're at peace." That was the first meeting. Four or five days later, we celebrated the festival of Shavuot [Pentecost]. The Samaritans of Holon came, and we celebrated Shavuot on Mount Gerizim; we celebrated together for the first time without asking permission from the Jordanians or anyone else except for the Israeli Army. We felt happiness that cannot be forgotten (Figure 21.6).

---

1   Ben-Zvi, 1935, p. 9.

2   Abed Cohen appears in figure 20.6 and 22.1.

22
Reflections of a Documentary Filmmaker

MOSHE ALAFI

The Samaritans: A Biblical People, ha-Shomronim: Edah. Torah. Har. tells the story of the Samaritan will to survive—to maintain, preserve, and "keep" their truth against all odds. Our team reveals Samaritan treasures and manuscripts that are seldom seen by outsiders, including the legendary Abisha Scroll. We present the lives of three key individuals within the Samaritan community, exploring the deeply religious and spiritual world of this ancient yet endangered biblical people in its heroic biblical quest for survival. Shadi Atlif is a thirty-two-year-old Samaritan priest, with no chance of marriage within the community. He met Natasha in Ukraine, after an Internet courtship. We follow this new couple from their initial meeting to Natashas arrival in Israel, their engagement, wedding, and the complexities of life as a mixed-Samaritan family. The tensions are immense, and the stakes are even larger.

Ḥefetz Marḥiv (seventy-eight years old) is a leader of the Mount Gerizim Samaritan community, the last Samaritan scribe for Torah books written by hand in Samaritan script. Ḥefetz teaches the youth to read and recite scripture. He knows that others have switched to computerized texts, but this is not allowed for the holy books in the synagogue. Who will write the holy books in the future? He has only five students and is afraid that the age-old scribal arts will be lost. Ḥefetz prays that they will keep to the ways of their people.

Benyamim Tsedaka (seventy-five years old) is a Samaritan scholar and leader of the Holon community. Benny travels the world in search of friends for his community and Samaritan books to redeem through scholarship—holy manuscripts sold for bread by the destitute Samaritans in centuries past. The future of his people is in his hands, and Tsedaka is desperately seeking a successor among the young, with slight success. Against the will of the high priest, Tsedaka has created communities of gentile Samaritans in Brazil—desperate that the Samaritans may survive.

The Samaritans: A Biblical People is no ordinary documentary film or ethnographic study. This project aims to be both a mirror and a voice for the Samaritans themselves, an expression of who they are: their past, their current struggles, and their hopes for the future. The leadership of the Israelite Samaritan community has fully supported our efforts. We see this documentary as both a "calling card" for the Israelite Samaritans and a window through which we may experience their endangered three-thousand-year-old tradition.

— From an early funding proposal for *The Samaritans: A Biblical People*

When I began this journey six or seven years ago, the Samaritans seemed distant and far away—both in time and in space. In fact, their centers on Mount Gerizim and in Holon are each only an hour's drive from my home in Jerusalem. The existence of these ancient biblical people seemed almost mythical to me, like something out of the *Iliad* or the *Odyssey*. Each spring, while gearing up my Passover preparations, my mind drifted to the Samaritans and their Passover sacrifice, which I had never seen. "We Jews," I thought to myself, "'merely' discuss the laws of the Passover sacrifice. The Samaritans actually perform them!" I had no idea then how deeply contact with the Samaritans would soon challenge my own assumptions about Judaism.

In 2012, I was invited to direct and produce a short film for a new visitor center at Mount Gerizim National Park—which is adjacent to Kiryat Luza, the Samaritan center, and home of the high priest. The name, I now know, has deep roots for Samaritans. Mount Gerizim is identified as the Beit-El of Genesis 28:19, "which was originally called Luz." This film was my opportunity to "ascend the mountain" and really understand the Samaritans—literally and figuratively, perhaps even spiritually. It would engage me as a documentary filmmaker and challenge me as an Orthodox Jew. I was very excited. In this sixteen-minute film, I was to tell the story of Mount Gerizim and its people not just for Israeli and international tourists, Jews, Christians, and Muslims—but for the Samaritans themselves. That was quite a tall order!

Journey to the Mount premiered at the Mount Gerizim Visitor Center in 2018 and was well received. I remained unsatisfied, however. The project just felt incomplete. The more I learned, the more I realized how little I really understood the Samaritan

22.1 Abed (Ovadia) Cohen Prepares the *Mezuzah* Plaque for Shadi (Ziv) and Natasha's New Home, Kiryat Luza, Mount Gerizim, June, 26, 2019 (Photograph by Moshe Alafi).

people—and the less I felt satisfied. I hadn't yet explored the inner world of the Samaritan community—its leading figures, historical personalities, ancient texts, contemporary challenges—and the ancient secrets that have preserved the community for over three-and-a-half thousand years. I wanted to know more.

In 2016, Benyamim Tsedaka called me excitedly. Benny and I had worked closely on *Journey to the Mount*. He told me about a call for proposals by the New Fund for Cinema and Television in Tel Aviv to produce a sixty-minute documentary film about the Samaritans. This was a serious project, with real academic and international support—not a promotional video, or a news report, but a full-length documentary! "Tell them you have my endorsement," Benyamim said over the phone. Little did I know that Benny was working quietly with Professor Steven Fine of Yeshiva University, promoting my application. Now I had to win the competition!

After a serious competition, the New Fund for Cinema and Television and the Yeshiva University Center for Israel Studies entrusted me with the project. It meant a lot that the Samaritan Community Council pledged to support my work. The community offered unparalleled access to the lives of both the Mount Gerizim and Holon communities—and to their community treasures. On top of that, Steven and I approached this project with the same intense enthusiasm, as we set out on this adventure together. I returned to my files and old footage and began dreaming.

As a documentary filmmaker, I connect deeply with people, and I tell their stories. The films that have been made about the Samaritans in the last few years view the community as outsiders looking in. My goal was to enter their world, to embed myself as best I could in their happiest and saddest moments. I hoped to document the life and the challenges of this small community with passion and com-

passion. It took time for members of the community to really trust me. Who would appreciate a stranger sticking his camera into their daily lives and most intimate concerns, and then producing a film? Over centuries, the Samaritans have rightly learned to be suspicious of outsiders like me. They have been hurt too many times.

After many cups of black coffee and conversations lasting long into the night, I was slowly made privy to the lives of the community and of the challenges the Samaritans face. Again and again, our conversations turned to survival. How would a small community of eight hundred and eighteen people (the population on January 1, 2020) survive? Most Samaritans are optimistic about the future and proud of their glorious history, enduring against all odds. They constantly worry about new challenges to their way of life. Our documentary tracks attempts by the Samaritans to ensure their own future—with pathos and pain.

SHADI (ZIV) AND NATASHA ATLIF: SURVIVAL AT WHAT COST? (FIGURE 22.1)

Survival is a complex thing. What happens when one person or one family's strategy for survival is a direct threat to other members of the community? These tensions can debilitate large nations, all the more a micro-nation like the Samaritans. Over the course of two years, I documented the story of Shadi and Natasha. Shadi (in Hebrew, Ziv) Altif searched and searched for a spouse within the community. He was desperate. Finally, he was introduced online to Natasha from Kherson, Ukraine. He traveled there often, and they spoke online even more. Shadi and Natasha married a year later. I shadowed this new couple—with and without my camera—for hundreds of hours. Deciding to bring a "foreign wife" was no easy decision for Shadi. Still, he understood that in light of the genetic problems of his inbred community, "new blood" was essential for the preservation of the entire Samaritan people. Beyond that, Shadi was alone, with no prospects for marriage. What was he to do?

The same devotion to the community that motivates Shadi is heard in the cries of Samaritan women elders in Holon. These leaders poured out their fears from the depths of their hearts, my cameras rolling. One woman said: "Those who intermarry are breaking apart our community; they will destroy us. The entire snowball will smash, and there will be nothing left of us." They have reason to worry. Thirty Ukrainian women and twenty other foreign women have recently joined the Mount Gerizim community. This is on top of the high intermarriage rate between Holon men and Israeli Jewish women—which became acceptable just a generation ago. A small number have left the community. The children of these new Samaritans will not be raised in Ancient Hebrew, as their fathers were. They will speak Modern Hebrew, Arabic, and Russian. They will have a completely different relationship to their ancestral traditions than any previous generation of Samaritans has had. In anguish, Matzliaḥ Cohen, a priest who lives on Mount Gerizim, told me on camera that "I would prefer a community of two-hundred-and-fifty real Samaritans over a community of eight-hundred-and-fifty people of which some are merely listed as Samaritans in their identity cards but are not actually Samaritan." My heart broke.

I, the Jewish filmmaker, listened and sympathized, and kept the cameras rolling. Sometimes, I even tried to help a bit. I often thought to myself: "This is what happened to us Jews. The barrier to conversion was lifted already in ancient times, and we were able to marry converts from outside of the Jewish community (albeit with certain limits and conditions). It was precisely this form of intermingling that saved Judaism from becoming a community on the verge of extinction." Still, I can say that as an Israeli. Intermarriage endangers the very future of even the great American Jewish community! Even Orthodox families are not immune. What will become of the Samaritans?

During one of my many days of filming, while my team and I were standing outside of the synagogue on Mount Gerizim, a young Samaritan approached me, and addressed me in Hebrew. He asked with a bitter smile: "You guys don't have this sort of thing, do you?" "What thing?", I asked him curiously. He answered: "Never-ending prayers lasting six, eight, or twelve hours straight, or prayers that begin on Shabbat at three in the morning. How can we go on this way? A lot of guys don't even come to the synagogue or just show up for a little bit. If the priests would only shorten the prayers, then everyone would come on time and everyone would be able to complete them."

I could only smile. "We all have the same challenges," I answered. In my heart, I continued: "These are exactly the same discussions that I have heard in my own community and in my own synagogue. For Sephardi Jews like me, the early morning Seliḥot [penitentiary prayers before the High Holy Days], parts of the Sabbath prayers, and other rituals are also really, really long. I often hear that "if we would just change, shorten … make them more accessible." Is it true? Perhaps the entire edifice of prayer would crumble if we begin to change it? Once again, I was struck by the relevance of the Samaritan

dilemma to my own thinking about contemporary Jewish culture.

I have often heard from my non-religious friends that "Judaism is frozen in the past." "Move on already," they jibe. "Why do you stick to customs that haven't been relevant for a thousand years?" In Samaritan culture, change comes very, very slowly, and the mimetic transfer of all things Samaritan from parent to child is at the core of Samaritan identity. Samaritans follow and fulfill the written Torah and rely mostly on oral teachings to know how to do it. This kind of transmission is so fragile! We Jews have a vast literature of "Oral Torah," and follow Jewish law as laid down in the *Shulkhan Arukh*, a compendium compiled by Rabbi Joseph Caro in 1563. Thousands of books of Jewish law and lore, *Halakha* and *Aggada*, have been written, each according to the practices of every Jewish community. Samaritans too have books preserved in manuscript, but few can read them. The Samaritans tell us that their tradition has stayed the same for over three-and-a-half thousand years. We say the same about Judaism. Continuity is at the center of our self-understanding. Their tradition does develop and adapt slowly—even slower than ours!

MATZLIAḤ COHEN: FILMING THE ABISHA SCROLL (FIGURE 22.2)

"They won't let you" is the documentary filmmaker's favorite expression. We filmmakers are like children: tell us that "they won't let you," and we take it as a personal challenge. Such was the case with the Abisha Scroll. Since I came to the community as an impartial listener, I will recount the story of the Abisha Scroll just as my Samaritan friends told it to me. The Scroll was written, I was told, by Abisha son of Pinḥas son of the high priest Aaron in the thirteenth year after Israel's entry into the Holy Land, led by Joshua son of Nun. It is only taken out of its safe in the Mount Gerizim synagogue on special and rare occasions, and even then it is kept in a glass box and only handled by the eldest priest.

I wanted to see and photograph this scroll, and Steven, cheering me on from New York and sharing insights from his own reading—was adamant that we must try. Many other Torah scrolls were copied from it, and these were the scrolls usually shown to visitors. Mention of the scribe of the Abisha Scroll is found at the end of the Scroll in the *tashqil* passage written in between the columns of the original text of the Scroll. I asked everyone who I thought could help to see and photograph the Abisha Scroll. The response was always a resounding "no." "The Scroll is not brought out for outsiders."

On one particular day, my team and I went to film Matzliaḥ the priest and his son Brito as they prostrated themselves before the synagogue ark and recited the five Samaritan articles of faith. I once again asked to see the Abisha Scroll. Once again, the answer was: "It is not brought out." I called Abed, the former head of the Community Council. He put me in touch with Aharon the priest, one of the synagogue officiants, the *ḥazzanim*. Aharon, like Matzliaḥ, was very clear: "It is not brought out." Then I got in touch with Benyamim Tsedaka. He said to Abed: "He's OK. Give him permission. Remember, we are working together."

The Abisha Scroll is kept in a double locked safe. Each lock has a separate key, and each key is guarded by a different priest. One

22.2 Cantor Matzliaḥ (Najah) Cohen examines the Abisha Scroll, Synagogue, Kiryat Luza, Mount Gerizim, 2019 (Photograph by Moshe Alafi).

of those priests was Abed, and the other was Aharon. I would need permission from both to see the Scroll. Needless to say, I was feeling the pressure. For months, I had been refused, but maybe now "the gates of Heaven would open." Aharon called back. This time the answer was: "Fine, but don't touch the Scroll, don't photograph the place where it is stored, don't ascend the altar, don't set up any lighting, and only the eldest priest may handle it." Upon receiving permission to view the Abisha Scroll, I noticed that the expression on Matzliaḥ's face had completely changed. Matzliaḥ, Pinḥas, and another priest approached the platform before the Holy Ark. They drew back the ancient curtain emblazoned in silver thread embroidered with images of the Tabernacle and its vessels. They then disappeared behind the screen. Brito remained with me. The scraping of keys and the squeaking of hinges could be heard from behind the curtain. Minutes later, the group emerged with the glass case containing the Abisha Scroll. Matzliaḥ was absolutely beaming. I became very excited. I felt as though I was being greeted by a distant ancestor, for Abisha was the grandson of the high priest Aaron, the brother of Moses. Abisha personally knew the prophet Moses.

They placed the case down on the table with reverent trepidation and removed the Scroll. The script was somewhat faded, and the parchment was crumbling a bit; after all, the Scroll is over three-and-a-half-thousand years old! Matzliaḥ held the Scroll in his hands, and Aharon the priest adorned it with stunning, thousand-year-old silver Torah finials, what Jews call *rimmonim*, pomegranates. Matzliaḥ spoke with a trembling voice: "Moshe thanks to you, really, thanks to you. "Thanks to me what?" I asked Matzliaḥ. "I have

served as a *ḥazzan* for over fourteen years, but this is the first time that I have handled this holy scroll with my own hands. Thanks to you, really, thanks to you."

ḤEFETZ MARḤIV: SCRIBE AND TEACHER (FIGURE 22.3)
Many Torah scrolls and codices have been copied by hand from the text of the Abisha Scroll. The oldest and most famous Samaritan scribe alive today is a wise and humble man named Ḥefetz Marḥiv. Ḥefetz Marḥiv is a Torah scribe, liturgical poet, and a schoolteacher who trains children for their *ḥitma* ceremony, a ceremony that marks religious maturity. My Samaritan friends were quick to tell me that it is "like a bar mitzvah." Ḥefetz opened for me the world of Samaritan education and also shared with me a painful story that he has in common with many other elders of the community.

Immediately following the fall holidays, all the children who have reached the age of seven are gathered into the community center. They study five days a week throughout the entire year. Preparing for class, Ḥefetz sets out for school from his home at the edge of the neighborhood, in the winter wearing a thick Bedouin *abaya* and in the summer holding a parasol to protect him from the bright sun. The children arrive at the community center at two thirty immediately after a long day of school in Nablus. Ḥefetz teaches the children everything from basic literacy in Samaritan Hebrew to a mastery of the five books of the Torah—from the first line of Genesis to the last line of Deuteronomy. At the end of the year, the *ḥitma* is organized for each child. This is a joyous family affair with a lot of refreshments. The child is expected to publicly recite the "Song of Moses" (Deuteronomy 32) by heart.

22.3 Ḥefetz Marḥiv, Scribe and Teacher, Kiryat Luza, Mount Gerizim, 2019 (Photograph by Moshea Alafi).

Ḥefetz has been a teacher for over thirty years. Hundreds of children from the community have studied with him. When I asked him if he recalled his own *ḥitma*, he smiled bashfully and answered: "I didn't have a *ḥitma*; we didn't have anything to eat at home, so we couldn't invite others to a party." It broke my heart. But the scales of justice prevail in this world. He who did not merit a *ḥitma* of his own has merited to train every Samaritan child on Mount Gerizim for this most important event of their lives for over thirty years.

Ḥefetz's inner passion was made evident to me in his home one day after he completed writing his fifteenth Torah scroll—this one before our cameras. He showed us how he, like Abisha before him, transmitted his legacy to the next generation. At the conclusion of his Torah can be found the *tashqil* ("The work of Ḥefetz Marḥiv"), which is just like the *tashqil* of the Abisha Scroll—a scroll bequeathed to all generations of Samaritans to come.

JAMIL COHEN: CHANGE FROM THE BOTTOM UP (FIGURE 22.4)

As I became more and more familiar with the Samaritans, I took note of the community's profound respect for the divinely appointed high priest. When the priestly line of Pinḥas ended several hundred years ago, the priesthood was transferred to the line of Ithamar in accordance with the Leviticus 21:10: "The priest who is greater than [*gadol mi*] his brother" is interpreted to mean "the priest who is older than his brother *in years*." A Samaritan priest might know if he was next in line for the high priesthood, but he would never know if he would actually achieve the office. The practical details of his appointment are left to Heaven.

A cultural gap between the older generation that experienced British, Jordanian, Israeli, and Palestinian rule and a more worldly and less traumatized younger generation is growing wider and wider. The younger Samaritans are thirsting for a less restrictive communal structure, one that can preserve their customs while allowing for the kind of personal development common to Israelis and even Palestinians of their generation. At the forefront of innovation is Jamil, named in Hebrew for Yefet, the third son of the biblical Noah. Jamil, a member of the Community Council, has a strong character and is a visionary. He is a bold man who permits himself to act first and ask questions later. Jamil fascinates me because of his dual commitment to the new and his absolute adherence to tradition. Jamil is a man of the "middle generation." He is a trained scribe who prepares marriage contracts (*mikhtav zivug*) and writes amulets, and he is also a successful Nablus businessman. "Changes," he says, "must come from the bottom up. Only afterwards will the community leadership accept them." Jamil understands that this film project will help the community to consider its current situation and its future more deeply.

SHMUEL SASONI: JUST ONE STORY (FIGURE 21.5)

Jamil sent me to meet one of the elders of the community, not a priest but an important and unique scholar, Shmuel Sasoni. When I entered Shmuel's house, I immediately noticed a pipe organ in the living room. This was an unusual sight. I had not seen a musical instrument in any of the other homes that I had visited. In the Samaritan tradition, all music is vocal. There are no instruments, nor is there a method of musical notation. But here in Shmuel's house, a musical instrument was on display!

22.4 Jamal Cohen, Member of the Community Council, in his Office, Kiryat Luza, Mount Gerizim, 2019 (Photograph by Moshe Alafi).

After I explained who I was and what I was looking for, Shmuel uncapped his wellspring of knowledge. Our conversation slid between history, culture, and textual variants between the Jewish and Samaritan versions of the Torah. He explained which Samaritan customs are of ancient origin and which of them developed later, due to practical circumstances (for example, the construction of the *sukkah* inside the home). From there, the conversation shifted to the challenges that the Samaritan community faces today.

Shmuel is a math teacher. I asked him if he could tell me a story that he would like to pass on to the next generation. The eighty-two-year-old sat in a big leather armchair and contemplated my question. "There are so many important stories that should be passed on to the next generation," he answered me. "How can I choose?" I did not answer him. I just looked deeply into Shmuel's eyes and said: "Please, my dear friend, just one story." A long silence passed, as I waited. Shmuel began his story, which he later repeated before our

cameras as part of our Tales of the Samaritan Elders Initiative, and we titled based upon the concluding line: "Happy Are Those Who Keep the Sabbath and Anyone Who Observes It Is Called a Samaritan [a Keeper of the Torah]." I stayed with Shmuel for another hour and a half to listen to many more stories, and just as I was about to leave, Shmuel said to me: "Until today I had two daughters and one son. Now, I have two sons and two daughters—you have become like a son to me."

I, of course, have no intention of becoming a Samaritan—even if I could. I am grateful that this community has opened up to me the doors of their houses, their synagogue, and, most importantly, their hearts. I look forward to the Passover sacrifice next year on Mount Gerizim, my personal "journey to the mount." There, I will watch my friends eat the meat of the Paschal lamb, while I film the event for posterity.

Translated by Baruch-Lev Kelman

23
Contemporary Jewish Artists Encounter Samaritan Culture: A Visual Essay

STEVEN FINE AND RICHARD McBEE

In the Fall of 2020, in the heat of the COVID crisis, we assembled an international group of Jewish artists over Zoom to think together about the Samaritans, their culture and our interactions with them over more than three millennia. Our plan was to integrate the results in the exhibition, *The Samaritans: A Biblical People.* While a considerable body of Christian art illustrating stories involving Samaritans of the New Testament exists, we were keenly aware of the almost complete lack of engagement by Jewish artists with Samaritans and Samaritanism. Our exhibition was the chance to explore this theme. Members of the Jewish Art Salon, an international association of artists creating contemporary Jewish visual art, studied textual, historical and visual sources with Steven via zoom over several weeks. All the while, each artist was imaging the kinds of art that she or he could make in conversation with what they were learning. All were surprised, most exhilarated, and a few dropped out. Each artist was keenly aware that this engagement with the Samaritans had to treat our new acquaintances with the deepest respect even as we strove to be true to our own identities. In a sense, the artists experienced in paint and metal and paper and leather what academics often experience in writing; photographers and filmmakers in pixels. The results are still coming in, and a more thorough discussion of this project will appear in *Images: A Journal of Jewish Art.*

Many of the works focus on the parallel paths taken by Samaritans and Jews. In *The Samaritan Series*, Mark Podwal sets Samaritan iconography in conversation with his earlier work on Torah imagery, Hebrew calligraphy (here, Samaritan), the flora and geography of the Land of Israel and the menorah as lighting fixture (a double entendre in Hebrew). The Abisha Scroll is particularly prominent in his effervescent images (Figure 23.1a-d). In "Tabernacles," Yona Verwer set imagery drawn from Samaritan Tabernacle drawings in conversation with medieval Jewish depictions of the Tabernacle (Figure 23.2). She printed her two tabernacles on a kind of vertical blind, so that each could be seen to varying degrees simultaneously— or separately. Andi Arnovitz is creating *Palimpsest* (a work still is progress) as an assembly of (almost) identical Samaritan and Jewish Torah texts printed back to back on rice paper then bound, rolled and shelved— as if in an ancient/modern book shelf (Figure 23.3). Arnovitz's work is a metaphor for the complexities and closeness of Jewish-Samaritan relations over millennia.

Hillel Smith, Richard McBee and Archie Rand interpreted the Samaritan-Jewish relationship in figurative terms. Smith drew on the visage of Jacob son of Aaron, creating a contemporary legend in Samaritan Hebrew that Samaritans can read, but others can only recognize (Figure 23.4). It reads *Hineni,* "Here I am," a reference to the Binding of Isaac (Genesis 22). This piece calls out through Jacob's stylized visage and Smith's bold colors for the attention of viewers. In *The Encounter* McBee presents the Binding of Isaac, with two "Abrahams"— an American Orthodox Jew and a Samaritan. The Samaritan "Abraham" bears the iconic features of high priest Jacob son of Aaron (Figure 23.5). Each ascends the mountain to sacrifice his only son, Isaac, as described in Genesis 22. The pairs walk side by side, without noticing one another, up the different mountains that in McBee's vision are the same peak. In *The Samaritans*, Archie Rand creates an iconic association between a Jewish and a Samaritan man, each in ritual garb and both set at the time of religious focus (Figure 23.6).

Judith Joseph and Joel Silverstein engaged Samaritan stories that we studied together directly. Judith created a homage to Badri Cohen's Passover tale, creating a bell reminiscent of those worn by the sheep (Figure 23.7). Titled *The Voice of the Bell,* Joseph's bell is engraved with flora typical of plants that sprout on Mount Gerizim each spring. Leather strands dangle small bells that tinkle in the wind, each strand punched with the text of Exodus 12, the biblical Passover sacrifice in Samaritan script. Above the bell, Hebrew letters ascend to heaven, like prayers or the smoke of the pascal sacrifice. In *The Death of Shobakh,* Silverstein engages the "Epistle of Joshua Son of Nun," a story preserved in the Samaritan chronicles that was absorbed into Jewish literature during the Early Modern period (Figure 23.8).[1] Drawing on comic book and other pop culture imagery, Silverstein tells the story of Shobakh, king of Armenia, who led a great legion to the valley of Shechem to take back the Land from Joshua and the children of Israel. He almost succeeds, after Shobakh's mother, a witch (styled after the Wicked Witch of the West), magically imprisons Joshua behind seven walls. Israel is saved by the hero of this Samaritan-come-Jewish tale, the biblical priest Pinḥas son of Eleazar, the son of Aaron. Sporting the "covenant of peace" and the "eternal covenant" promised to him in Numbers 25, Pinḥas rides in like the cavalry upon his steed. Silverstein's Pinḥas, with his characteristically Samaritan red cap, represents the institution of the high priesthood— which guides and protects the "the Keepers" to this very day.

---

1 Mentioned by Jesse Abelman in this volume; Fine, 2021.

23.1a-d
Mark Podwal, from *The Samaritan Series*, 2020
(Courtesy of Mark Podwal).

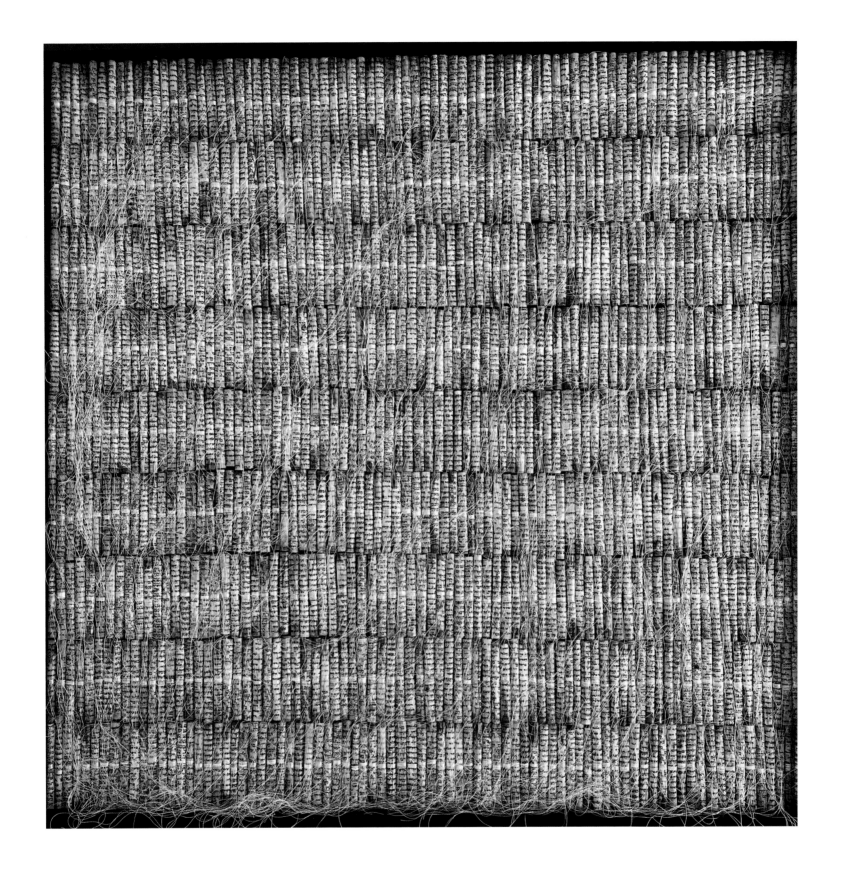

23.3 Andi Arnovitz, "Palimpsest," 2021 (Photograph by Andi Aronovitz).

STEVEN FINE AND RICHARD McBEE

23.4 Hillel Smith, *Hineni, Here I Am*, 2021 (Photograph by Hillel Smith).

23.5 Richard McBee, *The Encounter*, 2021 (Photograph by Richard McBee).

23.6 Archie Rand, *Samaritans,* 2021 (Photograph by Kevin Blumenthal).

23.7 Judith Joseph, *The Voice of the Bell,* Copper and leather, brass bells, 2021 (Photograph by Judith Joseph).

𐤉𐤌𐤒𐤃𐤔𐤅𐤓

23.8 Joel Silverstein, *The Death of Shobakh*, 2021 (Photograph by Joel Silverstein).

24
Afterword: Why the Samaritans?

STEVEN FINE

When my oldest son was in fourth grade, some time ago, he was studying in a Mishnah class at the start of the academic year. His small class was preparing for the Jewish New Year, and the rabbi—a young graduate of a Baltimore yeshiva—was guiding the boys through Tractate Rosh Hashanah. The group arrived at Mishnah Rosh Hashanah 2:2, the story of the nefarious *Kutim* discussed so beautifully by Joseph L. Angel in our volume. Rabbi Cohen (not his real name) began to explain how these awful *Kusim* (in Yiddish dialect) ruined the communication of vital information from Jerusalem to the Galilee, Syria, and ultimately Babylonia. He told the boys that the *Kutim* were descendants of false converts, always attacking "us."

Rabbi Cohen must surely have told this story many, many times to many children. After all, Rashi, the great commentator, *al ha-daf,* right there in the Talmud, calls *Kutim* "lion converts"—insincere converts who fell back into idolatry. A little way into the discussion, Elisha looked rattled, and Rabbi Cohen noticed. "What's wrong Elisha," the attentive and kind teacher asked. "Rabbi Cohen, my *abba* [dad] has a friend who is Samaritan. Calling Samaritans *Kutim* is like using the "N" word." The teacher had no answer and went on with the lesson. Soon after, though, he sought me out to tell me this story, and to ask for more information about Samaritans.

A second story: Elisha knows one Samaritan well—Benny Tsedaka (Figure 24.2). Benny is an occasional visitor in our home, as are we to his. We have been friends for years, having been introduced by our mutual teacher, Professor Dov Noy. Benny was kind and open to my then little boy. On one occasion, Benny was visiting us at the same time that a great Israeli scholar of midrash was visiting the small college, Baltimore Hebrew University, where I launched my career. I planned a public program, where we all would learn and teach about Samaritans and Jews in antiquity. The three of us, and the rest of my family, had a delightful dinner at our home before the program (which was well attended). As the meal was winding down, Leah, my wife, brought out small booklets of the blessings after meals to conclude the event.

Tsedaka was deeply engaged in conversation with Elisha, and the scholar, a dear man, and I were jabbering along separately—

in Hebrew. He looked at me wryly as the booklets arrived with a twinkle in his eye and asked me: *Mevarkhin alav?* That is, is he included in the call to say grace said at the beginning these blessings, traditionally pronounced when in the presence of three Jewish men. I smiled, knowing that my friend was citing a Mishnaic text in Tractate Berakhot (Chapter 7:1). It reads: "Three who dined together must say the call [to bless]?" The Mishnah goes on to mention the *Kuti* as one to include. I glanced in his eye, chuckled, and responded in English: "Leave me alone."

This second story, of two Jewish academics and a Samaritan, is more complex than it seems at first glance. Jews have not included Samaritans in the prayer call for a millennium and a half, as attitudes and relations between Samaritans and Jews hardened into enmity, name-calling, and separation. Friendship became rare if it happened at all. Our story is still more complicated, however. It should be recalled that Benny's mother was Batya Tsedaka, the daughter of Yefet Tsedaka—who was the first Samaritan to marry a Jewish woman. Her name was Miriam, a penniless widow introduced by Yefet's friend Izhak Ben-Zvi. According to the rabbinic matrilineal principle of Jewish descent, then, Benny is indeed Jewish. Our program was a success. More than that, at this meal Elisha once again saw, in the flesh, that his father has a friend "who is a Samaritan."

The negativity between Jews and Samaritans began to change in recent times, after the Jerusalem Chief Rabbi— *Ḥakham Bashi*— Ḥayyim Abraham (Mircado) Gagin (died 1848) saved the Samaritan remnant from destruction by asserting their Israelite lineage; the legendary high priest Jacob son of Aaron came into office; and then after Yefet Tsedaka took in a young Izhak Ben-Zvi in Jaffa in 1909. Ben-Zvi, who appears across this volume, was a friend, matchmaker, scholar, and the main benefactor of the Samaritans for over half a century. This connection had inestimable significance for the Samaritans. Having a leader of the Zionist movement as their patron had great benefits—and the president of the new state even more so. Ben-Zvi's last public act was the dedication of the synagogue in Holon in 1963. As Israel Tsedaka has taught us, the Israeli Samaritans declared the feud over, furthering their sometimes complex

© STEVEN FINE, 2022 | DOI:10.1163/9789004466913_026

24.1 Pilgrimage to Mount Gerizim during Covid, Passover morning, 2020 (Photograph by Zev Rothkoff).

integration into Israeli society. As far as the Israeli Samaritans were concerned, the Samaritans and the Jews were one nation once again.

Samaritans and Jews have come a long way together—from their biblical split through the reigns of the Persians, Greeks, Romans, Christians, and Muslims. This was a relationship that both sides saw as a kind of death dance—until Jacob son of Aaron, Yefet Tsedeka, and a wide range of Jewish and Samaritan figures decided otherwise. Reconciliation is not easy in our world—whether between Serbs and Croats, Protestants and Catholics, Trumpists and Progressives, or Samaritans and Jews. It is rare, and notable, especially for a thirty-six-hundred-year-old enmity. In a real sense, then, this complex attempt at reconciliation is a model for us all.

The Samaritans are neither Jews nor Arabs: in fact, they are both

and neither all at once. Thus, they pose a challenge to our sense of self. They are the "other Israel." For some of my students, this realization is close to the equivalent of hearing that humans are likely not alone in the universe. Meeting Benny on campus—three times so far—has been a point of real and unforgettable excitement for students and faculty alike. Our project is an opportunity on the largest possible stage for us all to reflect—Jews, Christians, Muslims, and Samaritans—to think about otherness and complexity, about core issues of who each of us is, and about what we hope to be.

A third story: a few years ago, an Israeli friend, an art historian, received a phone call from her granddaughter, a soldier in the legal department of the Israel Defense Forces. *Savta*, she asked, what is the difference between a Samaritan and a Karaite?" "Why do you

24.2 Benyamim Tsedaka and Steven Fine examine a Samaritan manuscript, Yeshiva University, 2018 (Photograph by Moshe Alafi).

24.3 *Har Bracha* [Mountain of Blessing] *Tahini*— Samaritan Tahini, ready to be shipped from the factory in Kiryat Luza, Mount Gerizim, 2020 (Photograph by Steven Fine).

ask," inquired the grandmother. "*Savta*, a Karaite soldier insulted a Samaritan soldier, and he beat him up. The case came to us, and we need to understand the difference between them."

Sometimes invisible to Israeli society, the Samaritans are a piece of modern Israel, of its "fabric," its cultural "mosaic." The Holon branch is completely integrated into Israeli society, while the Mount Gerizim community has a far more complex place in the web of relationships between Israel and the Palestinians. Some Mount Gerizim Samaritans work in family businesses, and earn their livings writing amulets for Arabs and Jews in Nablus, while still others work in factories in the Israeli city of Ariel. One works for a rent-a-car firm at Ben-Gurion Airport. Another is a school principal in Nablus. Samaritan tahini is world-famous, manufactured by the sons of the high priest on Mount Gerizim, featured in the Hebrew version of *Forbes* magazine, and is produced under rabbinical supervision (for our benefit. Figure 24.2). Yefet Tsedaka (named for his grandfather), Benny's brother and neighbor in Holon, is a member of the Central Committee of the Likud, the political party led by former prime minister Benjamin Netanyahu. A Samaritan seat is reserved on the Palestinian Legislative Council. The community, like all communities, also has its limits—played out publicly in the painful excision of popular Israeli actress Sofi Sarah Tsedeka, who converted to Judaism after an acrimonious separation from the community and who is now embracing something of her Samaritan roots. In a real sense, Samaritans are one of the many "tribes" of modern Israel, a piece of its complexity, a lesser-known and understudied element of a complex multicultural country.

For me as a cultural historian of Judaism in the Roman world, Samaritanism has great academic interest. For more than a century and a half, Samaritans have been studied and analyzed, their history discussed, artifacts uncovered, and texts published. Archeologist Leah di Segni nonetheless wrote in 1998 that the Samaritans are a "ghost people."[1] What she meant is that like ghosts they float through scholarship on ancient Judaism and Christianity, and are deployed as "explanations" for otherwise inexplicable questions, a side-subject that Jews and Christians use when convenient but one that they seldom actually know. There is much historical scholarship on rabbinic or Christian attitudes toward Samaritans, but it is the rare scholar of these fields who goes beyond that. There have been some, as we have seen. Michael Avi-Yonah included Samaritans in his story, as did midrashist Joseph Heinemann, Noy the folklorist, and more recently Menachem Mor and Hagith Sivan in their larger histories.[2] In general, though, actual Samaritans, their literature and material culture have been left to the Samaritanologists. The spotlight in historical scholarship instead has been on "non-rabbinic Jews," "Jewish followers of Jesus," Jewish–Christian relations in late antiquity, and Christian influence on Judaism.

The integration of Samaritan Studies into contemporary scholarship on the history and literature of late antiquity provides a third voice, the Samaritan, alongside the Jewish and that of Roman Imperial Christianity. The two "Israels" of the flesh are now together with the newer "Israel of the spirit." Samaritanism allows histori-ans like me to ask hard questions about Jewish and rabbinic identity and their "others" and get answers back from a second living community. We can now go beyond the modern construction of "non-rabbinic Jews"—people whom ancient rabbis called *ammei ha-arets*—"people of the land"—"ignoramuses," be they rich or poor, educated or not. I realized at some point that I could engage not only texts and artifacts (if that is not enough) but actual "non-rabbinic" Israelites—Sabbath-keeping, Torah-observing Israelites— many of them Levites, like me—and that they were willing to talk. When I first began this search, almost three decades ago, American scholars were wont to smirk ("there he goes again") when I suggested that Samaritan Studies and the integration of the "other Israel" into our work could transform and revive a field, just as they did when my dear departed friend Yaakov Elman began to explore the Babylonian Talmud within its Sasanian Persian environment.

As I was quietly collecting Samaritan *mezuzot,* books and ephemera, Yaakov was acquiring Zoroastrian documents and prayer garments. We were both making new friends and enamored with the parallel paths we were walking. The comparativist impulse has always been a trademark of Yeshiva University scholarship—from founder Bernard Revel's work on Karaite *halakha* (which included Samaritan law), second president Samuel Belkin's work on Philo of Alexandria, to Louis H. Feldman's studies of Josephus, Elman's work on the Talmud in its Iranian context, and my own interests in art, archeology, and now the Samaritans. Yeshiva scholars have always been contrarian in this way, bucking the majoritarian discourse in favor of comparative studies. This is a hallmark of our commitment to both *Torah* and *Madda,* to an integrationist impulse that looks out from and builds upon our core commitments to Judaism, the Jewish people, Zionism, and synthetic engagement with our neighbors.

More than a century ago, the great Zionist cultural sage Asher Ginzberg, known as Ahad Ha'am, "One of the People," called on his colleagues to overcome their prejudices and help the then-faltering Samaritans to survive. Enough Jews responded with funds and food and support and even teachers. After May 1948 and until June 1967, the early State of Israel—struggling itself— quietly supported the community in Nablus and helped the Israeli Samaritans to establish themselves in Holon. This support continues, though many in the Israeli religious establishment have always been understandably queasy about the relationship. Today prosperous beyond their dreams, the Samaritan community has reached out to us. In preparing our documentary, exhibition, and books, the community allowed us—meaning Moshe Alafi—to enter places where few have gone before. They have embraced us, supported us, and shared their deepest fears and hopes with us in a very public way. In a real sense, we have become a mirror for the community, as the Samaritans plot and imagine their own future—and they for us, as we plot ours. "Do we include him?" The answer for our project is an emphatic "yes!"

---

1   Di Segni, 1998, 51.
2   Avi-Yonah, 1984; Mor, 2003; Sivan, 2009.

Bibliography

A.B. – The Samaritan News. "Letter of Opposition to the Samaritans from the 19th Century," 584–586 (1993): 120–139. [Hebrew].

——. "The Priests Are in Unity of Mind Regarding Marriages with Non-Samaritans." *A.B. – The Samaritan News* 169 (September 15, 1976): 16.

——. "Thousands of Shechem Residents Visited the Exhibition of our Heritage and Were Enthusiastic about its Many Exhibits." *A.B. – The Samaritan News*, 379 (March 15, 1985): 1. [Hebrew].

Abū al-Fatḥ. *The Kitāb Al-Tarīkh of Abu 'l-Fath*, tr. Paul Stenhouse, Sydney, AU: Mandelbaum Trust, University of Sydney, 1985.

Abū Shafīq. "Ya'qūb b. ʿUzzi (The Priest Jacob the Samaritan)," *The Book of the Samaritans.* Nablus, 1960, Arabic.

——. *Tārīḫ ḥayātī*, Nablus, 1972, 1975 (manuscript). [Arabic].

——. *Waṣiyyatī wa-Tārīḫ ḥayātī*, Nablus, 1974 (manuscript). [Arabic].

Ahad Ha'am (Asher Ginzberg). "A Small Compilation." *HaShiloah* 1 (1897): 385–391. [Hebrew].

Adler, Elkan-Nathan, and Max Séligsohn. *Une Nouvelle Chronique Samaritaine.* Paris: Librarie Durlacher, 1903.

Akhiezer, Golda. "The Research Project of Abraham Firkovich as an Outcome of *Haskalah* and *Ḥokhmat Israel*." In *Studies in Caucasian, Georgian, and Bukharan Jewry: Historical, Sociological, and Cultural Aspects*, ed. Golda Akhiezer, Reuven Enoch, and Sergei Weinstein. Ariel: Ariel University Institute for Research of Jewish Communities of the Caucasus and Central Asia, 2014, 38–71.

——. *Historical Consciousness, Haskalah, and Nationalism among the Karaites of Eastern Europe.* Leiden: Brill, 2018.

Albert Edward, Prince of Wales, 1862, *The Prince of Wales's Journal: 14 February – 14 June, 1962.* London: Royal Collection Trust. https://www.rct.uk/collection/themes/exhibitions/cairo-to-constantinople/the-queens-gallery-buckingham-palace/the-prince-of-waless-journal-6-february-14-june-1862 (manuscript).

Alon, Gedaliah. "The Origin of the Samaritans in Halakhic Tradition." In *Jews, Judaism and the Classical World.* Jerusalem: Magnes, 1977, 354–373.

Anderson, Robert T. "The Museum Trail: The Michigan State University Samaritan Collection." *The Biblical Archaeologist* 47, no. 1 (1984): 41–43.

Arnon, Danchu. *The Samaritans, Recipes, Traditions and Customs.* Tel Aviv: Rosh Yarok Press, 1999. [Hebrew].

Avi-Yonah, Michael. *The Jews under Roman and Byzantine Rule: A Political History of Palestine from the Bar Kokhba War to the Arab Conquest.* New York: Schocken Books, 1984.

Barges, J.J.L. *Les Samaritains de Naplouse.* Paris, 1855.

Barton, William E. *The Old World in the New Century.* Chicago. The Pilgrim Press, 1902.

Bedford, Francis. *The Holy Land, Egypt, Constantinople, Athens, etc. etc. A Series of Forty-Eight Photographs, taken by Francis Bedford, for H.R.H. the Prince of Wales during the Tour in the East, in which, by command, he accompanied his Royal Highness, with Descriptive Text and Introduction by W.M. Thompson.* London: Day & Son, 1866.

Ben-Gurion, David. *Studies in the Book of Joshua.* Jerusalem: Kiryat Sefer Publications, 1960. [Hebrew].

Ben-Gurion, David, and Izhak Ben-Zvi. *Erets Yisroel in Fergangenheyt un Gegenvart.* New York, 1918. [Yiddish].

Ben-Ḥayyim, Ze'ev. *The Literary and Oral Tradition of Hebrew and Aramaic amongst the Samaritans. Volume III, Part 2: The Recitation of Prayers and Hymns.* Jerusalem: The Academy of the Hebrew Language, 1967. [Hebrew].

——. ed. תיבת מרקה [*Tibåt Mârqe]: A Collection of Samaritan Midrashim, Edited, Translated and Annotated.* Jerusalem: Israel Academy of Sciences, 1988. [Hebrew].

Benjamin of Tudela. *The Itinerary of Benjamin of Tudela: Critical Text, Translation and Commentary*, ed. and trans. Marcus N. Adler. London: H. Frowde, 1907.

Benjamin, Sandra. *The World of Benjamin of Tudela: A Medieval Mediterranean Monologue*, Teaneck, NJ: Fairleigh Dickinson University Press, 1995.

Ben-Zvi, Izhak. *The Samaritans.* Tel Aviv: A.Y. Stiebel, 1935; repr. Jerusalem: Yad Ben-Zvi Press, 1970. [Hebrew].

——. *Eretz Israel under Ottoman Rule.* Jerusalem: Bialik Institute, 1955. [Hebrew].

——. *The Exiled and the Redeemed.* Philadelphia: Jewish Publication Society, 1957.

——. *Essays and Reminiscences*, ed. Rahel Yanait Ben-Zvi and Yehuda Erez. Jerusalem: Yad Ben-Zvi Press, 1966. [Hebrew].

Botley, Paul, and Dirk van Miert, eds. *The Correspondence of Joseph Justus Scaliger.* Geneva: Librairie Droz, 2012.

Bourgel, Jonathan. "Roman Influence on Relations between Jews and Samaritans." *Cathedra* 144 (2012): 7–20. [Hebrew].

Boušek, Daniel. "The Story of the Prophet Muhammad's Encounter with a Samaritan, a Jew, and a Christian: The Version from Abu l-Fatḥ's *Kitub al-Turikh* and Its Context." In *The Samaritans in Historical, Cultural and Linguistic Perspectives*, ed. Jan Dušek. Berlin: De Gruyter, 2018, 105–130.

Bowman, John. *Samaritan Documents Relating to Their History, Religion, and Life.* Eugene, OR: Wipf and Stock, 1977.

Chen, Sarina. *Between Poetics and Politics: Vision and Praxis in Current Activity to Construct the Third Temple.* PhD diss., The Hebrew University of Jerusalem, 2007. [Hebrew].

Chiesa, Bruno, and Wilfrid Lockwood. *Yaqub Qirqisani on Sects and Christianity: A Translation of "Kitab al-anwar."* Book 1. Frankfurt: Lang, 1984.

Churgin, Pinkhos. *Studies in the Times of the Second Temple.* New York: 1949. [Hebrew].

Claridge, Amanda. *Rome. An Oxford Archaeological Guide.* New York: Oxford University Press: 2010.

Cohen, Yoel. "The Political Role of the Israeli Chief Rabbinate in the Temple Mount Question." *Jewish Political Studies Review* 11, no. 1–2 (1999): 101–126.

Corinaldi, Michael. "The Personal Status of the Samaritans in Israel." In *Samaritan Researches*, ed. Vittorio Morabito, Alan D. Crown and Lucy Davey. Sydney: Mandelbaum Publishing, 2000, 2.85–96.

Cowley, Arthur E. "Samaritana." *Jewish Quarterly Review* 16, no. 3 (1904): 474–484.

——. *The Samaritan Liturgy.* London: Clarendon Press, 1909.

Crown, Alan D., "The Abisha Scroll of the Samaritans." *Bulletin of the John*

Rylands University Library 58 (1975): 36-65.

——. ed. *The Samaritans*. Tübingen: Mohr Siebeck, 1989.

——. et al., eds. *A Companion to Samaritan Studies*. Tübingen: Mohr Siebeck, 1993.

Daube, David. "Jesus and the Samaritan Woman: The Meaning of συγχράομαι." *Journal of Biblical Literature* 69, no. 2 (1950): 137–147.

Deinard, Efraim. *Toldot Eben Reshef*. Warsaw, 1875.

Di Segni, Leah. "The Samaritans in Roman-Byzantine Palestine: Some Misapprehensions." In *Religious and Ethnic Communities in Later Roman Palestine*, ed. Hayim Lapin. Bethesda: University Press of Maryland, 1998, 51–66.

Dvir, A. *The Letters of Dr. HaLevi*. 1884. [Hebrew].

Elkin, Ze'ev, and Menachem Ben-Sasson. 2002. "Abraham Firkovich and the Cairo Genizas in the Light of His Personal Archive." *Pe'amim* 90: 51–95. [Hebrew].

Elmalih, Avraham. *HaRishonim Letzion*. Jerusalem: Rubin Mass, 1970. [Hebrew].

Even Shmuel (Kaufmann), Yehuda. *Midreshei Ge'ulah*. Tel Aviv: Dvir Publishing House, 1954. [Hebrew].

Feldman, Louis H. "Josephus' Attitude Toward the Samaritans: A Study in Ambivalence," *Studies in Jewish Civilizations-- 3: Jewish Sects, Religious Movements, and Political Parties,* Menachem Mor, ed., Omaha: Creighton University Press, 1992.

——. "Josephus' Attitude Toward the Samaritans: A Study in Ambivalence." *Studies in Jewish Civilization* 3 (1992): 23–45, repr. *Studies in Hellenistic Judaism*. Leiden: Brill, 1996, 114–146.

Fine, Steven, ed. *Sacred Realm: The Emergence of the Synagogue in the Ancient World*. New York: Yeshiva University Museum, 1996.

——. "'For the School House Is Beautiful': A Note on Samaritan 'Schools' in Late Antique Palestine." In *Shoshannat Yaakov: Studies in Honor of Professor Yaakov Elman*, ed. Shai Secunda and Steven Fine. Leiden: Brill, 2012, 66–76.

——. "When is a Menorah "Jewish"? On the Complexities of a Symbol under Byzantium and Islam." In *Age of Transition: Byzantine Culture in the Islamic World*, ed. H. Evans. New York: Metropolitan Museum of Art, 2015, 38-53.

——. "'They Remembered That They Had Seen It in a Jewish Midrash': How a Samaritan Tale Became a Legend of the Jews." *Religions* 12 (2021). https://doi.org/10.3390/rel12080635.

Finkel, Joshua. *Jewish, Christian, and Samaritan Influences on Arabia*. Princeton, NJ: Princeton University Press, 1933.

Finn, James. *Stirring Times*. London: C.K. Paul & Co., 1878.

Firkovich, Abraham. 1872. *Avnei Zikkaron*. Vilna. [Hebrew].

Frankl, Ludwig August. *The Jews in the East*, Vol. 2. Trans. P. Beaton. London: Hurst and Blackett Publishers, 1859.

Franz-Klauser, Olivia. "Samaritanerforschung im 19. Jahrhundert: Die Anfänge der historischen Kritik im Schatter religiöser Vorurteile, gezeigt an der Rezeption Moritz Heidenheims (1824–1898)." *Pardes* 12 (2006): 112–137.

Funkenstein, Amos. *Perceptions of Jewish History*. Berkeley: University of California Press, 1993.

Furstenberg, Yair. "The Rabbis and the Roman Citizenship Model: The Case of the Samaritans." In *In the Crucible of Empire: The Impact of Roman Citizenship upon Greeks, Jews and Christians*, ed. Katell Berthelot and Jonathan J. Price. Leuven: Peeters, 2019, 181–216.

Gafni, Isaiah. *Relations between Jews and Samaritans in the Period of the Mishnah and the Talmud*. MA thesis, The Hebrew University of Jerusalem, 1969. [Hebrew].

Gaster, Moses. "Jewish Knowledge of the Samaritan Alphabet in the Middle Ages." *The Journal of the Royal Asiatic Society of Great Britain and Ireland* (1913): 613–626, repr. *Studies and Texts in Folklore, Magic, Medieval Romance, Hebrew Apocrypha and Samaritan Archeology*. London: Maggs Brothers, 1928, repr. New York: Ktav, 1971, 1:600–613.

——. *The Samaritans: Their History, Doctrines and Literature*. London: The British Academy, 1925.

——. "The Story of the Daughter of Amram: The Samaritan Parallel to the Apocryphal Story of Susanna." In *Studies and Texts in Folklore, Magic, Medieval Romance, Hebrew Apocrypha and Samaritan Archeology*, London: Maggs Brothers, 1928, repr. New York: Ktav, 1971, 1:199–210.

——. "The Story of My Library." Trans. B. Sabin Hill. *British Library Journal* 21, no. 1 (1995): 16–21.

Gaster, Theodor H. "Prolegomenon: Moses Gaster (1856-1939)," *Studies and Texts in Folklore, Magic, Medieval Romance, Hebrew Apocrypha and Samaritan Archeology,* New York: Ktav, 1971, 1: xv-xxxxix.

Ginzburg, Mordechay Aharon. *Dvir: Including a Collection of Various Letters, etc.* Vilna: Menaheam Mann Ben Baruch and Simha Zimel Ben Menahem Nahum Press, 1844. [Hebrew].

Goitein, S.D. *A Mediterranean Society: The Jewish Communities of the Arab World as Portrayed in the Documents of the Cairo Geniza, Vol. 2: The Community*. Berkeley: University of California Press, 1972.

Goldhaber, Yechiel. *The Jewish Community in Nablus: Relations between the Jewish Community and the Samaritan Community*. Jerusalem, 2019 (manuscript).

Grafman, Rafi, *Crowning Glory: Silver Torah Ornaments of the Jewish Museum*, ed. Vivian B. Mann. New York: The Jewish Museum, 1996.

Guérin, Victor. *Description Géographique Historique et Archéologique de la Palestine 2: Samarie, pt. 1*. Paris: L'Imprimerie Nationale, 1874.

Hadar, Alon. "The Demons in the Most Famous Samaritan Family Break Out of their Bottle," *Makor Rishon*, October 10, 2009. [Hebrew].

Halpern-Amaru, Betsy. "The Journey of Susanna among the Church Fathers." In *The Judgment of Susanna: Authority and Witness*, ed. Ellen Spolsky. Atlanta: Scholars Press, 1996, 21–34.

Hamutovski, Yitzhak. "Rabbi Meir and the Samaritans: The Differences Between the Accounts in the Yerushalmi and the Bavli." *JSIJ – Jewish Studies, an Internet Journal* 8 (2009): 34–39 [Hebrew].

Har'el, Yaron. "On the Common Educational Initiative of the Jews and Samaritans in Nablus." *Cathedra* 119 (2006): 121–132. [Hebrew].

Haralambakis, Maria. "A Survey of the Gaster Collection at the John Rylands Library, Manchester." *Bulletin of the John Rylands Library* 89, no. 2 (1993): 109–110.

Harviainen, Tapani and Haseeb Shehadeh. "How Did Abraham Firkovich Acquire the Great Collection of Samaritan Manuscripts in Nablus in 1864?" *Studia Orientalia* 73 (1994): 167–192.

Hasan-Rokem, Galit. "Textualizing the Tales of the People of the Book: Folk Narrative Anthologies and National Identity in Modern Israel." *Prooftexts* 19, no. 1 (1999): 71–82.

——. *Tales of the Neighborhood: Jewish Narrative Dialogues in Late Antiquity*. Berkeley: University of California Press, 2003.

Heinemann, Joseph. "Anti-Samaritan Polemics in the Aggadah." *Proceedings of the World Congress of Jewish Studies* 1973 (1977): 57–69.

Heller, Chaim. *The Samaritan Pentateuch: An Adaptation of the Massoretic Text.* Berlin, 1923. [Hebrew].

Horesh, Priel. "The Synagogue and the Torah Scroll During the Eighteenth and Nineteenth Centuries" *A.B. – The Samaritan News* 454 (February 15, 1988): 14–15 [Hebrew].

Hutchinson, Walter. *Customs of the World.* London: Hutchinson, 1900.

Isser, Stanley. "Jesus in the Samaritan Chronicles." *Journal of Jewish Studies* 32, no. 2 (1981): 166–194.

Jacobs, Martin. *Orienting the East: Jewish Travelers to the Medieval Muslim World.* Philadelphia: University of Pennsylvania Press, 2014.

Jacoby, Ruth. "The Four Species in Jewish and Samaritan Tradition." In *From Dura to Sepphoris: Studies in Jewish Art and Society in Late Antiquity*, ed. Lee I. Levine and Ze'ev Weiss. Portsmouth, RI: Journal of Roman Archaeology, 2000, 225–230.

Justnes, Årstein. "Forfalskninger av dødehavsruller: Om mer enn 70 nye fragmenter—og historien om ett av dem (DSS F.154; 5 Mos 27,4–6) [Faking the Dead Sea Scrolls: On More than 70 New Fragments—and the Story about One of Them (DSS F.154; Deut 27:4–6)]." *Teologisk Tidsskrift* 6, no. 1 (2017): 70–83.

Kartveit, Magnar. "Samaritan Self-Consciousness in the First Half of the Second Century B.C.E. in Light of the Inscriptions from Mount Gerizim and Delos." *Journal for the Study of Judaism in the Persian, Hellenistic and Roman Periods* 45 (2014): 449–470.

Katz, Israel J. "In Memoriam: Johanna Spector (1915–2008)." *Musica Judaica* 19 (2009): 183–198.

Kelman, Baruch-Lev. "A Samaritan Torah Curtain in a Jewish Synagogue? A Responsum of Jacob b. David ibn Yaḥya, 1622." Forthcoming.

Kirchheim, Raphael. *Karme Shomron: The Vineyards of Samaria.* Frankfurt: I. Kaufmann, 1851. [Hebrew].

Knoppers, Gary. *Jews and Samaritans: The Origins and History of Their Early Relations.* Oxford: Oxford University Press, 2013.

Koester, Craig R. *The Dwelling of God: The Tabernacle in the Old Testament, Intertestamental Literature, and the Old [sic; read: New] Testament.* Washington, DC: The Catholic Biblical Association of America, 1989.

Lavee, Moshe. "The Samaritan May Be Included: Another Look at the Samaritan in Talmudic Literature." In *Samaritans: Past and Present*, ed. Menachem Mor and Friedrich V. Reiterer. Berlin: De Gruyter, 2010, 147–173.

Lebedev, Victor V. 1992. *Samaritanskie dokumenty Gosudarstvennoi Publichnoi biblioteki im. M. E. Saltykova-Shchedrina: Katalog [Samaritan Documents of the State Public M. Saltykov-Shchedrin Library: Catalogue].* Saint Petersburg: State Public M. Saltykov-Shchedrin Library.

Levine, Lee I. "R. Abbahu of Caesarea." In *Christianity, Judaism and Other Greco-Roman Cults*, ed. Jacob Neusner. Leiden: Brill, 1975, 4.56–76.

Levy-Rubin, Milka, ed. *The Continuatio of the Samaritan Chronicle of Abu l-Fatḥ al-Sumiri al-Danafi.* Princeton, NJ: The Darwin Press, 2002.

Lieber, Laura S. "Feasting, Fasting, and the Bounty of the Land: Rituals of Sukkot in Samaritan and Rabbinic Antiquity." In *Law and Spirituality in Rabbinic Literature*, ed. Shana Strauch Schick, Leiden: Brill, 2021, 138–159.

——. *Classical Samaritan Poetry in Context.* University Park: Pennsylvania State University Press, forthcoming.

Lieberman, Saul. *Studies in Palestinian Talmudic Literature,* ed. David Rosenthal. Jerusalem: Magnes Press, 1991. [Hebrew].

Loeb, Laurence D. "Review: *The Samaritans: The People of the Sacred Mountain.*

Filmed by Johanna Spector." *American Anthropologist* 77, no. 3 (1975): 694–695.

Ludwig August Frankl. *The Jews in the East*, Vol. 2. Trans. P. Beaton. London: Hurst and Blackett Publishers, 1859.

MacDonald, John, and A.J.B. Higgins. "The Beginnings of the Christianity according to the Samaritans." *New Testament Studies* 18 (1971): 54–80.

Magen, Yitzhak. *The Samaritans and the Good Samaritan.* Jerusalem: Staff Officer of Archaeology, Civil Administration for Judea and Samaria, 2008.

Mayer. Leo Ari. "A Samaritan Curtain from the Sixteenth Century." *Bulletin of the Israel Exploration Society* 13 (1947) 169-170. [Hebrew].

Megillat Taanit, ed. Vered Noam. Jerusalem: Yad Ben-Zvi Press, 2003. [Hebrew].

Meshorer, Yaakov. *City Coins of Eretz Israel and the Roman Period.* Jerusalem: The Israel Museum, 1985.

Miller, Peter N. *Peiresc's Mediterranean World.* Cambridge, MA: Harvard University Press, 2015.

Mills, John. *Three Months' Residence in Nablus: The Modern Samaritans.* London: J. Murray, 1864.

Montgomery, James. *The Samaritans: The Earliest Jewish Sect, Their History, Theology and Literature.* Philadelphia: J.C. Winston, 1907.

Mor, Menachem. *From Samaria to Shechem: The Samaritan Community in Antiquity.* Jerusalem: Shazar, 2003. [Hebrew].

——. and Friedrich Reiterer, eds. *Samaritans: Past and Present: Current Studies.* Berlin: De Gruyter, 2010.

Nachmanides, Moses. *Moses ben Nahman's Commentary on the Torah*, ed. Charles Chavel. Jerusalem: Mossad Harav Kook, 1960. [Hebrew].

Nasr, Seyyed Hossein, Caner Karacay Dagli, et. al., eds. *The Study Quran: A New Translation and Commentary.* San Francisco CA: HarperOne, 2015.

New York Times. "120 Israeli Samaritans Go on a Pilgrimage to Jordan." May 5, 1966, 12.

Niessen, Friedrich. "A Judaeo-Arabic Fragment of a Samaritan Chronicle from the Cairo Geniza." *Journal of Semitic Studies* 47, no. 2 (2002): 215–236.

Notley, R. Steven, and Jeffrey P. García. "Hebrew-Only Exegesis: A Philological Approach to Jesus' Use of the Hebrew Bible." In *The Language Environment of First Century Judaea: Jerusalem Studies in the Synoptic Gospels*, Vol. 2, ed. Randall Buth and R. Steven Notley. Leiden: Brill, 2014, 362–366.

Noy, Dov. "Introduction to the Collection," in Ratson Tsedaka, *Samaritan Legends: Twelve Legends from Oral Traditions*, ed. Dov Noy. Haifa: The Israel Folktale Archives, 1965, 5-9 [Hebrew], 93-85 [English].

——. "Ratson Tsedaka z"l and the Samaritan Renaissance." *A.B. – News of the Samaritans* 503–505 (February 15, 1990): 19–25. [Hebrew].

Ophir, Adi, and Ishay Rosen Zvi. *Goy: Israel's Multiple Others and the Birth of the Gentile.* Oxford: Oxford University Press, 2018.

Pennacchchietti, Fabrizio A. *Three Mirrors for Two Biblical Ladies: Susanna and the Queen of Sheba in the Eyes of Jews, Christians, and Muslims.* Piscataway, NJ: Gorgias Press, 2006.

Pummer, Reinhard. *The Samaritans.* Leiden: Brill, 1987.

——. "Samaritan Tabernacle Drawings." *Numen* 45 (1998): 30–68.

——. "The Samaritans in Egypt." In *Études sémitiques et samaritaines offertes à Jean Margin*, ed. Christian-Bernard Amphoux, Albert Frey, and Ursula Schattner-Rieser. Lausanne: Éditions du Zèbre, 1998, 213–232.

——. "Samaritan Synagogues and Jewish Synagogues: Similarities and Differences." In *Jews, Christians, and Polytheists in the Ancient Synagogue: Cultural Interaction during the Greco-Roman Period*, ed. Steven Fine. London: Routledge, 1999, 118–160.

——. *Early Christian Authors on Samaritans and Samaritanism: Texts, Translations, and Commentary,* Tübingen: Mohr Siebeck, 2002.

——. *The Samaritans in Flavius Josephus.* Tübingen: Mohr Siebeck, 2009.

——. "Samaritanism: A Jewish Sect or an Independent Form of Yahwism?" *Samaritans – Past and Present,* ed. Menachem Mor and Friedrich V. Reiterer. Berlin: De Gruyter, 2010, 1–24.

——. "The Mosaic Tabernacle as the Only Legitimate Sanctuary: The Biblical Tabernacle in Samaritanism." In *The Temple of Jerusalem: From Moses to the Messiah: Studies in Honor of Professor Louis H. Feldman,* ed. Steven Fine. Leiden: Brill, 2011, 125–150.

——. *The Samaritans: A Profile.* Grand Rapids, MI: Eerdmans, 2016.

——. "Synagogues – Samaritan and Jewish: A New Look at their Differentiating Characteristics." In *The Samaritans in Historical, Cultural and Linguistic Perspectives,* ed. Jan Dušek. Berlin: De Gruyter, 2018, 51–74.

Purvis, James D. "Ben Sira and the Foolish People of Shechem." *Journal of Near Eastern Studies* 24, no. 1–2 (1965): 88–94.

——. "The Sanctuary and Holy Vessels in Samaritan Art." In *Samaritan Researches,* 5 Vols., ed. Vittorio Morabito, Alan D. Crown, and Lucy Davey. Sydney: Mandelbaum Publishing, 2000, 4.27–38.

——. "Studies on Samaritan Materials in the W.E. Barton Collection in the Boston University Library." *World Congress of Jewish Studies* 1 (1969): 134–143.

Rabello, Alfredo Mordechai. "The Samaritans in Roman Law." In *The Samaritans,* ed. Ephraim Stern and Hanan Eshel. Jerusalem: Yad Ben-Zvi Press, 2002, 481–495. [Hebrew].

Reich, Ronny. "Samaritan Amulets from the Late Roman and Byzantine Periods." In *The Samaritans,* ed. Ephraim Stern and Hanan Eshel. Jerusalem: Yad Ben-Zvi Press, 2002, 289–310. [Hebrew].

Revel, Bernard. *The Karaite Halakah and Its Relation to the Sadducean, Samaritan and Philonian Halakah.* Philadelphia: Cahan Print, 1913.

Rogers, E.T. *Notices of the Modern Samaritans.* London, 1855.

Rogers, Mary Elizabeth. *Domestic Life in Palestine.* London, 1862.

——. "Books and Book-Binding in Syria and Palestine, Part 1." *The Art-Bulletin* (London, March 1, 1868): 41–43.

Roggema, Barbara. *The Legend of Sergius Baḥira.* Leiden: Brill, 2009.

Rossi, Azariah de'. *The Light of the Eyes by Azariah de' Rossi,* Trans. Joanna Weinberg. New Haven, CT: Yale University Press, 2001.

Sassoni, Avraham. *"Lifne She'at ha-Purqan.,"* *A.B. – The Samaritan News* (April 15, 1969): 3. [Hebrew].

Shapira, Dan. 2002. "From Our Exile to Shechem: Abraham Firkovich Visits the Samaritans." *Cathedra* 104: 85–94. [Hebrew].

Schechter, Solomon. "Higher Criticism—Higher Anti-Semitism." In *Seminary Addresses and Other Papers.* Cincinnati: Ark Publishing, 1915, 35–39.

Schiffman, Lawrence. "The Samaritans in Tannaitic Halakhah." *Jewish Quarterly Review* 75, no. 4 (1985): 323–350.

——. "The Samaritans in Amoraic Halakha." In *Shoshanat Yaaqov: Jewish and Iranian Studies in Honor of Yaakov Elman,* ed. Shai Secunda and Steven Fine. Leiden: Brill, 2012, 371–389.

Schorsch, Stefan. "Is a Qibla a Qibla? Samaritan Traditions About Mount Garizim in Contact and Contention." *Near and Middle Eastern Studies at the Institute for Advanced Studies, Princeton: 1935-1918,* ed. Sabine Schmidtke. Piscataway, NJ: Gorgias Press, 1918, 95-100.

Schuller, Eileen. "4Q372 1: A Text about Joseph." *Revue de Qumran* 14 (1990): 349–375.

Schur, Nathan. "Samaritan History: The Modern Period (from 1516 A.D.)." In *The Samaritans,* ed. Alan D. Crown. Tübingen: Mohr Siebeck, 1989, 113–134.

——. "The Origins of the Jews in Nablus in the Middle Ages and the Modern Era." In *Mehkarey Shomron,* ed. Shim'on Dar and Ze'ev Safrai. Tel Aviv: Hakibbutz Hameuchad, 1986, 229–301. [Hebrew].

——. "The Samaritans in the Mamluk and Ottoman Periods, and the 20th Century." In *Sefer HaShomronim,* ed. Ephraim Stern and Hanan Eshel. Jerusalem: Yad Ben-Zvi, 2002, 622–626. [Hebrew].

Sedaka, Israel. "Izhak Ben Zvi, David Ben Gurion and the Samaritans." In *Samaritans – Past and Present: Current Studies,* ed. Menachem Mor and Friedrich V. Reiterer. Berlin: Walter de Gruyter, 2010, 239-246.

Shayed, Eliyahu. *Memories 1883–1899.* Jerusalem: Yad Ben-Zvi Press, 1983. [Hebrew].

Shehadeh, Haseeb, " "A Case of Palestinian Arab Justice between Minority and Majority: The Samaritan High Priest Salāma b. Ṣadaqa and the Arab Tailors of Nablus in the Nineteenth Century," *Samaritans – Past and Present: Current Studies,* eds. Menachem Mor and Friedrich V. Reiterer, Berlin: Walter de Gruyter, 2010, 205–220.

Shelemay, Kay Kaufman. "In Fond Memory of Johanna Spector, Mentor and Friend." *Musica Judaica* 19 (2009): 199–202.

Shtober, Simon. "Present at the Dawn of Islam: Polemic and Reality in the Medieval Story of Muhammad's Jewish Companions." In *The Convergence of Judaism and Islam,* ed. Michael M. Laskier and Yaacov Lev. Gainesville: University Press of Florida, 2011, 64–88.

Sivan, Hagith. *Palestine in Late Antiquity.* Oxford: Oxford University Press, 2009.

Spector, Johanna L., and Dan Wolman. *The Samaritans: The People of the Sacred Mountain.* New York: Johanna Spector, 1970.

Spolsky, Ellen, ed. *The Judgment of Susanna: Authority and Witness.* Atlanta: Scholars Press, 1996.

Stein, Dina. "Diaspora and Nostalgia: Traveling Jewish Tales in the Mediterranean." *Mediterranean Historical Review* 34, no. 1 (2019): 49–69.

Stenhouse, Paul. "Further Reflections on the Falasha and Samaritan Versions of the Legend of Susanna." In *Between Africa and Zion Proceedings of the First International Congress of the Society for the Study of Ethiopian Jewry,* ed. Steve Kaplan, Tudor Parfitt, and Emanuela Trevisan Semi. Jerusalem: Yad Ben-Zvi Press, 1995, 94–102.

Stern, Ephraim and Hanan Eshel, eds. *The Samaritans.* Jerusalem: Yad Ben-Zvi Press, 2002. [Hebrew].

Stiebel, Guy D. "'A Light Unto the Nations' – Symbolic Architecture of Ritual Buildings." *Eretz Israel* 28 (2007): 219–234. [Hebrew].

Tal, Abraham. "The First Samaritanologist: Wilhelm Gesenius." In *Biblische Exegese und hebräische Lexikographie; das „Hebräisch-deutsche Handwörterbuch" von Wilhelm Gesenius als Spiegel und Quelle alttestamentlicher und hebräischer Forschung, 200 Jahre nach seiner ersten Auflage,* ed. Stefan Schorch and Ernst-Joachim Waschke. Berlin: De Gruyter, 2013, 139–151.

——. ed. and trans., *Tibåt Mårqe The Ark of Marqe Edition, Translation, Commentary.* Berlin: De Gruyter, 2019.

Tam ibn Yaḥya, Jacob b. David. *Sefer Tamat Yesharim.* Venice, 1622.

Times of Israel Staff. "A Modern First, Passover Sacrifice to Take Place in Old

City." *Times of Israel*, 5 April 2017. https://www.timesofisrael.com/in-first-passover-sacrifice-to-take-place-in-old-city/.

Tropper, Josef. "Die Samaritanischen Inschriften des Pergamonmuseums." *Zeitschrift des Deutschen Palästina-Vereins* 11, no. 1–2 (1995): 118–133.

Tsedaka, Benyamim. "Toward a History of the Synagogue Ritual: Between Jews and Samaritans." *A.B. – The Samaritan News* 357–358 (April 15, 1984): 9–16. [Hebrew].

——. (Sedaka, Ben). "The Israelite Samaritans, Lesson 100, The Newcomers Keep the Torah." *Facebook* post, June 4, 2019.

——. "Sukkot." https://www.israelite--samaritans.com/religion/sukkah/ (accessed August 3, 2021).

——. (Sedaka, Ben). "Text variants are not necessarily 'Jewish' or 'Samaritan,' but texts of the united Israelites," *Facebook* post, 17 February 2020. [Hebrew].

——. and David Selis. *Samaritan Manuscripts of the Mendel Gottesman Library of Yeshiva University*. New York: Yeshiva University, 2021.

——., and Sharon Sullivan. *The Israelite Samaritan Version of the Torah: First English Translation Compared with the Masoretic Version*. Grand Rapids, MI: Eerdmans, 2013.

Tsedaka, Miriam. "The Longest Way to Marry a Samaritan." *A.B. – The Samaritan News* 156 (March 15, 1976): 16.

Tsedaka, Ratson. *Samaritan Legends: Twelve Legends from Oral Traditions*, ed. Dov Noy. Haifa: The Israel Folktale Archives, 1965. [Hebrew].

Twain, Mark. *The Innocents Abroad*. Hartford: American Publishing Company, 1867.

Union of American Hebrew Congregations. *The Samaritans: Their Traditions and Customs*. New York: Union of American Hebrew Congregations, 1970 (filmstrip and guide).

Vilmar, Eduard, ed. *Abulfathi Annales Samaritani. Quos Ad Fidem Codicum Manu Scriptorum Berolinensium Bodlejani Parisini Edidit*. Gotha: Perthes, 1865.

Whiting, John D. "The Last Israelitisch Blood Sacrifice." *National Geographic* 37, no. 1 (1920): 1–46.

Yaniv, Bracha. *The Torah Case: Its History and Design* (Jerusalem: Bar-Ilan University and Yad Ben-Zvi. Press, 1997. [Hebrew].

——. "The Samaritan Torah Case." *Samaritan Researches*, 5 Vols., ed. Vittorio Morabito, Alan D. Crown, and Lucy Davey. Sydney: Mandelbaum, 2000, 3–13.

Yassif, Eli. "Moshe Gaster—A Groundbreaking Innovator in Folklore and in Judaic Studies." *Peamim* 100 (2004): 113–123. [Hebrew].

Young, Brad H. "The Samaritan: Love Your Enemies." In *The Parables: Jewish Tradition and Christian Interpretation*. Peabody, MA: Hendrickson Publishers, 1998, 101–118.

Zohar Production Company and Keren Kayemeth Leyisrael. *La Palestine en Marche*. Dir. Zalman Kotler and Yitzchak Berliand. Cin. Yaacov Ben Dov. Jerusalem, 1926. https://youtu.be/bx8TT_7DDCo (accessed August 3, 2021).

Index